# THE SPENCERS

*By the Same Author*

Althorp

# THE SPENCERS

*A Personal History of an English Family*

CHARLES SPENCER

ST. MARTIN'S PRESS

NEW YORK

www.stmartins.com

ISBN 0-312-26649-9

First published in Great Britain as *The Spencer Family*
by Viking, an imprint of the Penguin Group

First U.S. Edition: September 2000

10 9 8 7 6 5 4 3 2 1

# Contents

For Kitty, Eliza, Amelia and Louis
with all my love

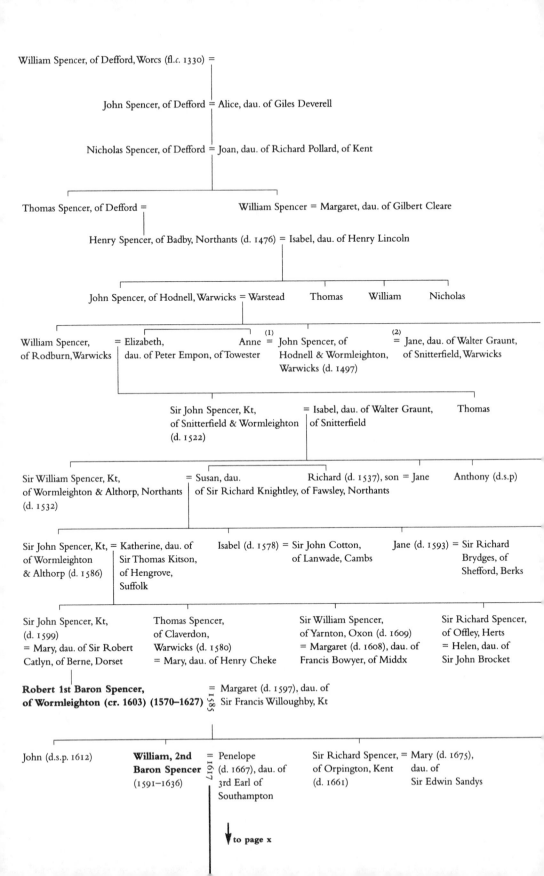

William Spencer, of Defford, Worcs (fl.c. 1330) =

John Spencer, of Defford = Alice, dau. of Giles Deverell

Nicholas Spencer, of Defford = Joan, dau. of Richard Pollard, of Kent

Thomas Spencer, of Defford =          William Spencer = Margaret, dau. of Gilbert Cleare

Henry Spencer, of Badby, Northants (d. 1476) = Isabel, dau. of Henry Lincoln

John Spencer, of Hodnell, Warwicks = Warstead     Thomas     William     Nicholas

William Spencer,     = Elizabeth,           (1) Anne = John Spencer, of        (2) = Jane, dau. of Walter Graunt,
of Rodburn, Warwicks  | dau. of Peter Empon, of Towester   Hodnell & Wormleighton,   of Snitterfield, Warwicks
                                              Warwicks (d. 1497)

Sir John Spencer, Kt,          = Isabel, dau. of Walter Graunt,     Thomas
of Snitterfield & Wormleighton  | of Snitterfield
(d. 1522)

Sir William Spencer, Kt,           = Susan, dau.      Richard (d. 1537), son = Jane     Anthony (d.s.p)
of Wormleighton & Althorp, Northants | of Sir Richard Knightley, of Fawsley, Northants
(d. 1532)

Sir John Spencer, Kt, = Katherine, dau. of     Isabel (d. 1578) = Sir John Cotton,     Jane (d. 1593) = Sir Richard
of Wormleighton       Sir Thomas Kitson,              of Lanwade, Cambs                       Brydges, of
& Althorp (d. 1586)   of Hengrove,                                                            Shefford, Berks
                      Suffolk

Sir John Spencer, Kt,        Thomas Spencer,           Sir William Spencer,          Sir Richard Spencer,
(d. 1599)                    of Claverdon,             of Yarnton, Oxon (d. 1609)    of Offley, Herts
= Mary, dau. of Sir Robert   Warwicks (d. 1580)        = Margaret (d. 1608), dau. of = Helen, dau. of
Catlyn, of Berne, Dorset     = Mary, dau. of Henry Cheke  Francis Bowyer, of Middx   Sir John Brocket

**Robert 1st Baron Spencer,**        = Margaret (d. 1597), dau. of
**of Wormleighton (cr. 1603) (1570–1627)** 1585 Sir Francis Willoughby, Kt

John (d.s.p. 1612)     **William, 2nd**    = Penelope        Sir Richard Spencer, = Mary (d. 1675),
                       **Baron Spencer**  1617 (d. 1667), dau. of   of Orpington, Kent   dau. of
                       **(1591–1636)**    3rd Earl of          (d. 1661)            Sir Edwin Sandys
                                          Southampton

▼ **to page x**

# The Spencer Family Tree

*Family Tree Layout*

| viii | ix | |
|------|-----|-----|
| x | xi | xii |

Thomas Spencer,  = Margaret Smith,
of Badby & Everdon    of Wold

Isabel = Sir Nicholas Strelly, Kt,        Dorothy = Sir Richard Catesby,
        of Strelly, Notts                           of Legers Ashby, Northants
                                                    (d. 1553)

Dorothy (d. 1575) = Thomas Spencer,            Anne = Sir John Goodwin, of        Mary = Thomas Bales,
                    of Badby & Everdon (d.1576)        Winchington, Bucks                 of Wallington,
                                                       (d. 1597)                          Herts (d. 1586)

Elizabeth          William,    (1)  (2)              (3)                  Ferdinando,  (1)   (2)
= George, 2nd      3rd Bn      =    Anne = Sir John Goodwin,  =   Robert,  5th Earl of  = Alice = Thomas, 1st
Bn Hunson          Moteagle    1575     of Winchington,   1592  2nd Earl  Derby                Visc. Brackey
(d. 1603)          (d. 1581)             Bucks (d 1608)         of Dorset  (d. 1594)           (1540–1617)

Sir Edward Spencer, = Mary (d. 1661),    Elizabeth = Sir George Fane,    Margaret    Mary (1588–1658)
of Boston, Middx      dau. of John       (d. 1618) 1617 of Buston, Kent  (d. 1613)   = Sir Richard Anderson,
(d. 1666)             Goldsmith,                   (d. 1640)                          of Pendley, Herts (d. 1661)
                      of Welby

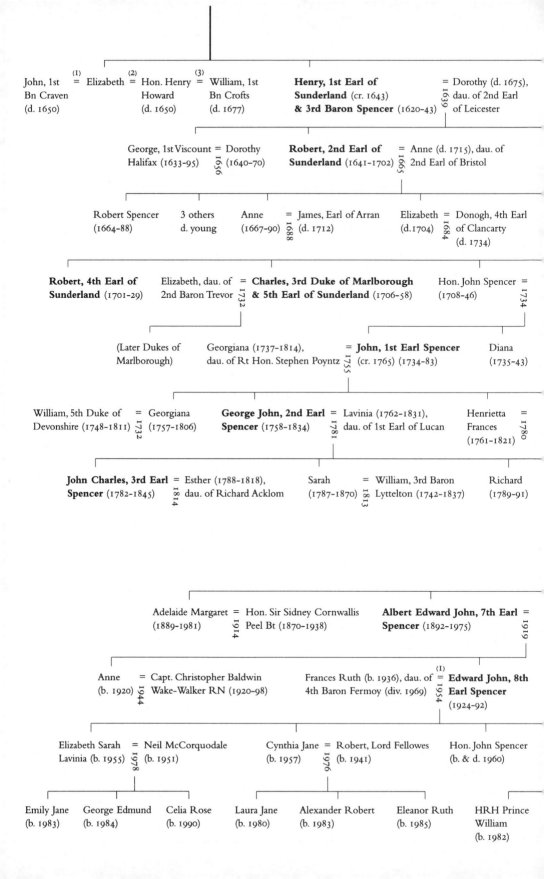

John, 1st Bn Craven (d. 1650) **(1)** = Elizabeth **(2)** = Hon. Henry Howard (d. 1650) **(3)** = William, 1st Bn Crofts (d. 1677)

**Henry, 1st Earl of Sunderland** (cr. 1643) **& 3rd Baron Spencer** (1620-43) = Dorothy (d. 1675), dau. of 2nd Earl of Leicester — 1639

George, 1st Viscount Halifax (1633-95) = Dorothy (1640-70) — 1656

**Robert, 2nd Earl of Sunderland** (1641-1702) = Anne (d. 1715), dau. of 2nd Earl of Bristol — 1665

Robert Spencer (1664-88)   3 others d. young   Anne (1667-90) = James, Earl of Arran (d. 1712) — 1688   Elizabeth (d.1704) = Donogh, 4th Earl of Clancarty (d. 1734) — 1684

**Robert, 4th Earl of Sunderland** (1701-29)   Elizabeth, dau. of 2nd Baron Trevor = **Charles, 3rd Duke of Marlborough & 5th Earl of Sunderland** (1706-58) — 1732   Hon. John Spencer (1708-46) = — 1734

(Later Dukes of Marlborough)   Georgiana (1737-1814), dau. of Rt Hon. Stephen Poyntz = **John, 1st Earl Spencer** (cr. 1765) (1734-83) — 1755   Diana (1735-43)

William, 5th Duke of Devonshire (1748-1811) = Georgiana (1757-1806) — 1732   **George John, 2nd Earl Spencer** (1758-1834) = Lavinia (1762-1831), dau. of 1st Earl of Lucan — 1781   Henrietta Frances (1761-1821) = — 1780

**John Charles, 3rd Earl Spencer** (1782-1845) = Esther (1788-1818), dau. of Richard Acklom — 1814   Sarah (1787-1870) = William, 3rd Baron Lyttelton (1742-1837) — 1813   Richard (1789-91)

Adelaide Margaret (1889-1981) = Hon. Sir Sidney Cornwallis Peel Bt (1870-1938) — 1914   **Albert Edward John, 7th Earl Spencer** (1892-1975) = — 1919

Anne (b. 1920) = Capt. Christopher Baldwin Wake-Walker RN (1920-98) — 1944   Frances Ruth (b. 1936), dau. of 4th Baron Fermoy (div. 1969) **(1)** = **Edward John, 8th Earl Spencer** (1924-92) — 1954

Elizabeth Sarah Lavinia (b. 1955) = Neil McCorquodale (b. 1951) — 1978   Cynthia Jane (b. 1957) = Robert, Lord Fellowes (b. 1941) — 1976   Hon. John Spencer (b. & d. 1960)

Emily Jane (b. 1983)   George Edmund (b. 1984)   Celia Rose (b. 1990)   Laura Jane (b. 1980)   Alexander Robert (b. 1983)   Eleanor Ruth (b. 1985)   HRH Prince William (b. 1982)

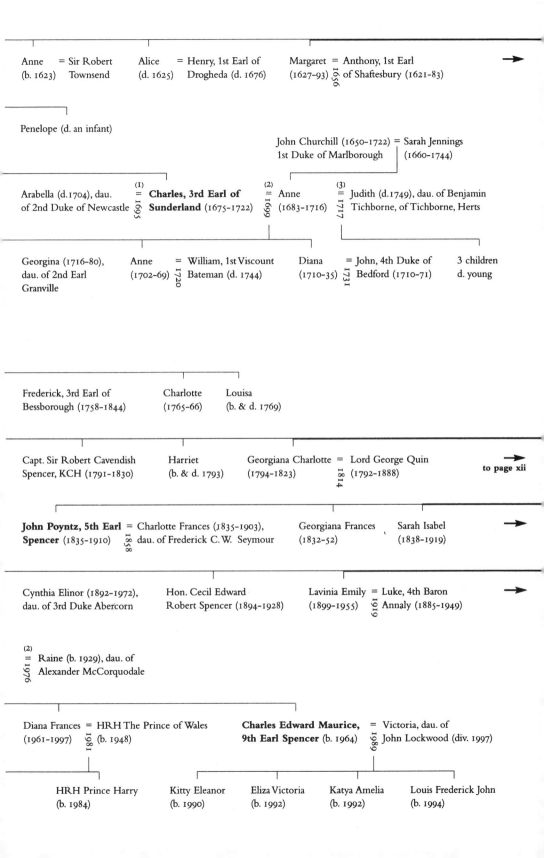

Anne = Sir Robert     Alice = Henry, 1st Earl of     Margaret = Anthony, 1st Earl
(b. 1623) Townsend     (d. 1625) Drogheda (d. 1676)     (1627-93) 1656 of Shaftesbury (1621-83)

Penelope (d. an infant)

John Churchill (1650-1722) = Sarah Jennings
1st Duke of Marlborough     (1660-1744)

(1)                                          (2)                  (3)
Arabella (d.1704), dau.  = Charles, 3rd Earl of  = Anne  = Judith (d.1749), dau. of Benjamin
of 2nd Duke of Newcastle 1695 Sunderland (1675-1722) 1699 (1683-1716) 1717 Tichborne, of Tichborne, Herts

Georgina (1716-80),    Anne     = William, 1st Viscount     Diana     = John, 4th Duke of     3 children
dau. of 2nd Earl       (1702-69) 1720 Bateman (d. 1744)     (1710-35) 1731 Bedford (1710-71)     d. young
Granville

Frederick, 3rd Earl of     Charlotte     Louisa
Bessborough (1758-1844)    (1765-66)     (b. & d. 1769)

Capt. Sir Robert Cavendish     Harriet     Georgiana Charlotte = Lord George Quin
Spencer, KCH (1791-1830)     (b. & d. 1793)     (1794-1823) 1814 (1792-1888)     **to page xii**

**John Poyntz, 5th Earl** = Charlotte Frances (1835-1903),     Georgiana Frances     Sarah Isabel
**Spencer** (1835-1910) 1858 dau. of Frederick C. W. Seymour     (1832-52)     (1838-1919)

Cynthia Elinor (1892-1972),     Hon. Cecil Edward     Lavinia Emily = Luke, 4th Baron
dau. of 3rd Duke Abercorn     Robert Spencer (1894-1928)     (1899-1955) 1919 Annaly (1885-1949)

(2)
= Raine (b. 1929), dau. of
1976 Alexander McCorquodale

Diana Frances = HRH The Prince of Wales     **Charles Edward Maurice,** = Victoria, dau. of
(1961-1997) 1981 (b. 1948)     **9th Earl Spencer** (b. 1964) 1989 John Lockwood (div. 1997)

HRH Prince Harry     Kitty Eleanor     Eliza Victoria     Katya Amelia     Louis Frederick John
(b. 1984)     (b. 1990)     (b. 1992)     (b. 1992)     (b. 1994)

Robert, Viscount Teviot = Jane, dau. of Sir Thomas
(cr. 1686) (1628-94)      Spencer, of Yarnton

William Spencer,          = Elizabeth, dau. of
of Ashton, Lancs (d. 1688)   3rd Baron Gerard

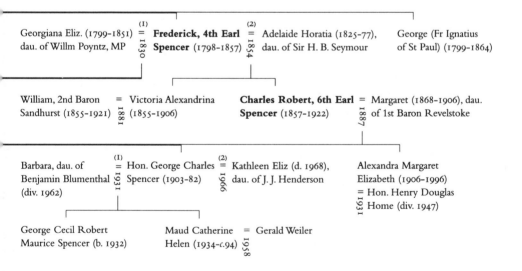

(1)
Georgiana Eliz. (1799-1851) = **Frederick, 4th Earl**
dau. of Willm Poyntz, MP   1830 **Spencer** (1798-1857)

(2)
= Adelaide Horatia (1825-77),
1854 dau. of Sir H. B. Seymour

George (Fr Ignatius
of St Paul) (1799-1864)

William, 2nd Baron   = Victoria Alexandrina
Sandhurst (1855-1921) 1881 (1855-1906)

**Charles Robert, 6th Earl** = Margaret (1868-1906), dau.
**Spencer** (1857-1922)   1887 of 1st Baron Revelstoke

Barbara, dau. of       (1) = Hon. George Charles (2) = Kathleen Eliz (d. 1968),
Benjamin Blumenthal 1931 Spencer (1903-82)   1966 dau. of J. J. Henderson
(div. 1962)

Alexandra Margaret
Elizabeth (1906-1996)
= Hon. Henry Douglas
1931 Home (div. 1947)

George Cecil Robert
Maurice Spencer (b. 1932)

Maud Catherine   = Gerald Weiler
Helen (1934-c.94) 1958

# Introduction

An obscure publication, with the less than exhilarating name of *Midland Halting Places*, turned its attention on Althorp in 1886, and gave the line on the occupying Spencer family – my family – which had, by then, become commonly accepted:

It is very seldom that when a great man is born into a family, that family continues to produce great men to represent it for generation to generation. Sooner or later a scapegrace is sure to come to the front and do his best to mar the renown won by his ancestors. As an exception to this rule the House of Spencer stands almost unrivalled. From the commencement of the Sixteenth Century one continuous line of rich, noble, and high-minded men have heaped up glory and honour around the illustrious name of Spencer . . .

It was a myth reinforced not only through the Victorian desire to find moral probity to respect and aspire to, but through comparison with other aristocratic families, whose black sheep were enthusiastically excoriated, just as the humble shepherding origins of the Spencers were admired – an unthreatening and vaguely respectable start for a family that had more than done its bit for its country, without often producing figures that would remain household names beyond their own lifetime.

This touchingly English celebration of modest do-gooders was perpetuated down the generations. It is the line I was brought up on, as a boy.

When my grandfather died, in 1975, cold and lonely in a nursing home, with him went a vast bank of knowledge about the Spencers. Some of his research I have managed to find in his handwriting – as thin and puny as he was spherical and formidable. He knew his ancestors intimately. I get the impression that he could hear their voices, and that he wanted more than anything to continue the dynasty as he saw it: a powerhouse of liberal Whig politicians, backed by their dutiful, beautiful, clever wives. He failed in all his aims except two: he married a truly exceptional woman, and he did magnificently in holding his inheritance together.

His chief failure was not in being denied the Knighthood of the Garter that so many of his predecessors had gained, although that hurt him deeply; nor in being the first Spencer for at least nine generations to make no political mark whatsoever in England's history. No, his chief failure was closer to home. It was in not carrying his only son, Johnnie, with him, so that my father never drank deep into the history of his ancestors, and came to see Grandfather's obsession with things Spencerian as something threatening; for they were matters about which he knew almost nothing, and that lack of knowledge led to his allowing his second wife, Raine Dartmouth, to sell much that was of a core importance to my family's heritage. Even after taking possession of Althorp, my father had little desire to get to grips with the minutiae of our family's story.

When I look back on my childhood, this sad truth is evident. I can remember how, in an effort to 'spring' me from boarding school for an extra afternoon each summer, my father resurrected the old custom of inviting the headmaster of Maidwell Hall to bring his twelve prefects round to Althorp, to see the house and its contents, and to enjoy a huge tea.

As we all strained to glimpse the gigantic cut-glass bowls of fresh raspberries and strawberries in the Great Dining Room, my father would end the tour – the highlights of which were the terrifyingly gloomy cellars, and the cabinet with the secret drawer that concealed a blackened farthing – with the following short speech:

The reason Althorp contains so many beautiful and wonderful things is because, throughout its 500-year history, my family has always had steady, sensible people in charge of it: unlike other families with similar houses, we have not suffered from having gamblers and alcoholics, ploughing through the contents in an effort to fund their addictions.

Again, a continuation of the myth that we were, as the Victorians termed it, 'the Good Spencers'.

Much to my relief as an author, let alone as someone with, I hope, a realistic view of human nature, it is clear that this is not a line that stands up to too much investigation. Certainly, there are many principled and decent people who were Spencers, but there are many more whose human foibles and weaknesses are at least as interesting as the successes of those who steered a firm course through life's temptations.

Over the following pages you will find Spencers who are, by turn, ambitious, capricious, devious and pious. Simply because they are relatives, they will not receive any special treatment from me. First, because I, like my grandfather, want to hear their voices, pure and true but also because, on balance, I find the more flawed characters the more interesting.

We live in an age when merit, in theory, is seen to be the key to success. It is therefore amazing to many that in previous generations – right up to the end of the nineteenth century – simply being born an aristocrat guaranteed power and influence by right, almost regardless of character or ability. You could be a drunk or a gambler, have venereal disease and no obvious talents, but if your provenance was sufficiently exalted, you were going to be prominent. It must have put enormous pressure not only on family loyalty, but also on the individual, knowing what was expected of him, and how far he was from being able to fulfil the expectations. This was as true for members of my family as it was for their peers.

There is a strong Spencer tradition, one of which I am proud, of women more than holding their own; of being remarkable people in their own right, with strength of character, the power of beauty and wit, and a strong sense of their own significance, all underpinning the ways in which they blazed ahead, independent and deeply confident. Georgiana Devonshire was a Spencer; so, through Georgiana's sister, was Byron's mistress, Lady Caroline Lamb; and, before them, Sarah, the extraordinarily powerful and contrary Duchess of Marlborough. Yet there were many more, from Dorothy Spencer, Countess of Sunderland, who was immortalized by Waller as his muse, 'Sacharissa'; through Georgiana Poyntz, First Countess Spencer, close friend of Sir Joshua Reynolds, David Garrick and a salon of the most able men of her day; to her daughter-in-law, Lavinia, confidante of Lord Nelson; and Charlotte, wife of the Fifth Earl Spencer, one of the most beautiful and glamorous figures of the Victorian age. There have been others, nearer to our own time.

I am conscious that it must look as if I have suffered from a raging case of wilful snobbery, writing about my own family in this way – especially as my only other book has been on my family's principal home, Althorp. However, I am not a disciple of ancestor worship. This is a book I have wanted to write for many years. I spent my adolescence and early adulthood surrounded by portraits of every leading character in the ensuing chapters, and I would have had to be singularly uninquisitive not to have wanted to explore further, to learn what these people thought and believed in, what they contributed to the world and to the Spencer name.

One concept that all my ancestors understood was the relationship between privilege and responsibility. Some of them may have shirked their duties, but they knew what they were shirking. Similarly, I understand what an enormous privilege it is to know so much about the people whose genes I carry; I can go back at least 500 years, through correspondence, official papers and diaries. That is no boast. It is merely a way of underlining the responsibility I feel, for I realize this is my one chance to do justice to the myriad characters who have carried my name before me, and it is quite sobering to think that, as I turn the spotlight on them one by one, I know that they will have their chance for all eternity to correct and chide me, should I do them wrong, for I will one day join them in the family vault, in the village next to Althorp, where I will be the twentieth generation of the Spencer family to be laid to rest.

# THE SPENCERS

# 1. The Despenser Debate

Though this is a book that purports to deal in definites, it needs to begin with a 'maybe'.

There has been much debate about where the history of my family can be seen to have begun. The version I was told, by Grandfather, was categorical: 'The word "Spencer",' he told me when I was a boy, 'derives from the Norman word for Steward, or Head of Household: "Despenser". Our common ancestor was Steward to the household of William, Duke of Normandy, joining his master at the Battle of Hastings, in 1066, and sub-sequently settling in England, when the Duke became King of England.'

Grandfather's forte was the Spencer family's history, and it was unwise for anybody to challenge him when he expounded on his specialist subject with confidence. The result was ill-disguised contempt and the risk of permanent banishment from Althorp. The fact is, he was nearly always right; and, in the rare instances when his interpretation of events was open to question, it was best not to pursue the matter too closely.

If we look at supporting evidence for Grandfather's Despenser claim, it is beyond doubt that one Robert Despenser was William's steward, and that he did accompany his master on his successful invasion of England. We also know that Robert, although head of William's household, was not a mere member of the domestic staff, but a powerful lord in his own right, holding his court position to augment his influence with his master. In England he was one of the most significant of the new class of magnate that the Crown was forced to rely on, in the late eleventh century, to ensure the ultimate success of the Norman conquest.

Thus we see Robert's name alongside those of other barons who assembled in Council with William I, in London, in 1082. The following year, when the same members of the Council 'set their Hands and Seals to the Charter of the King, for removing the secular Canons out of the Church of Durham, and placing Monks in their Stead', Robert's signature was on the document. The first recorded Despenser was also viewed as a powerful enough figure to act as witness to the King's Act, which granted the city of Bath, with its coinage and toll, to John, Bishop of Bath, for the better support of his see. As for the monks of Worcester, they termed Robert Despenser 'a very powerful man'. They should have known, since it was Robert who had seized the Lordship of Elmleigh from them, which they never regained.

Understandably, the Despensers jealously kept their senior court position in the family. Robert's son, William Despenser, became steward to Henry I; as did William's own son, Thurston, after him. On Thurston's death, his son Walter, Lord of Stanley and Usher of the Chamber of Henry II, maintained the Despenser tradition of being mighty courtiers. Walter's younger brother, Americus, settled in the tiny Midland county of Rutland, where he was sheriff in the 1180s, before following the family practice by becoming steward to Richard the Lionheart.

The close association between the Despensers and the monarchs of medieval England continued into the next generation, with Americus's son, another Thurston, a baron in King John's time, extending his influence into the reign of Henry III, when he was Sheriff of Gloucester, until his death in 1229.

It was at this stage, during Henry III's fifty-six-year reign, that the Despensers were transformed from being important figures in the royal court, to numbering themselves among the most powerful handful of men in the land. Hugh Despenser, Thurston's heir, was one of the twelve barons nominated by Henry III to amend and reform the laws of England. However, there were growing tensions between Henry and his barons, which were brought to a head when the monarch attempted to buy the kingdom of Sicily for his son, for a sum that the barons thought grossly inflated, and therefore contrary to the nation's – and their – interests. In the ensuing civil war, Hugh Despenser was chosen by his peers to be Justiciar of

England. This meant that he was entrusted with supreme control of the jurisdiction of the Law Courts of England.

Hugh fought against Henry III at the battles of Northampton and Lewes, at both of which he was noted for outstanding personal bravery. The military strength of the barons, under Simon de Montfort, resulted in Henry being taken prisoner at Lewes, giving the barons their greatest hold on power to date. To underline his humiliating loss of control, in 1265 King Henry was forced to send writs to all the cities, burghs and towns on the coasts of Norfolk and Suffolk, stipulating that he was no longer their effective master; instead, Hugh Despenser was to be obeyed in everything he instructed them to do.

Hugh and his allies had little time to enjoy their new-found power for, in that same year, 1265, they were vanquished at the battle of Evesham in the most crushing defeat on English soil since Hastings two centuries earlier. Despenser met his death on the battlefield, after again fighting valiantly.

The Despenser mantle was next taken up by Hugh's son and grandson, who shared the dead man's lust for power, as well as his first name. Given the plethora of Hugh Despensers at this stage, these two Hughs are often referred to as Hugh Despenser Senior, and Junior. They were two of the most able and ambitious men of their age. As their destinies would show, however, this was not an age noted for its compassion.

Hugh Despenser Senior was a successful soldier and diplomat under Edward I, serving him militarily in the four spheres of operations that dominated English foreign policy at the time: France, Flanders, Wales and Scotland. While Hugh Senior was summoned to Parliament as a baron, his son, also noted as a loyal servant to the Crown, received a knighthood. It was under Edward II, however, that both Despensers were to reach the peak of their power and influence.

I have always felt sorry for Edward II: his record as king is one of the more pitiful in British history. Sandwiched between the military triumphs of his father, Edward I, known to posterity as 'the Hammer of the Scots', and the equally rugged and successful

Edward III, the effete Edward II is only really remembered for two things: having his army trounced by Robert the Bruce at Bannockburn in 1314, and being put to death by his homophobic enemies through the insertion of a red-hot poker into his rectum. From such mishaps it is hard to salvage a dignified reputation for posterity.

It was Edward's close attachment to his royal favourites that was to be the chief focus of aggravation and destabilization throughout his adult life. Although those who would openly oppose Edward were to justify their rebellion as a just attack on 'the evil counsellors' who were perverting the King's mind, to the detriment of his subjects, the real issue was one of power, and who should exercise it.

By the time that Edward II came to the throne in 1307, the barons of England were once again attempting to chip away at the might of the monarchy. They resented the power that still lay with members of the royal household, and the King's prerogative that such a system of patronage reinforced. The barons believed that their might in the provinces should be recognized by the transfer of more executive authority into their hands. The result was friction, and revolt.

Edward II's blatant reliance on his deeply unpopular Gascon lover, Piers Gaveston, gave the opposition barons a focus for their self-serving discontent. However, it was the Despensers who, for the latter years of the reign, were to galvanize the King's enemies into open conflict with the Crown.

It has to be admitted that both Despensers were appallingly ill-advised choices as royal favourites. Early fourteenth-century Britain was not short of controversial figures, but they all had their apologists, who would write justifying the actions of the key personalities of the time. All, that is, except my supposed ancestors, the Despensers, who attracted not one page of defence from their contemporary chroniclers.

The universal contempt for the Despensers stemmed from their transparently rampant personal ambition, particularly after 1322, when they amassed an unseemly quantity of possessions and privileges for themselves, weakly handed to them by an increasingly dependent Edward. The two Hughs became, respectively, Earls of Winchester and of Gloucester, as well as owners of huge landed estates: at one stage, the Earl of Gloucester was calculated to own fifty-nine lordships in various English counties. There he kept his massive number of livestock, which amounted to 28,000 sheep, 1,000 oxen, 1,200 calving cattle, 40 mares with colts, 160 drawing horses, 2,000 hogs and 3,000 bullocks. In his various homes, there was estimated to be 40 tons of wine, 600 bacons, 80 carcasses of Martinmass beef, 600 muttons, 10 tons of cider; armour, plate, jewels and ready money, worth more than £10,000; as well as 36 sacks of wool and a great library of books.

This bountiful abuse of an ineffectual monarch was to spell the Despensers' doom: breaking point came when the younger Hugh prevailed on Edward to give him a barony, which it was contentiously claimed had reverted to the Crown. There followed an insurrection in the kingdom, in 1326, whipped up by the discontented lords, but soon spreading throughout the land. As the Abbé Millot recorded in his *History of England*: 'London revolted from Edward; the provinces followed the example of the capital; and the king, disappointed with regard to the loyalty of his subjects, took to flight.'

The beleaguered Edward II and the Despensers refused to break ranks with one another. Hugh Senior was cornered in Bristol, where he was handed over to the barons by his own men. The old man, being in his ninetieth year, might have expected a modicum of mercy; but it was not to be. Indeed, he failed even to be granted a trial, and was condemned to death, unheard. It was ordered that his execution should be that of a common criminal, and so he was hanged. The King and the younger Hugh were forced to watch his grisly end on the scaffold before them.

Despenser Junior had avoided the same fate by agreeing to surrender voluntarily, while holed up in the castle of Caerphilly. In return, his captors had solemnly guaranteed the safety of his life and limbs, hopeful that, after witnessing the demise of his father, Hugh would finally desert his king. However, this he would not do; so he was turned loose. He had overlooked the need, in such ruthless times, of extending his period of invulnerability, though, and he was almost immediately recaptured. This time the only guarantee he had was that he would be treated without mercy, and in that he was not to be disappointed: on 28 November 1326, he shared his father's fate; the only consolation, for a descendant, lies in the fact that it was very much preferable to sharing that of his monarch.

Unsurprisingly, given the brutal deaths of the three preceding heads of the family, the Despensers chose to adopt a lower profile over the following generations. There was a royal marriage of sorts, when Hugh Junior's grandson Thomas, Earl of Gloucester, wed Edward III's granddaughter, Constance. The only son, Richard, died when just fourteen, and with him was extinguished the senior line of the Despenser family.

Grandfather's contention was that our family sprang from a junior branch of the same family: from Geoffrey Despenser, in fact, the brother of the first of the three Hughs, the courageous figure slain at the battle of Evesham. We know little about Geoffrey, except that he was the first founder of Marlow Abbey in Buckinghamshire, and was a witness to Henry II's Confirmation of Lands to Bungey Abbey in Suffolk. Later in Henry II's reign, there is record of the donation by Geoffrey Despenser of the Church of Boynton to Bridlington Priory.

When he died, in 1251, Geoffrey left a son and heir, John, who was a minor. When he came of age, four years later, he was knighted by Henry III. This John was influential enough to obtain, in 1256, the Bull from Pope Alexander, which directed the Bishop of Salisbury to agree that

John Despenser be allowed to build a chapel, and have a chaplain in his manor of Swalefield, which John is prepared to endow, since the manor lies in a forest, making it unsafe for him and his family to go to the main church near-by, because of the amount of criminals lurking in the said forest.

John was a man of war rather than a man of God. He joined the barons against Henry III, and was taken prisoner at the Battle of Northampton. His manors of Castle Carton and Cavenby, in Lincolnshire, were confiscated. But the barons prevailed and Sir John was released in 1264.

His son and heir, William, has left behind almost no trace of his existence. All we know about him is that he styled himself 'William le Despencer of Belton'; and he lived at Defford, where he died during the reign of Edward III. His son, John, was a more remarkable figure, serving in the retinue of John, King of Castile, in his voyage to Spain, as a result of which he received the King's Letters of Protection for one year, dated 6 March 1386. On his return to England, he became a Squire of the Body to King Henry V, as well as Keeper of his Great Wardrobe. John accompanied his monarch, one of the most heroic English personalities of the Middle Ages, on his expeditions to fight in France.

John and his wife Alice had a son, Nicholas, who was the father of Thomas and William Despencer. The elder of the two, Thomas, produced Henry Spencer (the first time the name was used in the family without its Norman prefix of 'De-'), of Badby, Northamptonshire, the county which, beyond all others, has been associated ever since with the Spencer name.

Henry married Isabel, with whom he had four boys. When he died, in 1476, Henry's last will was sealed with the coat of arms that the family still bears today.

There have been those who have disputed Spencer claims to spring from the same blood as the mighty Despensers. Certainly, on the page, the case appears proven. I hope I can be forgiven for going through the family tree in such detail, but I feel it is a helpful exercise in order to explain Grandfather's thesis, while being aware that, at times, the preceding paragraphs must have all the appeal of one of those interminable chapters in Genesis, where so and so begets someone or other, seemingly *ad infinitum*.

It would not have been necessary to write down all the various links if the Despenser claim were undisputed; but that is not the case. At the time that the Tudor Spencers claimed such links with their presumed forefathers, they were accepted without question; indeed, as late as 1724, a contemporary chronicler was able to confirm that Althorp was 'the manor and seat of the noted Family of the Spencers descended from the ancient Barons Spencer of whom Hugh Spencer the Father and Son, favourites of King Edward II were'.

But in 1859, Evelyn Philip Shirley, in *The Noble and Gentle Men of England*, was a little more sniffy about the Despenser connection, although he failed to specify where the problem lay: 'The Spencers claim a collateral descent from the ancient baronial house of Le Despencer,' he wrote, 'a claim which, without being irreconcilable perhaps with the early pedigrees of that family, admits of very grave doubts and considerable difficulties.' Shirley concluded his judgement with a concession, though: 'It seems to be admitted that they descend from Henry Spencer [of Badby].'

The highly knowledgeable historian William Camden was convinced by the Despenser link, accepting the above family tree in full, and yet contemporary commentators still hold the claim as being open to question. In the course of compiling this book, I have studied the family papers in some depth, and fail to see where the problem lies. Perhaps, by the end of the eighteenth century, it just looked unnecessarily greedy and self-serving for the Spencers to claim prominence and position so very far back in the annals of the history of England?

Writing 200 years ago, Sir Egerton Brydges, the editor of Collins's Peerage, struck on a compromise position over this matter, which hints that my theory may hold some water: 'The present family of Spencer are sufficiently great,' wrote Brydges, 'and have too long enjoyed vast wealth and high honours, to require the decoration of feathers in their caps which are not their own. Sir John Spencer, their undisputed ancestor, and the immediate founder of their fortune, lived in the reigns of Henry VII and Henry VIII; and three hundred years of riches and rank may surely satisfy a regulated pride.'

I am happy to settle for that. I doubt whether Grandfather would be too pleased about it, though.

# 2. The Early Spencers

My family was never very imaginative with Christian names. Perhaps having a surname as solid as 'Spencer' led them to think that it had to be counterbalanced by something similarly uncompromising in its simplicity? At least this would explain the vast preponderance of 'Johns' in the family tree: my brother, who died soon after birth in 1960, was the thirteenth eldest son to be given the name in a little over 500 years.

As a result, prior to my family being created peers, and after they were established as rich landowners in the Midlands, we encounter a succession of Sir John Spencers. The first of these was the eldest great-grandson of Henry Spencer of Badby, who had first borne the modern Spencer name and coat of arms. By the time this Spencer – let us call him 'Sir John 1' – was a man, his branch of the Spencer family had begun to concentrate its land and talents in the heart of the English Midlands – specifically in Warwickshire, which was the centre of the burgeoning English wool trade.

By early Tudor times, at the end of the fifteenth century, sheep farming had become a significant industry. The weaving of wool, together with the manufacture of flax and hemp, was greatly improved by the arrival of cloth-dressers who had fled to England after persecution on mainland Europe.

To some, the trend of turning ploughed land over to grazing was deeply unsettling. Sir Thomas More, in his *Utopia*, written at the start of the sixteenth century, decried 'the increase of pasture, by which sheep may be now said to devour men and unpeople not only villages but towns'. Apart from the social upheaval implicit in this change of land usage, there was also resentment, again vocalized by More, that the sheep 'are in so few hands, and these are so rich . . .', allowing unscrupulous and greedy men to raise 'the price as high as possible'.

Sir Thomas may well have had John Spencer in mind when launching this attack, as his herds were famous throughout England for their size and strength. However, there is no record of Sir John I having been either unscrupulous or heartless. A shrewd marriage to Isabell Graunt had secured for the Spencers the addition of an excellent inheritance at Snitterfield, also in Warwickshire; but, otherwise, it was through skilful husbandry that he managed to build up his landholdings so consistently. Five centuries on, the two key estates – Wormleighton and Althorp – remain in my family's hands, both still demonstrating the fertility and quality that attracted Sir John's interest all those generations ago.

The family's association with Wormleighton dates back 530 years. It is a village close to the Three-Shire Stone which marks the junction of Warwickshire with Northamptonshire and Oxfordshire. On a clear day the Malvern Hills can be seen to the west, while from the roof of the tower in the village, Coplow in Leicestershire and the city of Coventry are both visible in the distance. My father told me that this beautiful hamlet marks the furthest point from the sea in all of England.

The earliest deed relating to Wormleighton in my family documents dates from the reign of King John, at the beginning of the thirteenth century, and is a record of a grant of services from seven acres of land by Cecilia, widow of Simon Dispensator. By coincidence, 'Dispensator' is the Latin word for 'Despenser', or steward.

It was not until John Spencer, father of Sir John I, that my family had direct dealings with the village of Wormleighton, and it was only with the agricultural expansion of Sir John I that the Spencers bought the land that was to become the centre of their sheep-farming empire. He paid William Cope, a financial officer of the royal household, £1,900 for the estate in 1508. In November of that year, all evidences, charters and other documentation relating to the estate were delivered to John Spencer. They remained at Althorp until they were sold in the 1980s.

The success of Sir John I can be gauged by his soon receiving a copy of a statute from London, condemning 'divers covetous persons, [who], espying the great profit of sheep, have gotten into their hands great portions of the ground of this realm, converting the pasture from tillage and keep some 12,000, some 20,000, some 24,000 sheep, whereby churches and towns be pulled down, rents of land enhanced, and prices of cattle and victuals greatly raised'. For Sir John, the figure was reputedly just under 20,000 sheep. Family legend has it that he was never able actually to reach the 20,000 mark because, every time his flocks approached that total, they were blighted by disease or accident.

Having failed to cut back on his sheep farming after receiving the statute, Sir John now received a direct order from the court, to grub up his fences and plough up the land. Unwilling to cut himself off from such a profitable form of farming without a fight, Sir John appealed to Henry VIII himself, to be allowed to continue his business, underlining several points that he insisted should be taken into consideration before a final decision about him and his sheep was made. First, that there had been no timber within fourteen miles of the manor of Wormleighton, whereas he had 'set all manner of wood and sowed acorns both in the hedgerows and also betwixt the hedges adjoining the old hedges'; secondly, that he had personally been responsible for 'building and maintaining of the Church and bought all ornaments as crosses, books, copes, vestments, chalices and censers . . . And where they never had but one priest, I have had and intend to have 2 or 3'; and, thirdly, that despite the danger and difficulty of the transport operation, he sold his fat cattle annually in London and in other towns and cities that required entrepreneurs like his good self to supply their urban needs.

Sir John's submissions were accepted. He continued with his accumulation of wealth undisturbed by central authority, and built Wormleighton Manor for himself and sixty relatives. It was a huge structure – old ground plans suggest it was perhaps three or four times larger than Althorp – and as such it remained the chief seat of the Spencers till the 1640s, when much of it was destroyed by the Royalists in the English Civil War.

What is left today shows that it was a classic piece of architecture of the time following the period of continued civil unrest that Sir

Walter Scott romantically termed 'the Wars of the Roses'. It was
a defensible structure, with castellations and narrow windows, and
yet it had no moat, indicating an increased expectation of peace.
The whole building was based around three courtyards, accessed
by an imposing gatehouse.

The two biggest rooms that remain in the sole surviving wing
are large – thirty-one foot long by twenty-two foot wide. The
brewhouse lies on the ground floor, with bay windows, and, above,
you can still see the Star Chamber, an early Tudor courtroom, its
oak lintels and panels originally painted with stars (it was the fashion
in Tudor times to paint oak). The dimensions of the rooms justify
the architectural historian Nikolaus Pevsner's conclusion that 'The
Manor house of the Spencers must once have been a grand affair,
perhaps as grand as Compton Wynyates.'

Like Compton Wynyates, one of the great treasures of early
English architecture, Wormleighton was to have its Northampton-
shire counterpart. Whereas the Comptons had Castle Ashby, the
Spencers acquired Althorp.

When Sir John Spencer I looked for further land to satisfy his desire
for agricultural expansion, his eye fell on the land of his cousins,
the Catesbys. Like the Spencers, they were an ancient family, with
roots in Warwickshire and Northamptonshire. John de Catesby
had been sheriff of the latter county in 1425, and by this stage he
had bought Althorp from the Lumley family; in a deed of 1421, he
styled himself 'lord of Olthorp'. But it was an estate that was to
remain in the Catesby family for only two generations, for John's
grandson allowed Sir John Spencer to lease Althorp for the grazing
of his sheep, from 1486. Twenty-two years later, convinced of the
supreme quality of the land, Spencer bought it from Catesby for
£800.

The rest of the Catesby family history at this stage was even less
happy than this unfortunate sale might indicate. The John Catesby
who last owned Althorp had a brother, Sir William, Sheriff of
Northampton during Edward IV's time, and subsequently Chancellor of the Exchequer to Richard III. Sir William, with Sir

Richard Ratcliffe and Viscount Lovell, effectively formed a trium-virate that governed King Richard's lands for him, giving rise to the following ditty:

> The Rat, the Cat, and Lovell our dog,
> Rule all England under the hog.

The hog being the hunchbacked Richard III, retribution for the neat but deeply libellous couplet was harsh: its author, Collingbourn, was 'hanged, headed, and quartered' on London's Tower Hill.

Richard III was subsequently slain in 1485, at the climax of the Wars of the Roses, the Battle of Bosworth, and the loyal Catesby was captured there, too. In the three days between the battle and his own execution, Sir William had time to sort out his affairs; and, in his will, he directed 'that John Spencer have his L.xli [£41] with the old money that I owe'.

Thanks to their active Catholicism, there was to be no peaceful retiring into the ranks of the growing gentry class for the Catesbys. We hear of another Sir William Catesby who, in 1581, was brought before the Court of the Star Chamber, a judicial innovation of the first Tudor monarch, Henry VII, for harbouring Jesuits, and for being present at the celebration of mass. Thanks to statutes recently brought in by Queen Elizabeth, both were serious offences, and Sir William was punished accordingly.

It was doubtless partly out of a feeling that his father had been harshly treated that Sir William's only surviving son embarked on a life of rebellion. Certainly, Robert Catesby was a man destined to make his mark somewhere, and it appears to have been a waste of his great potential that his religious convictions forced him into a life of sedition. As the historian Baker wrote:

He was a man of considerable talents, insinuating manners, and inflexible resolution; daring and fertile in expedients, but subtle and circumspect in the development of his purposes; and ready to sacrifice his life, his fortune, and every feeling of humanity, in defence of the Roman Catholic cause.

Contemporaries commented on his great height – 'above two yards high' – and his exceptional good looks, being 'one of the chief gallants of the time', as well as on his character, 'so liberal and apt to help of all sorts, as it got him much love'.

Robert had supported the Earl of Essex in his doomed rebellion, his subsequent pardon costing £3,000. In 1605, he garnered everlasting infamy through his involvement in the equally unsuccessful Gunpowder Plot, an attempt to blow up King James I and his Parliament which failed when Guy Fawkes was arrested before he could ignite his explosives.

Hearing that the plot had been compromised Catesby, with Rockwood, Percy and other fellow conspirators, fled from London, covering the first eighty miles in seven hours, heading for Holbeach, a house in Staffordshire owned by a sympathizer. From here there proved to be no escape: a sheriff and his posse kept them holed up in the house for two days, before it was accidentally torched. Catesby and Percy had to choose between burning to death and making a hopeless bolt for freedom. Percy was shot, and died two days later of his wounds; Robert Catesby was shot dead. He left behind a widow, Catherine, herself the daughter of a Spencer girl.

The pious first Sir John Spencer would have been appalled to think that a descendant of his – albeit remote – would try to murder God's anointed servant on earth. His loyalty and riches were the reason his monarch, Henry VIII, had honoured him with a knighthood, and everything about his recorded conduct justified his receiving such recognition. Not only Wormleighton, but also two Northamptonshire churches – those of Brington and of Stanton – were greatly improved by him, and supplied with vestments and chalices, and he made many bequests to other religious institutions.

So God-fearing was he that he stipulated in his will, read after his death in April 1522,

That he requires his Executors to recompense every one that can lawfully prove, or will make Oath, that he has hurt him in any wise, so that they make their Claim within two Years, tho' (as is recited) he has none in his Remembrance, but he had rather charge their Souls than his own should be in Danger: And requires his Executors to cause Proclamation thereof to be made, once a Month, during the first Year after his Decease, at Warwick, Southampton, Coventry, Banbury, Daventry, and Northampton.

Sir John I had, surprisingly, chosen to be buried in Brington, near to Althorp, rather than at Wormleighton. He had had a family vault built on the north side of the chancel of Brington church, designed by the priest he appointed to that parish in 1513, Thomas Heritage, a chaplain to Henry VIII, and Surveyor of the King's Works at Westminster. The first Sir John Spencer therefore established not only the wealth whereby his family was to prosper, but also the place where they would rest, once such worldly considerations were no longer relevant.

For ten years my family had at its head Sir John I's son, Sir William Spencer, who had been knighted by Henry VIII at York Place (now Whitehall) in 1529. Sheriff of Northamptonshire from 1531 to 1532, Sir William is chiefly remembered by my family for having had to endure particularly troublesome dealings with his in-laws.

Sir William had married into the Knightley family, from Fawsley, Northamptonshire, a village half-way between Althorp and Wormleighton. With Susan, his wife, he did not have a problem; but as for Sir Richard Knightley, his father-in-law, and Edmund Knightley, Sir Richard's brother – well, the records of the Court of the Star Chamber attest to strained, indeed violent, relations, while failing to tell us the original cause of such deep animosity.

The documents to be found in the Star Chamber's annals centre around Edmund Knightley's complaint to the King, concerning 'certain criminal offences committed and done in the county of Northampton . . . by one Sir William Spenser [sic] knight contrary to the laws of almighty God'. It was Sir William's contention that these offences had been reported by the Knightleys to the Bishop of Lincoln. This was totally unacceptable to Sir William, who had never liked Edmund, so he resolved to take a direct approach.

Coming out of a tavern one winter's day, Edmund and Sir Richard Knightley were confronted by the menacing form of a highly agitated Sir William, who told Edmund he had something to talk to him about, but it could wait till they were alone together. Edmund acknowledged the implied threat, and moved on. However, he was mistaken if he thought this was to be a temporary end to the matter.

Not far from the tavern, the Knightley party

came to a place called the Stokkes, beneath Chepe, [where] the said Sir William Spenser, in riotous manner, with six or seven persons with him, having their swords and bucklers in their hands ready to fight, overtook your said beseecher and his said brother, the said Sir William laying his hand upon his dagger, and saying these words: 'Edmund Knightley, what communication hast thou had with the Bishop of Lincoln concerning my vicious living?' To the which your said orator answered, 'My lord of Lincoln can report the truth; let him be the judge.' And therewith the said Sir William said to your said suppliant these words: 'Thou art a knave, a precious knave and a wretch!' And your said orator answered, and said: 'I am a gentleman and no knave'. And therewith the said Sir William said, 'Doest thou me nay? Then thou shalt have a blow!'; and therewith cast off his gown and his servants were drawing their swords. And one of the said servants, called Cartwright, being behind your said orator, violently and furiously with his sword drawn struck at your said orator. And if he had not been shoved back by the servant of your said orator's brother, in striking the said stroke he had utterly slain your said beseecher . . .

The outcome of this affray was a tactical retreat from the scene by both parties. But William had still to work off his anger. Soon afterwards, setting off from Wormleighton with a retinue of servants, he rode over to the Knightley home, and killed a buck in Fawsley Park. When a gamekeeper tried to apprehend the intruders, Sir William cut the man's bowstring with his sword, and would probably have run the gamekeeper through, had his own men not forcibly held him back. Riding away cursing angrily, Sir William told the gamekeeper that he would kill another twenty of the Knightleys' deer within a month, whenever and however he wished. At a time when the poaching of a single deer was a capital offence, this was provocation at its most extreme.

Sir William Spencer died in 1532, aged only thirty-four. He, too, bequeathed his body to be buried at Brington, and also ordered that his father's will should be complied with in every article, but his chief concern was that his young son, John, be well taken care of by the executors of his own will. Sir William was right to worry, for Edmund Knightley was not letting his feud die along with his adversary.

By the time of Sir William's death, Edmund had become a powerful man: a knight, a sergeant-at-law, and one of the commissioners for inspecting the religious houses, prior to their planned dissolution. However, he was to deprive himself of the opportunity to fulfil that last set of obligations, and it was his attempted undermining of Sir William's clear and simple will that was to lead to his ultimate disgrace. He made the mistake of trying to limit the monarch's claim to a share of the inheritance – something the Crown was entitled to because the heir to the estate was a minor.

As Thomas Cromwell, one of Henry VIII's chief advisers, reported to the King in September 1532, Knightley had

done his utmost to set the executors at variance and defect the King's title to the heir, to effect which he has presumptuously caused proclamations to be made in various towns in Co. Warwick, Leicester, Northants, in contempt of the King and his laws. My Lord Keeper has therefore committed him to the Fleet until the King's pleasure be known.

In the end, it was Knightley, not Spencer, who was the victim of royal retribution, although the battle was not resolved until after Sir William's death. His premature demise meant he could be the victor only from beyond the grave.

The little boy Sir William had been so desperate to protect became the second Sir John Spencer. In an act of political juggling of

considerable skill, he straddled the reigns of the Protestant Edward
VI, the devoutly Roman Catholic Mary and the Protestant Elizabeth I, holding office as Sheriff of Northampton at some stage
during each of the three monarchs' times. Sir John II was also MP
for Northamptonshire in 1553–4 and 1557–8.

An ardent Protestant himself, Sir John II was considered
sufficiently sound to be appointed a commissioner by Elizabeth I,
'to enquire about such persons as acted contrary to "An Act for
the Uniformity of Common Prayer, Service in the Church, and
Administration of the Sacraments"'.

He fitted into the ideal of the age, being a man of substance
noted for his care over his general expenditure, while never stinting
on entertaining in the grand manner, as is shown by his last will
and testament, of 4 January 1585. In this he ordered hospitality to
be kept to the same high standard at Althorp and Wormleighton
by his heir, as it had always been his own custom to do.

He was always busy: contemporaries commented on how active
he was, even after he could have adopted a more leisurely lifestyle
as owner of a great estate. His chief recreation was as a breeder of
cattle. However, professionally, he was an earnest fosterer of the
family's sheep-based wealth.

After his death in 1586, the instructions contained in his will
were obeyed: he was buried 'in a decent manner', in Brington
church, 'without pomp after the worldly fashion', next to his wife,
Dame Katherine. Sixty pounds was given to the poor, and money
was provided for the tomb that is still visible today, between the
South and North Chancels, under an arch of exquisite workman-
ship, embellished with roses and lozenges of various hues, a knight
in armour next to his lady, facing up to heaven, cut in marble.

# 3. A Poet in the Family

The second Sir John and Dame Katherine produced eleven children: five sons – of whom the youngest died soon after his baptism – and six daughters. Of the sons, four headed their own dynasties – their father's great business acumen resulting in three lesser landed estates, Claverdon, Yarnton and Offley, which were given to the younger sons. The Althorp and Wormleighton patrimony went to their eldest son, inevitably called John.

For the first time in the family annals, our attention now passes to Spencer daughters. Not the eldest, Margaret, who married Giles Allington, from whom the Barons Allington were descended; nor Katherine, the wife of Sir Thomas Leigh, of Stoneleigh in Warwickshire; and not Mary, whose marriage to Sir Edward Aston, of Tixhall, Staffordshire, was the only event of note recorded about her life. It is the other three – Elizabeth, Anne and Alice – who are of greater significance, bringing unwittingly to light the Spencer link to Edmund Spenser, the Elizabethan poet.

It is not possible to establish at this distance exactly how Edmund Spenser was connected to the Spencers of Wormleighton and Althorp. Certainly, the fact that the surname was spelt differently is of no real significance: spelling had yet to be standardized, and the use of 'c' or 's' in the middle of the name was an understandable variable. Indeed, the sixteenth-century stained glass windows from Wormleighton, now in the chapel at Althorp, spell the family name as 'Spenser'.

Interestingly, the claim of kinship came not from the Spencers, but from Edmund Spenser himself. As Evelyn Philip Shirley concluded, in *The Noble and Gentle Men of England*: 'The poet Spenser boasted that he belonged to this house; though . . . the precise link of genealogical connexion cannot now perhaps be ascertained.'

Edmund Spenser will be for ever remembered as the author of

the poem *The Faerie Queene*. Born in London in 1552, he described the city in his 'Prothalamion' as:

> My most kindly nurse
> That to me gave this life's first native source.

Educated at Merchant Taylors' School, and Pembroke College, Cambridge, he matriculated in 1569, leaving the university as a Master of Arts in 1576. Two years later he became a member of the Earl of Leicester's household, working from Leicester House in the Strand. For a man who has since become such a celebrated man of letters – the Prince of Poets in his Time – there is a measure of absurdity in the humble task he performed as deliverer of dispatches to Leicester's overseas correspondents.

In 1580 Spenser became secretary to Arthur, fourteenth Lord Grey de Wilton, who was then going to Ireland as Lord Deputy. Spenser stayed in Ireland – apart from a couple of visits to England – until the close of 1598. At various stages he was Clerk of the Munster Council – where he made, and enjoyed, the acquaintance of Sir Walter Raleigh – and Sheriff of Cork, an appointment that resulted in Spenser's house, Kilcolman Castle, being plundered by a discontented Irish mob. He fled with his family to London, died a month later in January 1599, and was buried in Westminster Abbey.

An interesting footnote to his time in Ireland lies in the identity of the man who shared his rooms in Chancery in 1593: Maurice, Lord Roche of Fermoy. Three hundred and sixty-one years later, Maurice Roche, Lord Fermoy, witnessed the union of his daughter Frances to Johnnie Spencer, Viscount Althorp – my parents' marriage – in the same abbey where Edmund Spenser was buried.

The question of kinship to the Spencer family was one that preoccupied Spenser throughout his working life. In one of his greatest works, 'Colin Clouts come Home againe', Spenser referred to Elizabeth, Alice and Anne as the 'sisters three':

> The honour of the noble family
> Of which I meanest boast myself to be.

Certainly, the kinship cannot have been over-close: in 'Muiot-potmos', a poem dedicated to Elizabeth Spencer – by then Lady Carey – Spenser expresses his gratitude that his claim is recognized by her, in the line '. . . for name or kindred's sake by you vouchsafed'.

Similarly, Spenser writes to Alice Spencer, in his dedication to her of 'The Teares of the Muses':

Most brave and beautiful ladie; the things, that make ye so much honored of the world as ye bee, are such, as (without my simple lines testimonie) are thoroughlie knowen to all men; namely, your excellent beautie, your vertuous behaviour, and your noble match with that most honourable Lord, the very Paterne of right Nobilitie: but the causes, for which ye have thus deserved of me to be honored, (if honor it be at all,) are both your particular bounties, and also some private bands of affinitie, which it hath pleased your Ladyship to acknowledge.

If the kinship had been intimate, then there would have been no need for the vouchsafing by Elizabeth, nor the acknowledging by Alice; indeed, if the blood link had been close, it would have appeared odd for Spenser to have harped on about it. However, similarly, the claim must have been logically sustainable, or else it would not have been presented by the poet, nor accepted by the Spencer ladies.

The reason behind dedicating poetry to influential ladies of breeding was flattery. Not content with fawning to their human charms, Spenser transformed the three Spencer girls into mythical muses – Phyllis (Elizabeth), Charillis (Anne) and sweet Amaryllis (Alice):

> Phyllis the faire is the eldest of the three:
> The next to her is bountifull Charillis;
> But th'youngest is the highest in degree,
> Phyllis, the floure of rare perfection,
> Faire spreading forth her leaves with fresh delight,
> That, with their beauties amorous reflexion,
> Bereave of sence each rash beholders sight.

> But sweet Charillis is the paragone
> Of peerless price, and ornament of praise,
> Admir'd of all, yet envied of none,
> Through the myld temperance of her goodly raies.

The Spencer daughters were the recipients of other dedications from contemporary writers. Milton wrote his 'Arcades' – a poem that could also be delivered as a masque – for Alice. It was first performed in 1602 for Elizabeth I, when she visited Alice and her husband at their home, Harefield Place; indeed, some of Alice's family were in the troupe at that début performance.

Alice's home was frequented by artists of all kinds. Her husband, Lord Strange, the grandson of Mary, Dowager Queen of France, a sister of England's Henry VIII, was a friend of poets, and even wrote some verse himself. He also was the patron of the company of actors who had previously been attached to the Earl of Leicester, 'Lord Strange's Company'. Spenser, keen to stay on the right side of such a benefactor of the arts, called Strange 'the very Paterne of right Nobilitie', and even praised the lord's amateur artistic efforts posthumously:

> He, whilst he lived, was the noblest swain
> That ever piped upon an oaten quill,
> Both did he other, which could pipe maintain,
> And eke could pipe himself with passing skill.

In a similar way Nash, the satirist, acknowledged the patronage of Elizabeth Spencer, Lady Carey, while also taking the opportunity to doff his hat with respect to a far greater literary talent than his own, when he recorded in his dedication to 'Christ's Tears over Jerusalem': 'Divers well-deserving Poets have consecrated their endeavours to your praise. Fame's eldest favorite, Maister Spencer, in all his writings he prizeth you.'

Later generations of the Spencer family were to honour their blood link with Edmund Spenser. When George John, Second Earl Spencer, found his vast collection of books was spilling out from the library at Althorp in the early nineteenth century, his wife, Lavinia, named one of the sitting rooms 'The Spenser Library', filled it with volumes of poetry, and had a portrait of Edmund placed above the fireplace there. The earl and his wife – both highly educated – seem to have agreed with the opinion of their friend, the historian Edward Gibbon, when he wrote: 'The nobility of the Spencers has been illustrated and enriched by the trophies of Marlborough, but I exhort them to consider The Faery Queene as the most precious jewel in their coronet.'

# 4. A Worthy Founder

Sir John Spencer II, father of these muse-like daughters, died in 1586. His eldest son, Sir John III, knighted on his father's death by Queen Elizabeth, followed him in January 1599. This ancestor of mine can have had little idea that evidence of his life at Althorp would still be visible in the Park 400 years on. However, that is the case, for Sir John III planted a large wood at the rear of Althorp, which is only now reaching the end of its natural life. The oldest oaks still growing there today were planted at his instruction in 1589. My father told me that, the Spanish Armada having been defeated the year before the wood was seeded, it was Sir John III's intention to boost the timber stocks, in order to be able to help the English Navy to build more ships, should such an invasion be attempted again in the future.

Other than that, he is remembered by my family for increasing the Althorp estate by buying Little Brington, a village a couple of miles from Althorp, in 1592. The vendor was Francis Bernard, and the price £2,150. Some property in that village, like the mighty oaks in the Park, remains in my family's possession today.

In stark contrast to his father's fertility, the third Sir John had but one son, by his wife Mary, sole daughter and heir of Sir Robert Catlyn, the Lord Chief Justice. Named after his illustrious maternal grandfather, Robert Spencer was a truly remarkable man, a lynchpin in the family's history, but also the object of great respect during his own lifetime.

Much of this esteem flowed from qualities that have been seen in generations of Spencers, both before and after Robert's tenure of Althorp: a keen and able participation in the family's farming enterprises, a lack of personal political ambition, and a relentless defence of the rights of the English citizen against the abuses of the Crown, as well as the ability to stand aloof from the self-serving infighting of the court. Soon after his death, it was said of Robert:

He made the country a virtuous court, where his fields and flocks brought him more calm and happy contentment than the various and unstable dispensations a Court can contribute, and when he was called to the Senate he was more vigilant to keep the people's liberties from being a prey to the encroaching power of monarchy than his harmless and tender lambs from foxes and ravenous creatures.

The Spencer family is perhaps unique, of the old English aristocracy, in tracing the roots of its noble title back to the relatively prosaic world of agriculture. The more usual paths to the House of Lords were via military distinction, or through royal blood links – legitimate or illegitimate. The humble farming ancestry of the Spencers was highly unusual, but so was the wealth that inspired husbandry had amassed for the family.

Robert, the fifth Spencer knight in succession, was able to cement his family's rise from gentry to nobility by building on his forefathers' endeavours. His personal involvement in the farming operation is shown by references to his attending markets in the West Country in 1597, accompanied by his bailiff, in a quest to improve the bloodline of his cattle, beasts of particular importance to the late sixteenth-century household: the Althorp domestic accounts of the time record that 200 lbs of butter were consumed every week the family was in residence.

We also know that Robert insisted on overseeing the entire agricultural operation on his home farm, at Muscot, five miles from Althorp, where he grew not only rye and barley, but also hops. He was a familiar sight, atop his horse, a small cob palfrey, constantly looking for ideas on how to improve the way tasks were handled, and with a reputation for being unusually approachable to his workers.

Writing in the 1860s, the vicar of Brington, the Reverend J. N. Simpkinson, working from the accounts and records in the Althorp Muniment Room, recreated the scene that would have been witnessed, if one could have been transported back to Robert's tenure of the Estate:

Lord Spencer never allowed himself to drop behind the agricultural improvements of the day: and the system he had adopted gave employment to many of the women of the villages around as well as to their husbands and fathers. He had introduced the cultivation of hops, both at Muscot farm and in Althorp park; and troops of women were wanted in the hop-grounds, in the spring and early summer, for weeding and tying. Then the meadows had to be 'clotted': and, in the parts of the park which were laid for hay, care must be taken to gather the sticks, and rake up the 'orts' – the litter, that is, that lay on the ground where the cattle had been foddered in the winter. And in the early part of June, the women were busy in weeding the young quickset hedges; fresh portions of which Lord Spencer added, year by year, to the enclosures on his estate . . . Lord Spencer treated his labourers liberally. Besides the regular pay (sixpence a day for men, and three-pence for women) he would kill two or three sheep to regale them on such occasions; besides supplying them amply with beer, and plenty of bread to eat with it – excellent bread, such as was not often to be had by labourers in those days, half of barley and half of rye; and at the conclusion would hire a 'minstrel', to make merry for them: often coming himself with a party from Althorp, to take part in the final rejoicings.

This enjoyment of a simple, rural life was maintained, despite his increasing importance as a man of influence in the country at large.

When Elizabeth I died, the new King James I was eager to cement his position, so he made it his business to identify the key men in the kingdom, to secure their loyalty. Robert Spencer, reputedly with more ready money than any other man in the kingdom, was clearly somebody whose support was desirable. This explains the honour that was paid to him and to his family when James's queen, Anne of Denmark, and his heir, Henry, Prince of Wales, stayed at Althorp during their progress to their new palaces in June 1603. It was repaid in full by Robert, who commissioned Ben Jonson to write a masque to be performed as a welcome for the royal guests, in the Park at Althorp. Queen Anne was intrigued by this novel art form – a marked improvement on the Danish court's idea of entertainment, which centred around the men present drinking enormous quantities of alcohol until they could consume no more – and it was thanks to this performance at Althorp that masques became a part of fashionable royal entertainment in the early seventeenth century.

Partly because of his wealth, partly because of the appreciation of the royal party for their gracious reception at Althorp, and partly because new men of note were needed to buoy up the Stuart hold on the throne of England, Robert was made Baron Spencer of Wormleighton later in 1603. His first task was to act as ambassador for the King, and to invest England's ally, Frederic, Duke of Württemberg, with the highest order of chivalry, a knighthood of the Garter. The baron and the duke vied with each other in the fabulousness of their retinues, and in their gifts to each other, dazzling those who witnessed their meeting with their displays of wealth and munificence.

Robert did not involve himself in court life back in England; it was of no interest to him. However, he took his duties as a member of the Upper House of Parliament seriously, trying to remain loyal to his monarch, while becoming increasingly perturbed by the royal inclination to be overbearing in its attitude to the people's representatives. James's belief in the Divine Right of Kings to rule – and raise money – as they saw fit, flew in the face of Spencer's belief in the need for respect for the people's elected representatives.

Diligent though Robert was, his agricultural provenance was not forgotten by some of his fellow peers. Once, while he was speaking in the House of Lords on the bravery displayed by former generations in guarding the liberties of England, the Earl of Arundel – conscious of four centuries of aristocratic blood in his own veins – interrupted contemptuously, 'My Lord, when these things were doing, your ancestors were keeping sheep!' Robert, apparently without missing a beat, retorted: 'When my ancestors were keeping sheep, as you say, your ancestors were plotting treason.' Arundel exploded with rage, to such an extent that he was sent to the Tower of London for his unseemly conduct, until he had calmed down and was ready to apologize to Robert for the rudeness of his insult.

Despite his misgivings about James's conduct as king, it is clear that James himself had only the greatest respect for Robert. Indeed, when it came to finding a suitable Midland home for his second son, Prince Charles, James was persuaded to choose Holdenby, across the valley from Althorp, in the hope that some of Robert's virtues would rub off on his boy. As the Reverend Simpkinson neatly phrased it, Robert was 'a nobleman who had attained a very great reputation and influence, not only in the midland counties, but also in the House of Lords, and in whom the king rightly believed that he should secure a most valuable neighbour and counsellor for his son'. The bond between the King and the baron was strengthened, when both lost their eldest sons in 1612 – the Spencer heir at Blois, in France, and Henry, Prince of Wales, after catching a chill playing tennis.

It was not Robert's first taste of family tragedy. His wife, Margaret Willoughby, was a lady of interesting pedigree. Her father was Sir Francis Willoughby, himself the son of Henry Willoughby and Anne, daughter of the Second Marquess of Dorset. Dorset was a landowner in the vicinity of Althorp, who had conveyed the manor of Newbottle (now Nobottle) to the first John Spencer in 1511. Dorset's son, the Third Marquess, has gone down in history as the man who pushed forward his daughter, Lady Jane Grey, on the death of Edward VI in 1553. The hapless Jane was queen for all of nine days, before being deposed by Mary Tudor. She was subsequently beheaded.

The first Baroness Spencer was, therefore, the first cousin once removed of Lady Jane Grey. This may explain why the only known portrait painted of Lady Jane during her brief life is at Althorp. She is shown as a devoted Christian, reading her Psalter, very much an innocent. There is nothing threatening about her, nothing ambitious or devious; just a naïve young girl, overtaken by other people's scheming, and unfairly paying for their manipulations with her life.

This link to royalty – albeit relatively obscure, and certainly extremely short-lived – did not spare Robert's wife from one of the common scourges of women at this time: death in childbirth; although the child, Margaret, survived. As the heartbroken widower recorded in his own hand in the first pages of his Account Book, after the details of the seven children that he had successfully fathered:

Anno Domi: 1597. At Allthrop. The xvii of August it plesed the Allmighty God to take to his mercy Margarite my most loving wife having borne to me all these children afore named they all now living and being married ix yeare and a halfe . . . her vertues surpassed all.

By coincidence, in 1906 my great-grandfather, another Robert Spencer, lost his wife, also a Margaret, in childbirth. Both children of the ill-fated births were daughters, and both were named after their deceased mothers. Although both Roberts lived for a considerable time after bereavement, neither remarried.

Robert, First Baron Spencer, died in 1627, choosing to have his bowels buried at Wormleighton – from where his baronial title gained its name – and his body at Brington, beside the beloved Margaret, who had died thirty years beforehand. In the sermon preached at his funeral, the congregation was reminded that it had been Robert's custom to feed fifteen poor persons every Monday, as well as giving alms at all other times, and relieving the distress of all who came to the gates of his mansions; that he had been a lenient landlord and a kind master, providing amply for his servants in their old age; that he had been held in such high estimation by his friends, that many of them entrusted their whole estates – and the education of their children – to his care; that his 'singular skill in antiquities, arms, and alliances' was not less noted than his constant integrity and uprightness of life and conversation; and also that, in the management of his great estates, he had made a 'careful frugality the fuel of his continual hospitality'.

# 5. The Washington Connection

William, Second Baron Spencer, was reputed to have inherited the qualities of his father just as suredly as he had inherited his estates. A monument to his memory was to record that he was a tender husband, loving father, faithful friend, a sincere worshipper of God, devoted to his king, and a patriot of his country. During his lifetime, with the tensions between Crown and Parliament increasing all the time, balancing the latter two demands became an ever more difficult task.

In the general celebrations at Charles Stuart's becoming Prince of Wales in 1616, William had been created a Knight of the Bath. Keenly involved in the political life of the nation, he was elected one of the Knights of the Shire for Northamptonshire in three different parliaments in James I's reign, and in two of Charles I's.

William's wife would have a marked effect on his political stance. She was Lady Penelope Wriothesley, daughter of the Earl of Southampton – the patron of William Shakespeare, and a figure known for his antipathy to the court faction.

By the second decade of his reign, James I was resorting to highly dubious means to raise money without suffering the intrusions and counter-demands of Parliament. The King was seen to be undermining the House of Lords, by selling peerages to fill his coffers. A letter of June 1618 from a Thomas Lorkin to an unnamed friend gives an indication of where Penelope stood on such questionable use of royal power, since her politics were known to have reflected those of her father and brother closely:

Ere long you are likely to hear of a new creation of my Lord Rich, my Lord Compton, Lord Peter, and Candish or Chandos, I remember not whether, are to be made Earles and to pay ten thousand pounds a piece, which is allotted for the expense of the progresse; my Lord Spencer likewise was nominated, but diverted as they say by my Lord of South-ampton (whose daughter his eldest sonne marryed) from accepting it.

Penelope was a considerable force for good at Althorp. Her father-in-law, lonely after his Margaret's death, invited her and William to live in the mansion with him, handing over day-to-day administration of the housekeeping to Penelope, while increasing the privacy that the young couple could enjoy through the provision of a drawing room for the new lady of the house and a closet for William. If the old First Baron had hoped the young couple would bring a bit of life to proceedings at Althorp, they did not disappoint, producing thirteen children, the old iron cradle, looked after by Nurse Detheridge, frequently coming out of storage, with its 'can-opy and a covering of silver velvet, laced with open spangle lace of gold and silver, and curtains of the same stuff suitable, fringed with crimson silk and silver'.

Running Althorp efficiently was a task Penelope took to with aplomb. Before her involvement, the accounts for the household had been kept by the bailiff, and by the steward of the household. These books showed the various items of expenditure pertaining to the kitchen, the stables, the park and the farms. Lord Spencer and William would inspect such accounts weekly. However, they were not precise enough for Penelope's liking. She introduced a more comprehensive and accessible system, whereby the rate, as well as the extent, of all household expenditure could be exactly monitored. Through a cursory glance, Penelope could discover what was in store, and what needed to be ordered. As Simpkinson admiringly wrote,

The estimated value of every bullock and sheep that was killed, and of every other article of farm produce which was brought into the house, appeared to her as important to know and to record, as the money which had gone to defray the purchases of the cater: while the last column of the book informed her practised eye every Saturday which of the stores was running low, and how soon it would need replenishing.

The Spencers were not short of money; far from it. Yet this skilful control of the accounts allowed the family to entertain in style, without worrying about wastefulness. The number and the calibre of domestic staff increased – there were soon over fifty, some from France, and others gentlemen in their own right – and they were sumptuously clothed. Penelope's readiness to pay for quality is demonstrated in the rate of pay of senior household figures – £6 per year, three times the conventional rate of the time.

Penelope wanted Althorp to be a byword for great hospitality and, despite the fact that it is almost as far from the coast as it is possible to be in England, she employed staff whose sole job it was to furnish the dining table with half a dozen barrels of oysters fresh from the east coast, on a weekly basis. Other fish came direct from London, brought by the wonderfully named carriers, Legg and Shortlegs, who also supplied groceries from the backs of their pack-horses. The journey took two to three days, Legg and Shortlegs 'freshening' their perishable goods on the way by hosing them with water.

Penelope's influence was to be seen in a more lasting manner through improvements to the gardens, and to Althorp itself. She had read Lord Bacon's Essays, and these persuaded her to redesign some of the avenues in the gardens, and to build a folly on a mound towards the rear of the main house. A new fruit and vegetable garden was initiated; and a pheasantry, too.

Inside the mansion, Penelope introduced forks, to be used with table knives, at meal times. Another practical change was the installation of a bell pulley in Penelope's bedroom, so she could summon her waiting-woman when she was required, without frequent breaches of her privacy.

Structurally, she helped William plan the enlargement of Althorp. A best drawing room was added in time for a royal visit by Charles I and his queen, Henrietta-Maria, in 1636, the windows constructed in the modish 'balconia' fashion.

The Spencers did not limit themselves to royalty and aristocracy when inviting house guests to Althorp. William's friends were an interesting mix: from his horse-racing and hunting friends (William, although he kept only a single racehorse himself, had an entire racecourse established in the park at Althorp), and those who attended the hawking parties, to learned and famous physicians of the day, especially one Dr Cotta, a Cambridge graduate practising in Northampton, and Doctors Ashworth and Clayton, from Oxford. Most noblemen of the time chose to socialize with people from their own background.

One group conspicuously absent from the guest list at Althorp, to judge from Penelope's household accounts, is that of the Puritans; William had no time for them. Indeed, one of his own friends was Charles I's controversial High Church Archbishop of Canterbury, William Laud. So, when it was time to appoint a new preacher for the parish of Brington, the man who William presented for the post had the full four surplices – something no Low Churchman would have contemplated.

William was so rigid in his Anglican beliefs that he rarely allowed his brother, Sir Edward Spencer, to visit Althorp. He considered Edward a traitor to his faith and upbringing for embracing Puritanism. Indeed, William refused to send his eldest son, Henry, to Sir Edward's alma mater, Balliol College, Oxford, in case his heir was similarly contaminated. Instead, William chose Magdalen, secure in the knowledge that it was under the presidency of Dr Accepted Frewen, later Archbishop of York, who, despite his name, was strongly anti-Puritan.

More welcome at Althorp in William's time was a family from the other side of Northamptonshire, who had fallen on hard times: the Washingtons.

The last English forebear of George Washington lies buried less than two miles from Althorp's front door, in the same churchyard – Brington – as the Spencer tombs.

In the early sixteenth century Lawrence Washington, of Warton in Lancashire, had decided to move south. A lawyer, Lawrence had become a member of the society of Gray's Inn. However, an uncle who was a successful London merchant told him to forget law for the time being, and to take advantage of the boom in the wool trade. As had been the case with the Spencers, the wish to profit from sheep had brought him to the Northampton area, where he settled, becoming mayor of the town in 1532.

When Henry VIII severed contacts with the Pope at the time of his first divorce, he decided to take control of the vast wealth of the religious houses across his kingdom. This decision was formalized in 1539 and, among those enthusiastic to benefit from the situation, was this same Lawrence Washington, who received a grant of the manor and lands of Sulgrave, which had previously been the property of a wealthy monastery, St Andrew's, in Northampton.

Later, people talked of a curse being attached to those who had profited from the monasteries' dissolution. Certainly, the speedy change in fortune of the Washingtons of Sulgrave Manor would give some credibility to such a theory, since the estate was effectively ruined by 1606; and Lawrence's grandson, another Lawrence Washington, was forced to sell Sulgrave soon afterwards, in 1610.

According to Reverend Simpkinson, the distressed Washingtons found a saviour in Robert, First Lord Spencer, who provided them with a small house in Brington. Not long after the move was made, Lawrence and his wife produced a son, Gregory, who died an infant, and was buried in Brington churchyard.

Why Lord Spencer should help the Washingtons is not clear. Perhaps it was because of a distant kinship: Spencer's grandmother, the wife to the third Sir John, was a daughter of Sir Thomas Kitson, the London merchant who was the Washington uncle who had advised the family to move to Northamptonshire so they could enrich themselves from the wool trade.

After Sulgrave's sale, the younger Lawrence Washington took his young family to London, while his brother, Robert, took on the house in Brington, with his older wife, Elizabeth. Apparently they were unable to have children of their own – Elizabeth was perhaps past her childbearing years – so they adopted Amy, one of their nieces. From the household records at Althorp, it is apparent that Amy was a frequent companion – and, quite possibly, a friend – of young Margaret Spencer, the sickly girl who had survived her mother's death in childbirth. As a result, her name appears frequently in Penelope Spencer's household accounts.

There are also other Washington references there: in mid-January 1622, we learn that there was, 'Given by Mr Robert Washington. Chickines 5, Casuall chickine 1, Chickine to the falkenor 1; given also by Mr Washington. Henns, cupp: 2, Flitch of bacon.' These may well have been by way of New Year's presents. They could never be repeated, since Robert died a month and a half later. His widow, Elizabeth, died nine days afterwards. Over the grave there is a ledger-stone marked with their names, telling all who see it that they sleep below, 'after they lived lovingly together many years in this village' of Brington.

By this stage the wider Washington family had risen considerably in importance, doubtless through James I's deep affection for George Villiers, whose sister had married Amy Washington's elder brother, William. James, always receptive to handsome young men, had met Villiers while on a progress through Northamptonshire in 1614. A younger son of a Leicestershire knight, George was lured to the royal court, where he was soon acknowledged to be the King's favourite.

As was his custom, James swamped his new love with gifts – including titular ones, advancing George to the rank of Viscount Villiers, and then, in rapid succession, to earl, then marquis, then finally Duke of Buckingham. The spin-offs for a favourite's family – while he remained in favour – were considerable and Villiers saw that his kin did not feel neglected in this regard. They became titled, or received sources of wealth in various forms, or were helped with promotion in their professions. By the time of simple Robert Washington's funeral in Brington, Amy's two eldest brothers found themselves styled Sir William and Sir John, and the latter was the owner of a landed estate in Yorkshire.

Although the Washingtons left Brington after Robert and Elizabeth's deaths, this was not the end of the links between the rest of the family and the Spencers. Sir John was a frequent visitor to Althorp, often staying for several weeks at a time. So close were the Spencers to him that, when he was widowed, it was to Althorp that he immediately retired for consolation, taking his three young children with him.

It was a friendship that crossed the generations. After Robert, First Lord Spencer's death in 1627, Sir John remained a welcome guest of William and Penelope Spencer's. Indeed, when their daughters were too old to need regular nannies, Lucy Washington, Sir John and Amy's little sister, assumed the role of their governess.

When the Spencer heir, Henry, required military instruction – particularly on how to master his charger ('the great horse') – Sir John and his son, Mordaunt, appear to have been sent for to help him learn. Henry, together with Sir John, and the latter's Washington nephew – another Henry – were all to fight on the Royalist side in the coming English Civil War. After the Parliamentary victory, Sir John, Mordaunt and Lawrence Washington decided to quit England, and set off for Virginia. There is speculation that they were forced to do so to save their lives, after being implicated in a Royalist conspiracy in 1656. Virginia, at this stage in its history, was known as a bolthole for disaffected Englishmen, eager to escape the government of the Commonwealth, which succeeded the reign of Charles I.

Sir John's great-grandson was George Washington.

# 6. Death for the King

The last time William, Second Lord Spencer's signature is to be found approving his wife's household accounts was on 9 December 1636. Nine days later he was dead, aged forty-four. Penelope was distraught. She refused several proposals in her widowhood, which lasted thirty-one years. In honour of the man she truly loved, Penelope erected 'a noble and stately monument of black and white marble' in Brington church.

On his father's death, the sixteen-year-old heir, Henry, was immediately brought to Althorp from his studies at Oxford. An extremely popular and able young man, Henry had already received a Master of Arts degree by this early age, his studies having initially been under the direct care of his father at Althorp. A contemporary wrote of Henry, during his Oxford days:

He had a tutor, crooked with age, who straitened the manners of his youth, arming him against those customs that are not knocked, but screwed, into the soul; inuring him to good discourse and company; habituating him to temperance and good order, whence he had the advantage of others, not only in health, but in time and business; and diverting him with safe, cheap, but manly and generous recreations; the result of which education was a knowing and a staid nature, that made him a lamb when pleased, a lion when angry.

He was then brought up under the charge of his mother, and the guardianship of his uncle, Thomas, Earl of Southampton, the son of Shakespeare's patron. The end product of this upbringing was a man of great renown and promise. He was only to have his potential increased through marriage to a woman in every way his equal. Dorothy Sidney was the eldest of the eight daughters of Robert Sidney, Second Earl of Leicester, and Dorothy Percy, herself daughter of the Ninth Earl of Northumberland. She was, like Henry, born in 1620. Unlike her eventual husband, she was brought up at the centre of court politics, where her parents were pivotal figures. Dorothy – her parents called her 'Doll' – was their favourite child.

Given her personal charms, as well as her parents' prominence, Dorothy was pursued by suitors as soon as she was old enough to become their prey. In the seventeenth century, this meant that her parents were having to fend off unwelcome attentions from the time she was fifteen. Her mother's concerns about two well-born but undesirable suitors are clearly shown in a letter to Dorothy's father:

Now considering Doll . . . I find my Lord Lovelace so uncertain, and so idle; so much addicted to mean company, and so easily drawn to debauchery; as it is now my study how to break off with him in such a manner as it may be said that we refused him . . . Many particulars I could tell you of his wildness; but the knowledge of them would be of no use to you, since he is likely to be a stranger to us; for, though his estate is good, his person pretty enough, and his wit much more than ordinary, yet dare I not venture to give Doll to him. And concerning my Lord of Devonshire I can say as little to please you; for, though his mother and sister made fair shows of good intentions to us, yet in the end we find them, just as I expected, full of deceit and juggling . . . My dear heart, let not these cross accidents trouble you; for we do not know what God has provided for her.

Of equally little interest to the Leicesters was the suit of the poet, Edmund Waller. A widower at the age of twenty-five, he directed his romantic yearning towards Dorothy. In his poems she was his 'Sacharissa', his sweet and perfect muse.

When it became evident that Dorothy was never going to be his, the distraught Waller threatened to quit England for ever. And yet Dorothy was still uppermost in the creative part of his mind when he wrote to a later love, Lady Sophia Murray, whom he termed his 'Amoret'. Lady Sophia was to be in no doubt that the best position she could attain in Waller's affections was a secondary one, as the poet explained in his 'To Amoret':

> . . . I will tell you how I do
> Sacharissa love, and you.
>
> If sweet Amoret complains,
> I have sense of all her pains;
> But for Sacharissa I
> Do not only grieve but die . . .
>
> Sacharissa's beauty's wine,
> Which to madness doth incline:
> Such a liquor has no brain
> That is mortal can sustain.
> Scarce can I to heav'n excuse
> The devotion which I use
> Unto that adored dame . . .

Hearing the news that Dorothy had married the nineteen-year-old Henry, Third Baron Spencer, at the Sidney family home of Penshurst in 1639, Waller was generous in accepting she had gone from him for ever, and wrote to one of Dorothy's sisters:

May my Lady Dorothy (if we may yet call her so) suffer as much, and have the like passion for this young Lord, whom she has preferred to the rest of mankind, as others have had for her; and may this love before the year go about make her taste of the first curse imposed on womankind, the pains of becoming a mother. May her first born be none of her own sex, nor so like her but that he may resemble her Lord as much as herself. May she that always affected silence, and retiredness, have the house filled with the noise and number of her children, and hereafter of her grand children; and then may she arrive at that great curse, so much declined by fair ladies, old age. May she live to be very old, and yet seem young; be told so by her glass, and have no aches to inform her of the truth: and when she shall appear to be mortal, may her Lord not mourn for her, but go hand in hand with her to that place where we are told there is neither marrying nor giving in marriage; that, being there divorced, we may all have an equal interest in her again. My revenge being immortal, I wish all this may also befall their prosperity to the world's end, and afterwards.

When the Spencers were married, they went to live with Dorothy's parents in France, where her father was ambassador. Only on the conclusion of Lord Leicester's mission in October 1641, did the family group return to England – an England that was in seething turmoil, since tensions between Charles I's court and the Parliamentarians were reaching their peak.

Within days of arriving back in the country, Henry had taken his seat in the House of Lords. He soon found himself being courted by both political factions with as much ardour as his wife had inspired among her many suitors. Henry's position was complex: his wealth, influence and human qualities were such that he could be assured of prominence whichever party he fell in with. His problem lay in deciding which should have his support. By inclination, he was liberal, against the Crown's increasingly frequent abuses of the burgeoning democratic system in England, and a believer in the inviolable rights of the people. However, taking a belligerent stand against his monarch was anathema to him.

In 1642 the Parliamentary party offered him the Lord Lieutenancy of Northamptonshire, in the hope that Henry would consolidate the sympathy that that Midland county was demonstrating for its cause. The turmoil of the times is shown by the fact that the Northamptonshire Lord Lieutenancy, a post that usually rested with an individual for several years, in 1642 was occupied by four different men.

Henry accepted the position, but not for the reason that the Parliamentarians had offered it. He abhorred the divisiveness that the extremists in the two opposing factions were trying to exacerbate, and hoped that the power he would enjoy as Lord Lieutenant would help him to bring about appeasement and understanding in his native county, while allowing him to push for the same in the nation's Parliament.

Those in the Parliamentary faction who wanted outright conflict with the court latched on to the fact that Charles I seemed to have become inaccessible to them and their grievances, and complained that this showed his inability to be a wise and considerate monarch. Henry, while wishing that the King would become more directly involved in addressing the Parliamentarians' grievances, was also appalled by the excessively aggressive stance that he thought Charles's opponents were taking. In the Lords, Henry was among the first to advise that a more conciliatory approach might harvest more positive and mutually satisfactory results.

From the snippets of his speeches that survive from this time, we hear Henry counselling that those who were worried by the King's apparent withdrawal from the centre of political life should 'lure him home by their loving behaviour, and not to do so as those troublesome women who by their hideous outcries drive their wandering husbands further off'. Later, angrier at the predicament that he believed some in Parliament were unnecessarily bringing about, Henry said that he did not pity 'them that bemoaned his Majesty's distance', even though they seemed to expect to be commended for their patience 'under so great a punishment'. In Henry's eyes, they deserved to be condemned for having sought the King's approbation.

By the summer of 1642, it was evident that Parliament and King were headed for almost certain armed conflict. In his final speech before leaving the Lords, Henry fired a parting salvo at those who had helped to foster an atmosphere that would bring the monarch and the people's representatives to such a state, through demands so unreasonable that they could never have been met: 'We had been satisfied long 'ere this, if we did not ask things that deny themselves; and if some men had not shuffled demands into our propositions on purpose that we may have no satisfaction.'

Henry left London accompanied by his kinsman, Spencer Compton, Earl of Northampton, to join the King at Nottingham, on 22 August 1642. Charles had raised his standard there, calling for his supporters to rally to him. Soon afterwards, Parliamentary forces from Northampton occupied Althorp, much to Henry's concern.

But the unreasonable stance of the Parliamentary leaders, combined with his belief in the obligation he had to protect his monarch, had persuaded Henry that his was the only right course, even though he had no personal sympathy with Charles or his advisers. Those who had been his closest colleagues ideologically in the House of Lords – Northumberland and Essex – went to take their places at the head of the Parliamentary cause.

If Henry Spencer had expected to find less selfish intent in the King's camp, he was quickly disappointed. A letter of 21 September 1642 to Dorothy displays his disgust at his new-found comrades-in-arms:

My dearest Hart,

The King's condition is much improved of late. His force increaseth daily, which increaseth the insolencie of the papists. How much I am unsatisfied with the proceedings here I have at large expressed in several letters; neither is there wanting daily handsome occasion to retire, were it not for gaining honour: for, let occasion be never so handsome, unless a man resolve to fight on the Parliament side, which, for my part, I had rather be hanged, it will be said a man is afraid to fight. If there could be an expedient found to salve the punctilio of honour, I would not continue here an hour. The discontent that I, and many other honest men, receive daily is beyond expression.

By this stage the royal army was comprised of 6,000 infantry, 1,500 dragoons and over 2,000 cavalry. Both sides were busy increasing their strength for the coming conflict. Henry hoped it would not come to actual bloodshed, but he despaired as he witnessed the determination of the Roman Catholics among Charles's close advisers not to have any conciliation with Parliament, with its significant Protestant sympathies. In desperation, Henry managed to see the King alone outside Birmingham in October 1642, and spent over an hour pleading with him to reach a settlement with the enemy. Charles was not strong enough to ignore the self-serving persuasions of his less honest advisers, and politely thanked Henry for his counsel, while putting it firmly to one side.

Later that same month, the first major battle of the English Civil War took place near Wormleighton, at Edgehill. An inconclusive affair, the encounter was marked by the success of the Royalist horse in sweeping through its Parliamentarian counterpart. Henry, serving in the King's Life Guards, was conspicuous in his bravery that day, taking a prominent role in the dramatic cavalry charge.

Henry Spencer's loyalty, combined with a gift of £10,000 to the royal coffers to help fund the war, led to his being raised to the earldom of Sunderland, on 8 June 1643. It was a title that had briefly belonged to the Scrope family, which had first achieved prominence in the reign of Edward II, when William, Lord Scrope, of Bolton, had been Chief Justice of the King's Bench. His descendant, Emmanuel, Lord Scrope, was made President of the King's Council in the North in 1618, under James I. Charles I had promoted him to become Earl of Sunderland in 1627, but Emmanuel died without a legitimate heir in 1640, leaving the title extinct. Charles decided to revive it by conferring it on his Spencer supporter. However, Henry did not enjoy his elevation for long.

The new Earl of Sunderland attached himself to the forces of Prince Rupert of the Rhine, Charles's flamboyant nephew and commander, and was present when the Prince's forces captured the important city of Bristol in the summer of 1643. From there, Henry rode to join Charles at the siege of Gloucester – even though he thought the King wrong to be side-tracked by the attempted reduction of a county town, when the Royalists should have been trying to bring the Parliamentarians to a conclusive set battle. Henry reported his reservations to Dorothy: 'The King's going to Gloucester is, in the opinion of most, very unadvised: the Queen unsatisfied with it; so is all the people of quality.' The siege had not been properly planned, and the King's lack of judgement and leadership convinced Henry that the war was an increasingly regrettable, unnecessary affair.

Above all, Henry missed his Dorothy. On 25 August 1643, from his quarters outside the besieged Gloucester, he transmitted his utter loneliness to his wife:

Writing to you, and hearing from you, being the most pleasant entertainment I am capable of receiving in any place, but especially here, where, but when I am in the trenches (which place is seldom without my company) I am more solitary than ever I was in my life . . .

Many of the soldiers are confident that we shall have the towne within this four days, which I extremely long for; not that I am weary of this siege, for really, though we suffer many inconveniences, yet I am not ill pleased with this variety, so directly opposite as the being in the trenches, with so much good company, together with the noise and tintamarre of guns and drums, with the horrid spectacles, and hideous cries, of dead and hurt men, is to the solitariness of my quarter, together with all the marks of peace, which often brings into my thoughts, notwithstanding your mother's opinion of me, how infinitely more happy I should esteem myself quietly to enjoy your company at Althorp than to be troubled with the noises, and engaged in the factions of the Court, which I shall ever endeavour to avoid.

Henry's colleagues were wrong about the vulnerability of Gloucester. It successfully survived the Royalist siege, and Charles ordered his army to strike camp in the first week of September. Henry was in no doubt as to the significance of the setback, and its accompanying waste of valuable campaigning time:

I am afraid our setting down before Gloucester has hindered us from making an end of the war this year, which nothing could keep us from doing if we had a month's more time which we lost there, for we never were in a more prosperous condition . . .

Increasingly disillusioned, Henry had by this stage made two resolutions to himself: the first was never to be parted from his King during the war, so he could help protect the monarch whenever Charles was commanding his forces in person; the second was never to accept a commission in the Royalist army. His conscience told him he, personally, must serve his monarch, but he had no wish to take a commanding role in an army whose aims and ethics ran counter to his own and led him into direct conflict with people whose values were closer to those of his own conscience.

The Royalists regrouped in their stronghold of Oxford, the scene of Henry's student days a few years earlier. From here, on 16 September 1643, Henry wrote to Dorothy:

I cannot, by walking about my chamber, call any thing more to mind to set down here; and really I have made you no small compliment in writing this much, for I have so great a cold that I do nothing but sneeze, and my eyes do nothing but water, all the while I am in the posture of holding down my head. I beseech you present his service to my lady, who is most passionately and perfectly yours, Sunderland.

Four days later, Henry was dead.

The Battle of Newbury was fought on 20 September 1643. It was not one of the more significant encounters of the Civil War, but it did see the deaths of several young noblemen. Henry Spencer, First Earl of Sunderland, was struck by a cannon ball in the groin, dying in slow agony. His body was taken to The Chequers coaching-house at nearby Speenhamland, where it was laid out with those of Lords Carnarvon and Falkland, prior to being taken away to be buried, his bowels interred on the battlefield itself, his heart preserved for posterity in a lead casket packed with mortar.

Lord Clarendon, the great contemporary historian of the war, recorded that the King's cavalry at Newbury 'charged with a kind of contempt of the enemy, and with wonderful boldness, upon all grounds of inequality; and were so far too hard for the troops of the other side, that they routed them in most places'. With sadness, he also recorded Henry's demise:

The Earl of Sunderland, a Lord of great fortune; tender years, being not above three and twenty years of age; and an early judgement; who, having no command in the army, attended upon the King's person, under the obligation of honour; and, putting himself that day in the King's troop, a volunteer, was taken away by a cannon bullet.

It was agreed among commentators that this was a great loss to the country, as well as to the King. In his *Memoirs of the Loyalists*, Lloyd wrote of the qualities that had died with Henry, calling the fallen young nobleman 'a good patriot upon all other occasions as one of them at Westminster observed; promoting the trade, manufactures, and privileges of this country; and now standing by his Majesty as he evidently saw him stand for his kingdom'.

The all-round virtues of this 'true nobleman' were trumpeted, as his death was mourned:

A good neighbour; the country about him, when he had occasion to make use of it, being his friends that loved him, rather than slaves that feared him; A discreet landlord, finding ways to improve his land, rather than rack his tenants: A noble housekeeper, to whom that ingenuity that he was master of himself was welcome in others: An honest patron, seldom furnishing a church with an incumbent till he had consulted the college he had been of, and the Bishop he lived under: An exemplary master of a family; observing exactly the excellent rules he so strictly enjoined; consecrating his house as a temple, where he ordered his followers to wrestle with God in prayer, while he wrestled with the enemy in fight.

Dorothy's devastation was total; on learning of Henry's fate, she lost the baby girl she had been carrying. Her physical and mental health plummeted, and her family feared for her wellbeing. Dorothy refused to leave Althorp, or to see anyone. Lord Leicester, her father, wrote to her in an attempt to bring her out of her misery:

Your reason will assure you that, besides the vanity of bemoaning that which hath no remedy, you offend him whom you loved if you hurt that person whom he loved. Remember how apprehensive he was of your dangers, and how sorry for any thing that troubled you. Imagine how he sees that you afflict and hurt yourself. You will then believe that, though he look upon it without any perturbation, for that cannot be admitted by that blessed condition wherein he is, yet he may censure you, and think you forgetful of the friendship that was between you, if you pursue not his desires in being careful of yourself, who was so dear unto him.

Her father's advice seems to have had an impact on Dorothy: she took over the running of Althorp herself, and ensured that it remained a bastion of Royalist support in a county that was predominantly Parliamentarian. Lloyd wrote of Dorothy: 'She is not to be mentioned without the highest honour in this catalogue of sufferers, to so many of whom her house was a sanctuary, her interest a protection, her estate a maintenance, and the livings in her gift a preferment.'

State papers of the latter 1640s bear this out, regularly referring to problems encountered by Parliamentary troops with the Althorp Estate:

October 27, 1646. Deposition of Capt. John Warren – That about St James' tide, 1643 Capt. Otway with his troop was marching from his quarters from Northampton to Coventry by Althorpe House, in Co. Northampton when a horse being tired he sent to Lord Spencer's house, who was an active enemy to the parliament and slain in the King's army at Newbury fight, for another horse, but being refused, the Captain marched thither, who also being refused he conjectured that some eminent cavalier might be in the house, and resolved to force an entrance, which was with some danger effected . . .

By 1649 the Royalists had lost the English Civil War, and Charles was imprisoned across the valley from Althorp, at Holdenby, the Midland palace his father had given to him in order to bring his royal son under the influence of Robert, First Baron Spencer. Holdenby was a huge mansion then, but it did not have a bowling green. Bowling – along with chess and praying – being one of Charles's favourite pastimes, the King was a frequent guest at the green at Althorp. Indeed, it was during such a visit as guest of Dorothy Sunderland, that Charles learned that a force of Parliamentarian troops had arrived to take him away to London. Charles was subsequently tried, and then beheaded at Whitehall –

where, thirty-odd years earlier, he and William, Second Baron Spencer, had innocently celebrated Charles becoming Prince of Wales.

We get a glimpse of Dorothy's defiant attitude to the Puritan masters of England, who dominated the country in the 1650s, in her appointment in 1654 of Thomas Pierce as rector of Brington. At a time when the military and religious forces of Cromwell's Commonwealth were happy to resort to violence in an effort to eradicate dissension from the state-approved practices of religion, Dorothy patronized one of the most able and eminent contro-versialist writers of the time. Pierce was known to be unashamed in his outspokenness, and to be possessed of a fiery temper. Cham-pioned by Dorothy Sunderland, he never shirked from attacking other, more compliant preachers in the locality, with considerable effect.

By the time the Stuarts were restored to the throne in 1660, Pierce's reputation was so well established that Charles II sub-sequently made him King's Chaplain. He went on to become Canon of Canterbury, and then President of Magdalen College, Oxford – Henry Spencer's alma mater. When he died in 1691, it was as Dean of Salisbury. He could trace his rise in the Church back to the bold endorsement of Dorothy Sunderland, who gave him a living when a more timid patron would have plumped for a less controversial candidate.

Dorothy's self-assuredness was also evident in the way in which she looked after Althorp, while her son Robert was in his minority. The lack of respect that both warring parties had for great houses was shown to her in 1646, when Royalist troops from the Banbury garrison burnt down the Hall at Wormleighton. By that stage the Warwickshire family home was a massive affair – occupying several times the square footage of Althorp – and the Royalists feared that it might be taken by the Parliamentarians and used as a fortress by them. With nobody from the family there to protest, the original home to the Spencer family was all but annihilated. Today, one wing survives, and that has had to be made whole again with stone, leaving only one side in the original Tudor red brick.

Althorp's neighbouring mansion, Holdenby, also suffered appallingly during the war. After its sale by order of Parliament in 1650, the bulk of it was destroyed in an attempt to eradicate such a dramatic symbol of royal power. A small section of the house and two gateways where the principal court had been, together with a range of lesser buildings, were all that remained, along with various obelisks and arcades in the grounds. The parkland around Holdenby was stripped of its timber, to complete the desecration of what had been one of the great houses of the English Midlands.

Dorothy managed to see that no such devastation overtook Althorp. In this she was aided by her husband's uncle, Sir Edward Spencer, whose conversion to Puritanism had so appalled his brother William, but whose influence was now used for the preservation of the family home and its contents. Edward did not fight in the Civil War, but he was still of sufficient influence on the Parliamentarian side to be able to protect his nephew's widow and children. When he learned of Henry's death, he had immediately gone to Dorothy to console her in her bereavement. Further compassion and practical support from the Parliamentarian side was provided by Dorothy's brothers, Lord Lisle and Algernon Sidney.

Dorothy was close to her family and deeply respectful of her parents. When her father, Lord Leicester, decided that the best thing for his grieving daughter would be remarriage, she yielded to his request to end her widowhood with a second husband. Dorothy married Robert Smythe, of Roundes, in the parish of Bidborough, Kent. Smythe was from the family of the Viscounts Strangford, of Ireland, and was considered a safe second husband for the countess, although his social standing was not as exalted as her own. There was a child: Robert, who became Governor of Dover Castle during the reign of Charles II. However, this was not the love match that she had enjoyed with Henry.

There was to be no distracting Dorothy from looking after her first husband's bequest. She was responsible for the dramatic transformation in Althorp, from Tudor to Stuart style, covering over the old open courtyard in the centre of the house with a roof, and ordering the construction of the broad and handsome wooden staircase that has been the main feature of the Saloon over the last three centuries.

Smythe predeceased Dorothy. In her second widowhood, she met the poet Edmund Waller again and teasingly asked her erstwhile admirer when he would write more fine verses to her, his 'Sacharissa'. Waller looked at the elderly figure before him, and replied, perhaps jokingly, but also perhaps with the satisfaction of the avenged: 'Oh madam! When your ladyship is as young again.'

After her death in 1684, Dorothy was laid beside the remains of her beloved Henry, in Brington church – final recognition of the fact that her true loyalty had remained with him throughout the four decades that they had been forcibly separated.

Of all my ancestors' tales, the doomed love story of Henry and Dorothy has always been the one that has moved me the most. When I was young, I would look at his portrait at the head of the Saloon staircase, his long dark hair flopping down round his handsome pale face, his torso encased in the armour that proved inadequate against the fateful cannonball that ended his life so prematurely. In his death, the futility and horror of civil war is encapsulated, for this was a man fighting to the end for a cause that he abhorred, but prevented by his concept of chivalric honour from drawing his sword for his political ideals.

As for Dorothy, left without her soulmate for two-thirds of her life, and persuaded to enter a marriage that in every sense was a secondary one, pity merges with sympathy for her truly tragic plight, while respect and admiration are due to her for the pride, confidence and aplomb with which she marked her remaining years.

# 7. Products of their Age

Henry and Dorothy Spencer, First Earl and Countess of Sunderland, were people of the highest possible character, prized by contemporaries for their ability to conform to the ideals of nobility and graciousness expected of the aristocracy at that time. It is therefore puzzling that their combined genes produced an heir as far removed from all that they individually stood for as can be imagined, a man so shameful in his conduct that, nearly 300 years on, my father would talk about him with an ashamed, resigned chuckle. I was brought up to be proud of my ancestors, but here was an exception that brought shame and dishonour cascading down the bloodline.

Two living children came from Henry and Dorothy Sunderland's four-year marriage. The daughter, also called Dorothy, married Sir George Savile, afterwards the Marquis of Halifax. The son, Robert, who inherited his mother's great beauty, was to become perhaps the most politically powerful Spencer of them all – while simultaneously ensuring his name would be a byword for deviousness and self-interest. Macaulay captured the spirit of the man with three words, 'cunning, supple, shameless', adding that Robert Spencer, Second Earl of Sunderland, was endowed with 'a restless and mischievous temper, a cold heart, and an abject spirit'. In this, he was the product of his age.

The latter half of the seventeenth century and the first half of the eighteenth was a time of great insecurity in England. The concept of the republic as demonstrated by the Commonwealth under Oliver Cromwell, which dominated the 1650s, was discredited, and there was widespread joy at the coronation of Charles II in 1660. Parliament and King co-existed with tolerance until the mid-1670s, when well-founded doubts arose about Charles's trustworthiness and intentions. These tensions were increased by Charles's financial difficulties, and by the prospect of his brother and successor, James, Duke of York, being increasingly flagrant in his attachment to Roman Catholicism. In time, this was to lead to revolution, the second Stuart king in three generations being removed from the throne, this time not through execution, but by replacement by a foreign prince. The consequent presence of an entirely plausible rival court, across the Channel in France, made generations of politicians in England decide that the only way they could pursue power while not risking their lives, should the Stuarts return, was by openly displaying loyalty to their monarch, while secretly pandering to his greatest enemy.

Robert Sunderland's character was perfectly suited to this unethical code of self-preservation and self-advancement. Some excuse for his character defects may perhaps be found in his fatherless upbringing. Certainly his tutor would have been surprised at how his charge turned out, if we judge by his glowing assessment of the young Robert:

His choice endowments of nature, having been happily seasoned and crowned with grace, gave him at once such a willingness and aptness to be taught, that reconciled his greatest ease and pleasure; and made the education of his dear lord, not so much his employment, as his recreation and reward.

It is hard to pinpoint exactly when Robert's personality took its decisive turn for the worse. As a young nobleman, he had shown himself greatly appreciative of the treasures of European civilization, during his 'Grand Tour'. This was a traditional finishing off of the young aristocrat's education, giving him a chance to learn artistic sensibilities which would, it was hoped, stand him in good stead in later life, encouraging the patronage and acquisition of fine objects for the family collection.

Some privileged young men saw the opportunity of travelling on the Continent with a tutor and servants, and without direct family supervision, as an opportunity to enjoy the brothels and bars of Europe, and the conduct of such 'milords' was infamous throughout France, Italy and Germany. Robert, however, was genuinely intrigued by the art he saw, extending his time abroad repeatedly, and he was imbued with a taste for collecting, the results of which are still to be seen on the walls of Althorp today. Apart from Sarah, Duchess of Marlborough, he was the main contributor to the collection there. Indeed he designed the dominant style of frame to be seen at Althorp – the 'Sunderland frame', with its swirling swathes of gold.

But even the aesthete in Robert was to be tainted by his lack of scruples. For he found that his expensive tastes could not be readily funded by his Spencer inheritance, and so he became susceptible to bribery and corruption of the worst kind, even resorting to treason in his quest to afford great art.

Robert's early career did not allow him to fall prey to such temptations, for his influence was not at that stage worth buying. It did, however, increase his exposure to European culture: in 1671, he became ambassador extraordinary to the court of Madrid, followed, in the autumn of 1672, by a similar posting in Paris, in the footsteps of his maternal grandfather.

By this stage, he was already marked out as a man of potential, attracting this secret assessment from Louis XIV's minister, Colbert:

The Earl of Sunderland will without fail depart tomorrow to wait on your Majesty. He is a young gentleman of high family; has a great deal of frankness, courage, parts, and learning; is also extremely well intentioned, and strongly disposed to become a Roman Catholic.

The following year, 1673, Robert was appointed one of the plenipotentiaries for the Treaty of Cologne, and, in 1674, he achieved his initial ambition of becoming a member of the Privy Council – the key royal advisory body – in London. This was a stepping-stone to his ultimate goals, the highest offices in the land. Robert realized that he must be patient; attaining them would require a careful strategy. Between 1674 and 1678, he enjoyed no official court or political role other than his Privy Councillorship, but he used those years to watch and to learn, to see who was allied with whom, and whose influence he should harness for his own ends. He saw that the Treasurer, Thomas Danby, was a man worth cultivating, and became one of his allies.

By the mid-1670s, Charles II was in a position that would have been quite familiar to his father and grandfather. The Stuart kings' reluctance to be beholden to Parliament was contrary to the desire of the Members of Parliament to establish themselves as an integral part of the government of the nation. James I and Charles I had summoned Parliament only in order to use its tax-raising powers. This they had done with increasing reluctance, as Parliament's reciprocal demands became increasingly bold.

Charles II was to suffer from the same dilemma: he needed money, and yet he could not abide what he believed to be the intrusions of mere Members of Parliament in his God-given privileges. While Charles had enjoyed the services of the Earl of Arlington as his secretary of state from 1662 to 1674, it had been possible for him to exercise some indirect royal control over many in Parliament. However, between 1674 and 1679, there was nobody to take a forceful role on the King's behalf.

Determined to bypass the need for money, and therefore the necessity of asking Parliament to fund him, Charles II decided to enter into a secret arrangement with his country's greatest enemy, Louis XIV of France. This was because Louis shared two things with his English counterpart and cousin: first, a belief in the complete autonomy of the monarch; and, secondly, the Roman Catholic faith. Both principles struck the majority of English Parliamentarians, and the wider landed and middle classes of England, as dangerous threats to the wellbeing of the nation. Well into the eighteenth century, until his death after the War of the Spanish Succession, Louis was therefore perceived to be the greatest threat to England's safety and stability. He actively fought Protestants abroad, and forcefully exiled them from his own kingdom. Of even greater concern to the English, he was to provide a welcome home for the displaced Stuart claimants to the English crown, even funding various forays to try to place the exiled James II, and his son, born the Prince of Wales, back on the throne. For Charles to enter into a financial deal with the greatest enemy his people had was the most treacherous act he could have performed. To ensure that it remained secret, he needed to find somebody who not only would treat the matter with the utmost confidentiality, but who also would not be so smitten by his conscience that he simply could not go through with such a betrayal of his compatriots. On both counts Robert Spencer, Second Earl of Sunderland, proved to be the perfect go-between.

In July 1678, Sunderland returned to Paris in an ambassadorial role, but with Charles II's underhand scheme as his prime concern. He duly arranged the secret payments to Charles from Louis, giving himself the power over the King that was to lead to his becoming, in 1679, the main secretary of state to the monarch. At the same time, Robert established links with the French court that were to be highly lucrative for himself, when he, too, became available for sale to his country's arch enemy. In Sunderland's case, this was to be an annual bribe of £5,500.

The influence that Louis was securing, through this payment, was that of Sunderland as the more powerful of the two secretaries of state. There was no prime minister of England during the Stuart age. Nor, in the modern understanding of the word, was there a cabinet: the 'cabinet council' that existed was not reflective of the majority opinion of the House of Commons, as it is designed to be today; neither was it of crucial importance in policy-making. Its lack of importance as a force and as a concept is shown by the fact that the king could ignore its advice when it met; and, with both Charles II and James II, this was what often happened. Indeed, the standing of the cabinet council could hardly have been lower in the three years of James II's reign, when the King preferred to consult just Sunderland and a posse of Roman Catholic advisers: the Jesuit, Petre, and Lords Arundel and Powis.

Louis XIV was therefore not buying Sunderland in order to gain control of the cabinet, since that would have been money wasted. Secretaries of state could not deliver up a pliant cabinet through the power of their office. And, as we have seen, persuading the cabinet to unite was neither an easy objective nor a decisive conclusion. What Louis wanted was Sunderland's direct access to the King of England's ear – something he enjoyed completely from

1679 to 1680 and from 1683 to 1685 under Charles II, and from 1685 to 1688 under James II. There were other periods when he was a force in the kingdom, but these were his glory years – in terms of his power, that is, rather than of the ethics of his conduct.

For an example of how dependent such a senior government figure was on the King's favour, one has only to look at the ease with which the mighty Sunderland was dismissed in 1680. This was because he had voted in favour of the Exclusion of the future James II from the English throne for his Catholic beliefs. A political miscalculation of this magnitude on Sunderland's behalf – Sir William Temple noted that the secretary of state was acting not only 'against his master's mind, but his express command' – led to Charles II going so far as to order that Sunderland's name be erased from the list of the Privy Council; this, even though probably no secretary had previously enjoyed such power before, having established an unprecedented control over the Privy Council. This had been achieved through starting to institutionalize his position at the head of a recognizable hierarchy, through the initiation of a recognizable structure of public government, which involved regular salaries being paid to political office holders, the concept of a proper business organization, and continuity of tenure of office.

Sunderland was aware that as much control as possible over the Privy Council was an effective way of consolidating his influence. This, combined with the control of intelligence information that came to the secretaries of state, was the cornerstone of Robert's power, but his real gift was in making his ruler believe that he was indispensable. The proof of his success lay in the fact that he persuaded three such different monarchs – the outwardly Anglican but secretly Catholic Charles II, the fervently Catholic James II, and the Protestant champion, William III – all to turn to a man they knew to have no scruples, but whose political gifts they needed, just as surely as he craved the trappings and financial benefits of office they gave him in return.

There are several pivotal moments in Robert Sunderland's career which demonstrate his extraordinary lack of principles and his ability to survive politically. The first came in the wake of the Duke of Monmouth's unsuccessful rebellion against James II. Monmouth had been one of the conspirators in the Rye House Plot of 1683, in which the prospect of murdering Charles II and James had been entertained. While two of the leaders of the plot, Russell and Sydney, were executed, Monmouth was sent into exile.

Monmouth was a royal bastard, the natural son of Charles II, which largely explains this leniency. He had joined with Sunderland and the Duchess of Portsmouth to bring down Danby after Sunderland had been appointed principal secretary of state in 1679. However, he had clearly learned little about his erstwhile political ally, if he expected their past unity of aims to count for anything when he truly needed Sunderland's help.

On James II's accession in 1685, Monmouth planned a rebellion to place himself on the throne. His forces arrived from the Netherlands in June of that same year. Sunderland, as administrative director of the army, passed James's orders to his forces in the west. On 6 July, Monmouth was routed at the Battle of Sedgemoor, and he was captured and sent to the Tower of London, while his forces were brutally dispatched by the victorious Stuart army and judiciary.

Monmouth was not over-concerned by his incarceration, for he felt confident that he would once again be spared the ultimate sanction for treason. But this confidence was misplaced, because it relied on Sunderland standing by his word – for Sunderland had secretly promised Monmouth a pardon, should he confess nothing during his interrogation. Doubtless this was because, had Monmouth told the entire truth about his plans, he would have revealed that Sunderland had been secretly negotiating with him, in case he was successful in his insurrection.

By the time Monmouth had destroyed his own credibility by contradicting himself repeatedly during questioning, Sunderland realized that he needed to be rid of a man who could expose his own double-dealing, and quickly. Sunderland intercepted a letter written by Monmouth to the King, and had it destroyed, ensuring James never knew of its existence. There was to be no question of Monmouth's being allowed to live any longer than was strictly necessary. His execution was not long in coming; this for a man who had had a personal guarantee from Sunderland, the King's chief minister, that his life would never be in danger because of his sworn protection.

The second illustration of Robert's true character took place in 1686, the second year of James II's reign, when Sunderland was locked in a power struggle with Edward Hyde and his supporters, to become James's chief adviser. Robert had lost favour under Charles II for voting publicly against the possibility of a Catholic heir succeeding to the English throne. However, with such a prize as supreme political power in the nation within his grasp, Sunderland was happy to convert to Catholicism – something the more principled Hyde just could not bring himself to do. Grateful that his minister had come over to what he sincerely believed to be the true faith, James duly invested Sunderland with the pre-eminence that he sought. However, James was well aware of the depths of treachery Sunderland was capable of, writing in the same year that he promoted him: 'Sunderland, besides having a pension from the Prince of Orange, had one also from the King of France. He was the most mercenary man in all the world: veered with all the winds.'

James was not so fickle. However, his dogged promotion of Catholicism was bringing him into ever sharper conflict with the predominantly Anglican political class, as well as with the Church of England itself. The position became strained beyond breaking point when the two Protestant daughters of the King, Princess Mary and Princess Anne, were superseded in the succession by the birth of a little boy, the Prince of Wales, on 10 June 1688. It was believed that James would doubtlessly bring him up to be a Catholic king. As a result, an invitation was sent to Princess Mary's Dutch husband, William of Orange, to come to England to usurp his own father-in-law.

To some extent, William and Mary were to owe their throne to Sunderland's treachery. James found out only after William was on his way to England that his most senior and most highly rewarded adviser had been playing his usual double game, and dismissed him on 27 October 1688. James later discovered that Sunderland had been communicating regularly with William via Sunderland's uncle, Henry Sidney, who was James's representative at The Hague, in the Netherlands. In order to cover his tracks, Sunderland had persuaded James to command that all foreign ministers, including Sidney, correspond solely and directly with Sunderland.

In what became known as the 'Glorious Revolution', James II and his supporters slipped off to France, and the reign of William and Mary began, with remarkably little English blood having been spilt.

This could have marked the end of Sunderland's life, let alone his career. He was widely hated, and was known to be a man of the lowest possible moral calibre. However, he was merely disgraced, and exiled. Almost unbelievably, within five years he had inveigled himself back into royal favour, not only as William III's confidant, but also as a key figure in the control of the liberal Whig politicians, with whom the Spencers were to identify strongly over the next 230 years.

There were no official parties in English politics at this time, but the definable difference between Whigs and Tories was becoming apparent: the Whigs, keen to check abuses of royal power and champions of the rights of the people at large; the Tories, ardent royalists and stolid supporters of the Anglican Church as a cement for the Establishment as a whole.

Before Robert, the Spencers had long shown sympathies that would later be termed Whig – hence the ghastly irony of the death of Robert's own father, fighting beside people whose cause he decried, while being slain by his ideological compatriots – but it was the Machiavellian Robert Spencer, Second Earl of Sunderland, who established his family as one of the key Whig aristocratic dynasties over the succeeding quarter of a millennium.

His Whig sympathies alone would have been enough to have made Princess – later Queen – Anne uneasy about Robert Sunderland. Although, during her own reign, Anne did support a Whig ministry while Sarah Churchill, Duchess of Marlborough, was her favourite, Anne felt more at ease with the Tories. Yet her dislike of Sunderland went way beyond the political; it was deeply personal.

Her letters on the man are as damning as it is possible to be. During her father James's reign she wrote to her sister Mary:

You may remember I have once before ventured to tell you that I thought Lord Sunderland a very ill man, and I am more confirmed every day in that opinion. Everybody knows how often this man turned backwards and forwards in the late King's [Charles II's] time, and now, to complete all his virtues, he is working with all his might to bring in Popery. He is perpetually with the priests, and stirs up the King to do things faster than I believe he would of himself.

Princess Anne's opinion of Robert's wife was equally low. Anne was the daughter of George Digby, Second Earl of Bristol, who had been a Royalist general in the English Civil War, and of Lady Anne Russell. According to Louis XIV's envoys in England, Barillon and Bonrepaux, Anne Sunderland was the lover, during her marriage, of Henry Sidney, reputedly the handsomest man of his time, but also her own husband's uncle. Sidney was a renowned ladies' man, and was, according to Burnet, 'a man of sweet and caressing temper, and had no malice in his heart, but too great a love of pleasure'. Extramarital affairs were certainly not uncommon at court at this time, though Sidney's and Anne's lack of discretion over the matter was considered shoddy. But it was not Lady Sunderland's questionable sexual morality that attracted the Princess's condemnation, but rather her general character; reservations she was prepared to communicate to her sister, Princess Mary, with the utmost candour:

His lady [Anne] too is as extraordinary in her kind, for she is a flattering, dissembling, false woman; but she has so fawning and endearing a way that she will deceive anybody at first, and it is not possible to find out all her ways in a little time. She cares not at what rate she lives, but never pays anybody. She will cheat, though it be for a little. Then she has had her gallants, though may be not as many as some ladies here; and with all these good qualities she is a constant Church-woman, so that to outward appearance one would take her for a saint, and to hear her talk you would think she was a very good Protestant; but she is as much one as the other, for it is certain that her lord does nothing without her.

This led to Princess Anne's withering conclusion that, 'Sure there never was a couple so well matched as she and her husband, for as she is throughout all her actions the greatest jade that ever was, so is he the subtellest workingest villain that is on the face of the earth.'

It was not to be long, though, before even she would be drawn into Robert Sunderland's web of influence. First, he managed to secure for one of his daughters, Lady Anne Spencer, a court position with the Princess. This was a less than successful appointment: not only did Lady Anne spend months unable to perform her duties, being constantly ill, but, even when in healthy attendance, she was treated with open distrust by her employer, 'knowing from whence she comes'.

Secondly, during the reign of William and Mary, which began in 1688, there were strong tensions between the rival royal courts of the two sisters. To Robert, a divided royal house was something to be avoided. He meant to straddle the current and future reigns with the minimum of fuss, so he made it his mission to smooth over the differences. Unsurprisingly, when one takes into account his previous record of being able to ingratiate himself even with those who knew he was totally untrustworthy, Robert managed to bring about a measure of reconciliation in the mid-1690s. According to Anne's favourite, Sarah Churchill, Sunderland 'showed himself a man of sense and breeding' in his dealings with her mistress at that time.

The death from smallpox of Queen Mary in December 1694 was seen by Sunderland as the perfect opportunity to bring a full *rapprochement* between King William III and his sister-in-law Princess Anne. With Sunderland's encouragement, Anne wrote her brother-in-law a letter of condolence. Soon after, again at Sunderland's behest, William offered Anne the use of St James's Palace, as fitting accommodation for the monarch-in-waiting.

Given Anne's hatred of Sunderland, clearly stated in her correspondence of a few years earlier, it is testimony to his diplomatic skills that, on her own accession to the throne in 1702, Queen Anne settled a £2,000 per annum pension on Sunderland, out of gratitude for his help during the previous years.

As a family man, Robert was less successful than in his professional life. He and Anne suffered the loss, as was common at the time, of children in infancy: their third son, Henry, and fourth daughter, Mary, dying soon after their respective births. And Isabella, the third of the four daughters, died before marriage. Of the four children who survived into adulthood, the eldest son – and heir – Robert, Lord Spencer, was to be one of the most dissolute young men of his generation. The eldest of seven children, he was born in 1666 and went up to be educated at Oxford in 1680.

We learn something of his character at that stage from his grandmother, Dorothy, First Countess of Sunderland, in a letter to Lord Halifax:

He has no good nature, nor good humour: he is scornful and too pretending . . . He comes to me seldom, seems weary in a minute, talks of my company as if I picked them up off the streets. My Lord Sunderland [her son, Robert, Second Earl of Sunderland] at his age did nothing like it. He will be spoiled, I can see it.

In 1688, the diarist John Evelyn reported good things of the second Spencer son, Charles – 'a youth of extraordinary hopes, very learned for his age and ingenious, and under a Governor of extraordinary worth' – but he qualified that praise with a less sanguine look at the heir to the Sunderland title:

Happy were it could as much be said of the elder brother, the Lord Spencer, who, rambling about the world, dishonours both his name and family, adding sorrow to sorrow, to a mother who had taken all imaginable care of his education: but vice, more and more predominantly, gives slender hopes of his reformation . . .

Evelyn was put in an invidious position when he had to judge between his allegiance to Anne, Second Countess of Sunderland, and his justifiable disregard for her first-born. Robert and Anne's high living had left the Spencer family finances in some disarray, Robert's taste for gambling compounding the problems brought about by their extravagant lifestyle and constant pursuit of artistic acquisitions.

Anne decided that the simplest solution would be to marry her eldest son to an heiress. She therefore asked Evelyn to effect an introduction, with a view to a match being made, between Robert Spencer and Jane Fox, the daughter of Sir Stephen Fox, a millionaire financier. Evelyn, though always keen to stay in favour with prestigious society hostesses, judged that Robert was such a liability that he simply could not get involved, even if it meant incurring her ladyship's displeasure. As he himself recorded:

Come my Lady Sunderland to desire that I would [make] a match to Sir Stephen Fox for her son, Lord Spencer, to marry Miss Jane, Sir Stephen's daughter. I excus'd myself all I was able for the truth is I was afraid he would prove an extravagant man: for though a youth of extraordinary parts, and had an excellent education to render him a worthy man, yet his early inclinations to extravagance made me apprehensive that I should not serve Sir Stephen by proposing it like a friend: this now being his only daughter, well bred, and likely to receive a large share of her father's opulence.

Robert Spencer's remaining years were to show that Evelyn deserved the undying gratitude of Sir Stephen Fox, as Robert degenerated into a life of boorish – indeed, drunken and violent – behaviour. In August 1685, with his father one of the most important people in the kingdom, Robert and two friends went round to the home of the Earl of Carnarvon – whose forefather had perished with Robert's own grandfather at Newbury – and whipped him. According to Sir Edmund Verney, the aristocratic trio also indulged in 'some other peccadillos in his [Carnarvon's] castle besides'.

This escapade resulted in Robert being sent abroad by his family, in temporary banishment. But if the Spencers had hoped he would return a changed man, it was to prove a forlorn hope. Within a year, we find Sir John Reresby noting, 'My Lord Spencer is not well by the ill usage he and the rest of his company received from the constables and watch three nights ago, being upon a high ramble.' Far from bridling at the thrashing his son had received from these officers, Robert Sunderland only grumbled, 'It was pity it was not worse.'

Robert Spencer's life was now unravelling fast. His father tried to channel his aggressive instincts, and put some structure into his son's life, by buying him an officer's commission in the army. It was not enough. In March 1687, young Robert exceeded even his usual ability to disgrace himself, interrupting a church service in Suffolk with his sword drawn, uttering profanities, and attempting to pull the preacher out of the pulpit. The congregation rushed to the priest's defence, pummelling the errant young aristocrat, stripping his clothes off his back, and subjecting him to further humiliations.

Robert had inherited a modicum of the persuasive charms of his father, and he knew how to ingratiate himself to his monarch. He showed great contrition for his appalling behaviour, and simultaneously claimed that he had been converted to Roman Catholicism. This was – as Robert well knew – bound to be a popular development with James II. Sure enough, the King now asked Spencer to represent him on a diplomatic mission to the Duke of Modena, brother to the Queen, Mary. But this was trust unwisely placed. Robert headed straight for the whoring and drinking places of Paris, and indulged himself to such an extent that, by the time he reached Turin, tales of his excesses were widely known.

Living at such a pace took its inevitable toll. Spencer was unable even to reach Modena, being too ill to complete his mission. He stayed for several months in Turin, before retracing his steps to Paris. It was to be his final trip; and it was suitable that he should end his days in this city, which had witnessed the most excessive behaviour of a truly spoilt and irresponsible youth. He died on 16 September 1688, the Marquis de Dagneau recording in his diary:

'Milord Spencer, fils aîné du Comte de Sunderland, est mort cette nuit à Paris pour avoir trop bu d'eau de vie.'

Anne, Second Countess of Sunderland's match-making skills may have been stymied by John Evelyn's good judgement, with regard to her eldest son, but she got her way with her daughter Elizabeth, whom she forced into a child marriage with Lord Clancarty, an Irish nobleman of enormous landed wealth. The lack of love in the relationship is underlined by the fact that, after several years, the union remained unconsummated.

Clancarty was a Jacobite sympathizer, supporting the deposed James II against William III and Mary in Ireland. With the failure of the Jacobite campaign, Clancarty was declared an outlaw, and so he fled to the exiled Stuart court at St Germain. The Clancarty estates in Ireland were confiscated, and handed to William III's favourite, Portland.

Anne Sunderland was appalled that her daughter's marital wealth had been taken from her, and planned ways of having it restored to her through the pardoning of Clancarty. It was decided to encourage Clancarty to come to consummate his marriage, the assumption being that his father-in-law, Sunderland, could then persuade William III to grant him a pardon, which, in turn, would lead to the restitution of the Clancarty estates.

At the end of 1698, Clancarty sneaked into England to fulfil the marital obligations that had previously been beyond him. However, his brother-in-law, Charles Spencer, reported the whereabouts of the outlawed Clancarty to the authorities, and the latter was arrested while in the unaccustomed position of being in bed with his wife.

With his usual inclination for self-preservation over integrity, Robert Sunderland publicly distanced himself from the ensuing scandal by disowning the innocent in this sorry tale, his daughter Elizabeth. However, Sarah Marlborough joined Anne Sunderland in seeking clemency for Clancarty, and she being the right-hand woman of Princess Anne, William yielded, pardoning Clancarty, while allowing him a pension on the condition that Irish peer remain abroad for the rest of his life, and that he no longer base himself in the enemy Jacobite camp.

Elizabeth Clancarty decided that the scandal had made her continued life in England too grim to contemplate, so she accompanied Clancarty into exile in Hamburg. She was never happy there, but it was where she spent the remainder of her very sad life. At least her marriage was consummated and she did become a mother, although she died before her eldest reached the age of six.

The Clancarty affair had occurred after Robert Sunderland's retirement from active political life. He had resigned his positions in 1697, the year in which he had been made Lord Chamberlain and a Lord of Regency, much to the disappointment of William III, who still believed him an indispensable adviser and ally, despite the cries of the Tories, who never left their monarch in any doubt as to their horror that such a man should have the King's ear.

Robert Sunderland lived out the remaining five years of his life at Althorp, surrounded by the spoils of his treacherous, self-seeking career. On his death, in September 1702, even a supporter such as Sarah Churchill, Duchess of Marlborough, had to concede that Robert 'had really a great many good qualities, with some bad ones'.

Bishop Burnet was similarly generously disposed to the wily statesman in death, summing up his gifts and shortcomings thus:

Lord Sunderland was a man of a clear and ready apprehension, and a quick decision in business. He had too much heat, both of imagination and passion, and was apt to speak very freely both of persons and things. His own notions were always good, but he was a man of great expense and . . . he went into the prevailing counsels at Court, and he changed sides often, with little regard either to religion or to the interests of his country. He raised many enemies to himself by the contempt with which he treated those who differed from him. He had indeed the superior genius to all the men of business that I have yet known; and he had the dexterity of insinuating himself so entirely into the greatest degree of confidence with three succeeding Princes, who set up on very different interests, that he came by this to lose himself so much that even those who esteemed his parts depended little on his firmness.

Within a few years of Robert Sunderland's death, Queen Anne's Whig ministry decided to commission the writer Edmund Smith to chronicle the history of the 1688 Revolution, showing the Whig influence in the event to its best possible effect. When being told his task by Addison, Smith retorted, 'What shall I do with the character of Lord Sunderland?' The implication was clear. Smith would have to address the deviousness and treachery of this most eminent of Whigs, if he were to give the full and true version of events; and yet that would show the Whigs in such a poor light, that the point of the propaganda exercise would clearly be severely compromised. Rather than deal with Sunderland and his disgraceful conduct, it was agreed that the history should not be written.

Perhaps that is, in itself, the most fitting and eloquent testimony to a man about whom 'too much cannot be said of his talents, nor too little of his principles'.

# 8. The Spencer–Churchill Match

Charles Spencer, Third Earl of Sunderland, was tall and plain, his skin pitted with scars from smallpox. Very highly sexed, he was to have three wives, several mistresses, and at least one illegitimate child. Contemporary gossip also had it that he was bisexual.

Although free from the hard living that had resulted in his elder brother's premature end, he had his own particular shortcomings, among which his hot temper was perhaps the most marked. Charles had incurred the grave displeasure of his father when, in his capacity as Member of Parliament for Tiverton, the young man had exploded during a debate that he 'hoped to piss upon the House of Lords'. Sarah, Duchess of Marlborough, assessed him as having 'no more genteelness than a porter'. Even his own mother – who doted on her children – conceded that Charles had too much 'heart and overearnestness' in his politics.

And yet his father's intellect and statesmanship had been inherited in full. He was to prove almost as significant a political force in the reigns of Queen Anne and, later, King George I, as his father had been in those of Charles II, James II and William and Mary. Although he was to be accused of financial impropriety, his character was superior to his father's in terms of his having a genuine sense of public duty.

Charles's initial political career was certainly hindered as much as it was helped by his father's notoriety. Queen Anne, although she had become respectful of the influence Robert Sunderland had wielded, and had agreed to pay him a pension on her accession, had never wavered in her personal hatred of the man, and this intensity of feeling she readily transferred to his only surviving son.

In terms of the history of the Spencer family, as opposed to the history of England, Charles Sunderland's true significance lies in the choice of his second wife; or, more accurately, in the identity of his second mother-in-law: for Sarah Marlborough was the greatest benefactor, in material terms, that the Spencers have ever prospered from, and her manipulative machinations set the tone for the conduct of the family for generations after her death, helping to establish them in parallel splendour at Blenheim and at Althorp.

Having been unexpectedly widowed in July 1698, losing the former Lady Arabella Cavendish – daughter of the Second Duke of Newcastle – when he was in his early twenties, Charles Sunderland found himself once again one of the most eligible bachelors in the country.

By this stage, John and Sarah Churchill, First Duke and Duchess of Marlborough, had achieved the pre-eminence that was to make them dominant figures in court and in foreign policy over the next dozen years, until they fell out with Queen Anne in a spectacular and irreversible manner.

Charles Spencer's mother, Anne Sunderland, never shy of pushing forward her children when a good match was in the offing, did not even have the patience or decency to allow her daughter-in-law's death a month's mourning before going to see Sarah Marlborough about the possibility of her giving one of her four daughters to Charles as a second wife. Lady Anne Churchill was only fifteen but, apart from clearly being a frail girl, she allied the eminence of her parents with their very fine looks, to make her a more than worthy match for the Spencer heir.

As for Sarah Marlborough, she was keen to establish her family as a dynasty, her four adult daughters clocking up two dukes and two earls as husbands. Indeed, of her seven granddaughters, five would become duchesses, one a countess and one a viscountess. In Charles Spencer, she smelt not only aristocratic lineage, but also huge political potential. What was more, that potential was as a leader of the Whig party, of which she thought herself a champion.

The Spencer–Churchill marriage took place in January 1700, both families having retreated to Althorp the preceding September to negotiate a suitable financial settlement. Sarah Marlborough, now at the peak of her influence over Princess Anne, managed to persuade the future queen to help to fund the match – a considerable achievement, bearing in mind Anne's dislike of the groom and his family. Given that another Churchill daughter was already married to the son of Lord Godolphin, who was to be Anne's Treasurer, Sarah Marlborough had ensured that her family, in its broader sense, now contained a core of the most able and significant Whig politicians of the time. No wonder that Robert Walpole predicted that the Spencer–Churchill union would 'certainly be turned to politics as every thing is'.

It would be fair to say two things at this stage: first, that the marriage into the Churchill family was the most significant that the Spencers were to make until the late twentieth century, for the matriarch under whose strict control the Spencers now found themselves for forty-four years did more to shape the family's fortune than anyone had done since the very early Warwickshire sheep farmers of the fifteenth and sixteenth centuries. And secondly, that Sarah remains one of the most intriguing and controversial women in British history.

Sarah Marlborough's dynastic ambitions can be traced back to her own family background. Born a week after the day of Charles II's Restoration in 1660, Sarah was the daughter of an impoverished gentleman from St Albans, Richard Jennings; in turn he was one of the twenty-two children of Sir John Jennings and Alice Spencer, a daughter of Sir Richard Spencer of Offley, a cousin of the Spencers of Althorp. There is no suggestion that this Spencer link in any way disposed Sarah to be as generous to her kinsmen as she was to be, but given the way in which she focused on her Spencer grandchildren as the key to her hopes and aspirations, it is a link worth noting.

The feistiness, independence and pride of Sarah, together with her inability to control her own passions, were themes that would resurface sporadically in generations of Spencer women. Also, Sarah's ravishing, glowing looks, with her golden-auburn hair, her fine skin and her natural *hauteur*, were to cascade down the female generations to follow. It seems her genetic stock has been as powerful as her character, and I believe that, in Sarah Jennings, you have the blueprint for the second half of the Spencer family history.

Her early years were conventional enough. Like any pretty daughter of a county family eager to increase its financial and social standing, she was sent to court to find a suitable match. Aged only thirteen, she was appointed one of the four maids of honour to James, Duke of York's, second wife, Mary of Modena. Vivacious and fine-looking, Sarah was extremely popular in court circles, but she was also clever enough not to become one of the many girls who were seduced and discarded – often pregnant – by the nobles and courtiers who preyed on the naïve young things who could be easily flattered and deceived.

It was during her teens that Sarah's dissatisfaction with the falseness and emptiness of court life first emerged, and with it a growing questioning of the wisdom of monarchs who oversaw and indulged in what she perceived to be a meaningless existence. Although not formally educated to any standard at all, Sarah was naturally intelligent enough to find the gossip and endless card-playing stultifying, and the constant waiting on the whims of spoilt royals, who assumed it was a privilege merely to be at the beck and call of their Highnesses and Majesties, was insulting and tedious to her. As a letter in middle age to Lady Cowper reveals, it did not take the spirited Sarah long to see through the sham that was court life:

I think anyone that has common sense or honesty must needs to be very weary of everything one meets with in Courts . . . I protest I was never pleased but when I was a child, and after I had been a Maid of Honour some time, at fourteen I wished myself out of the Court as much as I had desired to come into it before I knew what it was.

If court life did have one invaluable consolation for Sarah, it was in fulfilling the hopes of the family that had sent her there. She met, fell in love with and married a man who would rise to high rank and huge fortune, but his successes would be as much thanks to his wife's abilities as to his own. Indeed, his gifts may well have been largely ignored were it not for Sarah's unstinting efforts on behalf of both of them.

John Churchill was twenty-five, and Sarah Jennings fifteen, when they met. He was one of the eleven children of a Dorset gentleman, Sir Winston Churchill. As a young man of twenty-two, John Churchill had been caught in bed with the Duchess of Cleveland, one of Charles II's mistresses, who had taken a liking to the handsome youth ten years her junior. Banished from court by the furious King, Churchill embarked on a military career which Napoleon himself later esteemed one of the seven most distinguished in world history.

Ironically, given the fact that Churchill's later successes were to be against Louis XIV, he served what was effectively his military apprenticeship under the French marshal, Turenne. From 1672 to 1674, Churchill developed his huge talents in the service of this great general, and particularly distinguished himself at Maastricht. Even more ironic was the fact that Louis XIV, watching this engagement, personally congratulated Captain Churchill for his bravery at the head of his troops, and promised that he would commend Churchill to Charles II. On his return to England, he was promoted to the rank of lieutenant-colonel in the Duke of York's regiment, a step closer to the commander-in-chief's role that was to cost Louis's army so dear thirty years on. He was also awarded the court position of Groom of the Bedchamber, in which role he was to meet the ravishing Miss Jennings, who described her beloved as 'handsome as an angel'. They married in 1681.

The secret to Sarah's power lay in the closeness of her friendship with Princess Anne. Where Sarah was beautiful, Anne was plain; where Sarah was a life-enhancing force, Anne was plodding and dull. Anne, as princess and queen, craved the approval and support of her glamorous friend, and made her her most intimate confidante. Sarah used her favour to secure posts in the court, politics and the army for her wider family and friends, enriching herself considerably in the process – chiefly through the custom of selling favours and positions.

There was something of the schoolgirl crush about the Anne–Sarah relationship. The letters they wrote to one another were very intimate, and the two women even used pseudonyms for one another, to heighten the feeling of conspiratorial intimacy: Anne was 'Mrs Morley', while Sarah was 'Mrs Freeman'.

Sarah and John Churchill, despite the material benefits they had derived from the goodwill of James II, were prepared to side with the invading William of Orange in 1688's 'Glorious Revolution'. To James, this was a betrayal almost on a par with that of Robert, Second Earl of Sunderland's. Whereas Sunderland had been a key political adviser, Churchill was one of his senior army officers, as well as a companion who had accompanied James in his exiles to Scotland and Flanders, prior to his accession to the throne. It was also Churchill who had, during Monmouth's rebellion, been largely instrumental in the decisive royal victory at Sedgemoor.

Sarah justified her decision to side with William by choosing to present it as one of religious principle, rather than the pursuit of further advancement for her and her husband under the new regime; a regime under which, it was already evident by the mid-1680s, Princess Anne was probably to be heir, since William and Mary were childless. 'I had seen so much of the cheats and nonsense of that religion,' she claimed in 1704, when blaming James's overt Catholicism for his unacceptability as monarch, 'that it gave me a greater prejudice to it, than it is possible for any body to have that has never been in a Catholic country.'

Sarah's Whig beliefs also made her implacable in her hatred of Charles II's and James II's abuses of royal power, in particular their treacherous acceptance of secret 'pensions' from the French Crown. As Dr Frances Harris observed of Sarah, 'It was her lifelong conviction that no sovereign was to be trusted and that Parliament remained the true guardian of the constitution by its power to punish erring ministers . . .' The manner in which the later Stuart kings behaved only reinforced her beliefs in this regard.

Sarah strengthened her position further with Anne during the revolution, by helping her to escape the guards that James had had posted outside his own daughter's quarters. It was a key moment in the success of the Glorious Revolution and, in 1689, grateful for the support shown to his cause by the couple, William made the Churchills the Earl and Countess of Marlborough.

William III's readiness to accept the invitation of the English throne was largely tied in with his own ambition to stop Louis XIV of France becoming Catholic conqueror of Europe. The French armies had to be stopped, and the Netherlands and England were the cornerstone of an alliance that needed inspirational leadership if it was to withstand Louis's expansionist aims.

Marlborough was to be a key figure in the allied forces, and he left with William for the Low Countries in 1691, to take up his command. However, his and Sarah's positions were severely damaged early in 1692 when Marlborough was discovered to have been corresponding with the Jacobite sympathizers of the deposed James II. William took the opportunity to dismiss Marlborough from all his posts, and briefly send him to the Tower of London as a prisoner. It was not just the supposed Jacobite link that led to this, but also Marlborough's outspoken criticism of the Dutch monarch's promotion of his compatriots and other non-Englishmen to senior posts in the English military.

William was also wary of Sarah Marlborough because of her influence over his sister-in-law, Anne. With some reason, William saw Sarah as being behind Anne's increasing distance from, and hostility to, his court, while pressing her employer to establish her own party of politicians, along Whig lines.

And yet William's attempt to sideline the Marlboroughs was unsustainable. Sarah was so much her mistress's favourite that Anne proclaimed to Sarah that she herself 'had rather live in a cottage with you than reign empress of the world without you'. As long as Sarah could receive such love and loyalty from Anne, then there could be no ignoring the Marlboroughs. Consequently, they remained a force throughout the 1690s, and it was at the end of that decade that William agreed to allow Marlborough to become governor to Anne's son, the Duke of Gloucester, telling Marlborough, 'My lord, teach him to be what you are, and my nephew cannot want accomplishments.'

Indeed, William himself was forced to turn to Marlborough in 1701, when an army of 10,000 English troops was sent to the Continent to fight Louis XIV. Despite not trusting the moral integrity of Marlborough, William made him his commander-in-chief, and also invested him with powers to negotiate any peace treaty that might result from the military campaign. In William's reign the indispensability of Sunderland and Marlborough could not be ignored, whatever the King's misgivings about the loyalty of both.

The royal favour enjoyed by both members of the golden Marlborough couple was increased tenfold when Anne came to the throne on 8 March 1702. Within five days, Marlborough was made a Knight of the Garter – an honour pointedly refused him by William, who did not think Marlborough worthy of England's highest order of chivalry – as well as, the following day, receiving the appointment of captain-general of the country's military forces.

Meanwhile, Sarah's elevation was similarly dramatic. She became ranger of Windsor Park, a position which gave her a beautiful house within the grounds surrounding Windsor Castle. In addition she received the two senior court positions of Groom of the Stole and Mistress of the Robes, while also becoming Keeper of the Privy Purse. This marked the peak of Sarah's favour through Anne, for the basic differences between the two women – both in terms of temperament and of politics – began not only to be clear now, but, thanks to Sarah's power and pre-eminence, could no longer be ignored as eccentricities of little consequence.

Politically the two most powerful women in the kingdom were now further apart than ever. Whereas Anne felt secure with Tory support, with the ancillary bolstering she received from the Church of England, Sarah was convinced that the Tories were closet Jacobites, eager to restore the line of James II through his son, the Old Pretender, the one-time Prince of Wales. Sarah's other great fear was the French. However, while her husband was dealing so effectively with them on the battlefield, Sarah and Anne's differences could be subsumed through the mutual joy and relief they felt through Marlborough's great victories.

The first of these, Blenheim, in 1704, was the most devastating defeat ever suffered by Louis XIV. A combined French and Bavarian force was poised to overrun Vienna, and to knock the

Austrians out of the War of the Spanish Succession. But Marlborough's allied forces swooped down through central Europe and annihilated the enemy, driving many of them to their death in the waters of the River Danube, and capturing the two French commanders, Marshals Tallard and Marsin.

A grateful nation thanked Marlborough for delivering the balance of power in Europe to England by granting him and his heirs a pension for life, and by giving him what was to become the magnificent Blenheim Palace. The inscription on the monumental pillar in the grounds talks of Marlborough as 'the hero, not only of his nation, but his age', and goes on to describe how he

became the fixed important centre, which united in one common cause, the principal states of Europe, who, by military knowledge, and irresistible valour, in a long series of uninterrupted triumphs, broke the power of France, when raised to the highest, when exerted the most, rescued the empire from desolation, asserted, and confirmed the liberties of Europe.

Two years after the Battle of Blenheim, in 1706, Marlborough brought about the surrender of the greater part of the Spanish Netherlands by defeating the French at the Battle of Ramillies, although the duke was nearly killed during the two-hour engagement.

These were Marlborough's two greatest military achievements. One of the reasons why he had been able to act so decisively in both campaigns was because he knew, through his wife's unrivalled position, that he enjoyed enormous power and prestige, and this was respected by his allied opposite numbers. Similarly he had the undoubted support of Godolphin, a very close personal friend of his and Sarah's, and a minister whom Anne trusted and relied on above all others.

But the whole issue of Anne and Sarah's relationship, along with their political differences, was to be highlighted in 1706, a few months after Ramillies, through the question of how best to deal with the political ambitions of Charles Spencer, Third Earl of Sunderland.

By this stage, Charles Sunderland had established himself as a political force in his own right, having succeeded his notorious father in the House of Lords in 1702, after seven years in the Commons. Anne had recognized his growing importance in June 1705, when she sent him as Envoy Extraordinary and Plenipotentiary to the Emperor of Germany, to present her condolences on the death of Emperor Leopold I. In this role Charles had attempted to help sort out the differences between the new emperor and his subjects in Hungary. Out of these negotiations evolved the Treaty of Tyrnau.

Charles's involvement with European leaders continued when he accompanied Marlborough to the court of Berlin in November 1705. The victor of Blenheim and his Spencer son-in-law were received at the Prussian court with great reverence and respect. A similar trip to the Elector of Hanover's court was the first occasion on which Sunderland met the man he was later to serve as first minister – the future George I.

Back home in London, Queen Anne was becoming nervous of the increasing influence that she perceived the Whig party had established; for she believed that this could only be achieved at the cost of her own authority. Her worries were given greater urgency by the insistence that Charles Sunderland be appointed as one of the secretaries of state of the nation. The Whigs wanted this appointment as confirmation that Tory influence could be indefinitely kept in check. As Sarah Marlborough recorded in her memoirs, the Whigs 'chose to recommend him to Her Majesty, because, as they expressed themselves to me, they imagined it was driving the nail that would go'. The Whigs presented their request to Anne more palatably, as due reward for loyal support for the Crown. It was clearly hinted that such support could not be expected to continue long, without Sunderland's promotion to a post that had been familiar to his father.

For all the high regard that Anne had for Godolphin, not even he could initially persuade the Queen to make such a firm signal that she favoured one political faction over the other. In September 1706, Anne wrote to her Treasurer thus:

I do fear, for the reasons I have told you, we shall never agree long together, and the making him [Sunderland] secretary, I can't help thinking, is throwing myself into the hands of a party. They desire this thing be done, because else they say they can't answer that all their friends will go along with them this winter. If this be complied with, you will then in a little time, find they must be gratified in something else, or they will not go on heartily in my business. You say yourself, they will need my authority to assist them, which I take to be the bringing more of their friends into employment, and shall I not then be in their hands? If this is not being in the hands of a party, what is?

Anne had every justification in writing so strongly, and it is clear she had grasped how important it was for the Crown to remain above party politics for as long as was possible. Flair and intelligence Anne may have lacked, but her sense of the dignities and privileges attaching to her high office was very strong. The Queen was keen to profess herself an independent and determined lady, and this was one matter where she felt it important to let the strength of her feelings be known. As early as November 1704, she had written to Sarah Marlborough:

I have the same opinion of Whig and Tory that I ever had, I know both their principles very well, and when I know myself to be in the right nothing can make me alter mine. It is very certain there is good and ill people of both sorts, and I can see the faults of one as well as of the other.

Her instinctive feelings were reinforced by the subtle encouragement she was receiving from Robert Harley, Sunderland's enemy, and a self-avowed hater of a political scene comprising strong, self-serving rival parties. Harley claimed his own ambitions extended merely to wanting to promote 'the Queen's service'. Although he was later to be seen as one of the architects of the party political system in England, in 1706 he was able to write that to avoid

the rocks on both sides is to be the care of the Government and that it may not be like a door which turns upon its hinges from one side to another, or to shut out always somebody, ought to be the care of those that love the Government: for it is certain in such a country as ours [that] the going over to the extremes of one party only makes way to go again to another. For if a man can be turned out or put in for being of a party, that party is the government and none else.

When viewing the case for Charles Sunderland's promotion, an added worry for both Queen Anne and Harley lay in the fact that Sunderland was not some moderate – like Newcastle or Cowper – but a Junto leader; that is, one of the handful of key, fully committed Whig grandees, whose aims were undoubtedly party political in the modern understanding of the phrase.

Not being a committed Whig himself, Marlborough, deeply concerned that the question of Sunderland's appointment might result in his foreign campaigns not receiving the ready funding that they had enjoyed to date, took a conciliatory approach with his Queen, in an attempt to make her see his son-in-law's promotion as a necessary sacrifice, so that England could continue its pressure on Louis XIV on the field of battle. Marlborough wrote to Anne:

Madam, the truth is, that the heads of one party have declared against you and your government, as far as it is possible, without going into open rebellion. Now, should your majesty disoblige the others, how is it possible to obtain near five millions for carrying on the war with vigour, without which all is undone?

Marlborough hoped that the Whig Junto could be appeased by securing Sunderland his secretaryship, which would, in turn, result in him, as captain-general, being able to push ahead with the war. If the price of funding the campaigns was to be the Sunderland concession, then Marlborough was for that course of action.

Queen Anne saw this matter as a fundamental point of principle. The pressure on her to yield to the Whigs was immense: from the Junto, from Sarah Marlborough and from her two most powerful advisers, Godolphin and Marlborough. She felt the pressure so keenly that it reduced her to tears and nervous exhaustion. However, when Godolphin told the Queen that he would resign if she did not appoint Sunderland, she gave way.

The major political crisis was over, and Sunderland had achieved his aim on behalf of his fellow Whigs. Indeed, his new status allowed him to take a leading role, as a commissioner, in the union of England and Scotland in 1707. However, the cost was higher than was immediately realized by the triumphant Junto for the alienation between the Queen and Sarah Marlborough, from whose friendship the Junto's ascendancy could be traced, was no longer something lurking in the shadows, but was now out in the open for all to see, and for Sarah's enemies to begin profiting from.

Sarah Marlborough was famous for her temper. It was a passion that she never learned to control. The ultimately unacceptable side of her beguiling exuberance and freshness, it proved to be her undoing, both at court and in her dealings with those she professed to love.

There are several portraits of Sarah at Althorp, one of which captures her just after one of her furious outbursts, her long hair cut from her head, limply held in her hand. The artist, Godfrey Kneller, has caught Sarah in the aftermath of one of her attacks of spiteful anger, this time directed at the husband she knew loved her dearly, and who would frequently compliment her on the beauty of her hair. This explains why she had chopped the hair off – the thoughtless act of a spoilt girl, now a woman rich enough to commission an artist to capture her momentary madness for posterity. The slightly bug eyes are red-rimmed from tears, and the attempted expression of haughty disdain falls flat, and merely looks very sad. Apparently the conclusion of the tale behind this painting was to take place after the duke's death. Sorting through a chest of her husband's most treasured items many years after this tantrum, Sarah was deeply moved to find that same swathe of her hair carefully stored away with loving care, by a man who adored her despite her temperamental failings.

As she got older, and as she felt more powerful, Sarah's moods became more extreme and more frequent. They depressed and distracted Marlborough, as shown in a letter he wrote to her while in the campaign field in 1708: 'I do not say this to flatter you,' he wrote, 'nor am I at an age of making fond expressions, but upon my word, when you are out of humour, and are dissatisfied with me, I had rather die than live.'

This claim was borne out the following year, 1709, when Sarah was becoming obsessed with the way Anne was apparently slighting her. Sarah urged her husband to rally to her assistance; this, while the captain-general was trying to deliver a final knockout blow to the French. Marlborough was reportedly deeply distracted by Sarah's attention-seeking antics from across the Channel, and the expected victory, when it came at Malplaquet, was inconclusive and accompanied by an appalling loss of life on both sides. Marlborough himself was stunned by the bloodiness of the struggle, mourning 'so many brave men killed with whom I have lived these eight years, when we thought ourselves sure of a peace'.

Marlborough, aware that the allied losses at Malplaquet gave the Tories great scope for calling for an end to the war, and conscious that Sarah's less than respectful behaviour towards the Queen would only undermine the war effort further by driving Anne into the Tories' arms, eventually did write to Anne on his wife's behalf. The reply, written on 25 October 1709, shows how far matters had unravelled between the two women in three years:

I believe nobody was ever so used by a friend as I have been by her ever since my coming to the Crown. I desire nothing but that she will leave off teasing and tormenting me, and behave herself with the decency she ought both to her friend and Queen, and this I hope you will make her do.

The decisive break between Anne and Sarah came in 1710, with far-reaching consequences not only for the Marlboroughs, but also for their Spencer offshoots. Charles Sunderland saw the end might be coming, and urged Marlborough to see to it that Sarah prime Godolphin to stand fast, which, he hoped, would guarantee Anne would have to back down from any plans she might have to turn away from the Whigs. As Sunderland wrote to Marlborough at the end of March 1710:

Besides the danger to the whole, none of our heads are safe, if we can't get the better of what I am convinced Mrs Morley [Anne] designs; and if [the] lord treasurer can be persuaded [by Sarah] to act like a man, I am sure our union and strength is too great to be hurt.

In this assessment, Charles Sunderland was woefully mistaken. Within two months, he himself had been dismissed from his secretaryship of state. It was one of a series of changes that signalled the ascendancy of Harley and his Tories, and the demise of the Whigs; for Anne's new favourite was Abigail Hill, a cousin of Sarah's whom the duchess herself had brought into Anne's court, but who now enjoyed the Queen's confidence. Abigail was a Tory, as well as a relative of Harley's, and she helped encourage the transition of power that was to see the Marlborough–Godolphin–Sunderland triumvirate reduced to impotence.

Anne was aware that she risked losing her captain-general and her Treasurer, through the Sunderland dismissal, in a domino effect. The two men who had brought so much honour to her reign and her country had told her it would be an 'insupportable' move, in their view, to dispense with Sunderland's services. But Anne's fears of appearing weak made her stubbornly resolute. Dismissing a man as powerful as Sunderland had many attractions, one of which was being able to flatter herself that she had, four years on, stamped her royal authority on her overbearing politicians in a decisive and responsible manner. Informing Lord Somers, another member of the Whig Junto, of his colleague's demise, Anne told him 'that she was entirely for moderation, yet she did not intend to make any other alterations, but this was a resolution [that] she had taken for a long time, and that nothing could divert her from it'.

The Tories rejoiced at Sunderland's dismissal. Abel Boyer reported at the time: 'The High Church party were wonderfully pleased, and elated, upon this alteration, which they looked upon as a sure earnest, and forerunner of greater changes.' The Whigs retreated to Althorp in September 1710 to discuss their future tactics, knowing that they would be out of power after the inevitable dissolution of Parliament. As it transpired, this was the end of Marlborough and Sunderland's influence for the remaining four years of Stuart rule.

It is worth mentioning that, on his dismissal, Queen Anne offered Sunderland the sop of a £3,000 pension for life. In a gesture of noble self-denial that would have been anathema to his father, Charles proudly retorted that he was glad Her Majesty was satisfied he had done his duty, but if he could not have the honour of serving his country, then neither would he plunder it. This was a rare flash of selfless decency from an early eighteenth-century Spencer.

Meanwhile Sarah was utterly furious at what she perceived to be the cruel and ungrateful treatment of herself, her husband, their greatest friend and her son-in-law. In truth Sarah's own erratic behaviour was largely responsible for the mass fall from royal favour, yet Sarah refused to accept that she was to blame, preferring to believe that Anne had acted dishonourably and unjustly. The breakdown between the weak Queen and the arrogant courtier was formally recognized by both sides when, on 18 January 1711, Marlborough surrendered Sarah's key of office to Anne.

Sarah Marlborough has been seen as an early feminist, and it is indisputable that she did forge an independent course by the standards of the time. Her mother, Frances – a hatchet-faced crone, if her portrait at Althorp is a fair likeness – had insisted that her daughters be brought up with a sense of self-sufficiency as one of their central beliefs. In Sarah, this lesson manifested itself in her insistence on mastering her own business affairs; she always kept her burgeoning wealth separate from the considerable fortune of her husband.

Similarly, Sarah saw no reason why she could not be fully involved in politics, once declaring, in 1714: 'I am confident I should have been the greatest hero that ever was known in the Parliament House, if I had been so happy as to have been a man.' On another occasion she was to assert with bitter resignation: 'The things that are worth naming will ever be done from the influence of men.'

In her middle age, deprived of her influence at court, Sarah was more determined than ever to make her own independent mark as a woman by other means, acquiring property on a huge scale, and forcing herself, as a meddling matriarch, on the lives of those relatives around her who hoped to benefit from her wealth when she was gone. She was to become reputedly the richest woman in England, outside the royal family she so despised. This money gave her plenty of scope for her favourite pastime: dynastic scheming and manipulation.

The Marlboroughs' favourite child was Anne Spencer, Countess of Sunderland. As a couple, they had always been less than enamoured of their son-in-law, Charles Sunderland; increasingly so, as he treated their daughter more and more shoddily. There were political differences, too, which came to the surface particularly after the 1710 dismissal. Yet it was Sunderland's taste for prostitutes, his fathering of an illegitimate daughter, and the growing rumours of his bisexuality, which were the greatest causes of his alienation from the Marlboroughs.

Both Marlborough and his son-in-law headed families who had suffered greatly after their dismissals by Anne. The Marlboroughs had even felt obliged to spend an increasing amount of time overseas, knowing they were more appreciated there than they were in the homeland which they believed they had served so well. The enemies the couple had made in their years in favour now mercilessly attacked yesteryear's golden couple, particularly in print. In a sentiment that would not have been unfamiliar to one of her ill-fated descendants nearly 300 years later, Sarah, exhausted by the unremitting nastiness of the English press, left London in January 1713, saying: 'I really long as much to be out of this horrid country as I used to do to come into it.'

They returned on 1 August 1714 to find that Queen Anne had just died. Marlborough's military talents were acknowledged by the new King soon enough, and he was once again made captain-general of land forces, as well as colonel of the first regiment of foot-guards and master of the ordnance – the threat of a Jacobite invasion overcoming George I's initial fears as to how best to control Marlborough's famously rampant ambition.

The position was not made easier when both Marlborough and Sunderland were unexpectedly excluded from the core of George I's court. To their astonishment, neither was even on the list of Lord Justices, who were to oversee the wellbeing of the nation in the month and a half between the death of Queen Anne and the arrival of the first Hanoverian king of England.

Suspicion hung over Charles Sunderland, and it took rare diligence as a Privy Councillor, followed by a spell as Viceroy of Ireland, to reinstate him as a trusted royal adviser. Remarkably, Sunderland oversaw the obligations of his Irish position from England. He claimed he could not go to Ireland itself, because of problems with his wife's health – doubtless true, but also a convenient excuse for not being kept away from the hub of political life in London.

It was said that it was Sunderland who, at this pivotal stage in the Hanoverian attempt to establish themselves in Britain, was personally responsible for making it impossible for the Jacobites to mount a rebellion in Ireland in 1715, to coincide with the unsuccessful one that broke out then in England. As a reward, in February 1716, Sunderland was appointed a joint Vice-Treasurer of Ireland – a post he received for life, in a sole capacity, four months later.

At this juncture Sunderland was invited by George I to go to Holland and Hanover in the royal party. He clearly took the opportunity to ingratiate himself with the King for, in April 1717, Lord Townshend was ousted, and Sunderland was asked to form a new administration, along with Stanhope and Cadogan.

It was either side of this reinstatement in the political élite that Sunderland's problems with the Marlboroughs reached a climax. In 1716 his wife died. Anne Sunderland, her health always frail, had developed pleurisy. The ineptness of her physicians had led to a botched blood-letting, which left her suffering from a fatal exposure to septicaemia. Marlborough was devastated by the death of his daughter, and his sorrow may well have contributed to the debilitating stroke he suffered later in the same year, the effects of which he was never to overcome.

As for Sarah Marlborough, her grief was compounded by furious outrage when Charles Sunderland seemed altogether too hasty in remarrying, after her Anne's death. Only eighteen months into his second widowhood, he wed Judith Tichborne, a fifteen-year-old – the same age as his second oldest child – who was 'without a shilling and without a name'. With her customary fertility of imagination when angry, Sarah somehow convinced herself that Charles was partly responsible for Anne's death. She decided it was now her responsibility to take an active interest in the children of her dead daughter on her behalf, to see that their irresponsible father could not compromise the plans she had for them.

There were five children in this generation of the Spencer family: Robert, Lord Spencer, the heir to the earldom of Sunderland, born in 1701; Lady Anne Spencer, a year his junior; the Honourable Charles Spencer, four years younger than Anne; the Honourable John Spencer, born in 1708; and the baby of the family, destined to be the favourite of Sarah's twelve grandchildren, Lady Diana Spencer, two years John's junior.

In 1716, in a eulogy written on Anne Sunderland's death, J. C. Gent wrote of the Spencer quintet:

> Loving may they Live, mature in ev'ry charm,
> Strike ev'ry Eye, and ev'ry Fancy warm;
> Let Art and Nature join their forms to grace,
> And call the Mother forth in ev'ry Face;
> To them may Heav'n impart thy Virtues too,
> And teach them thy Example to pursue,
> Thy bright Perfections into each transfuse,
> And make thy Race the Theme of ev'ry Muse.

In only one of the five could it be said that Gent's hopes were successfully met.

# 9. The Manipulative Matriarch

When Charles Sunderland became Lord Commissioner of the Treasury in March 1718, the Spencer family that he headed was in financial turmoil. This was largely thanks to his own expenditure. Charles's particular weakness was not paintings, like his father, but books; he was the first Spencer bibliophile, and his excessive spending at book sales was famed throughout the literary world. He was also, like his father, a compulsive gambler. Sarah Marlborough was aware of both extravagances, and was most concerned that, with Charles clearly set on a third marriage, and with the prospect of yet more children, her daughter's offspring would not be sufficiently well provided for to fund the ambitions she had for her Spencer grandchildren.

Charles Sunderland had expected the Marlboroughs' vast wealth to provide for the children from his marriage to their daughter. He was to be disabused of this idea when the time came for a £10,000 marriage portion to be found for his elder daughter, Anne, to William Bateman, the son of a director of the very prosperous, but ultimately ill-fated, South Sea Company.

Although Bateman was not a choice that appealed to Sunderland, Sarah insisted that the father of the bride provide £5,000 of the marriage settlement himself. Sarah felt she had done more than enough by persuading George I to make Bateman a viscount, a concept that the King found very amusing, saying, after meeting the newly ennobled young man, that he could make Bateman a peer, but not even he could turn him into a gentleman.

Given the source of his new son-in-law's wealth, it was, ironically, the South Sea Company's disastrous collapse that was to be the dominant event in the remainder of Sunderland's ministry. Established in 1711 in a Tory attempt to bypass the Whig-dominated Bank of England, the South Sea Company, by the time of its demise, purported to be an attractive long-term investment for those prepared to stake their money against England's National Debt. The early investors made huge gains. Sarah Marlborough was one of the larger beneficiaries of the scheme, selling her and her husband's stock for £100,000 profit, just before many investors were totally ruined by the dramatic collapse in the company's value. She had recognized that it was not a process of investment based on any sound principles, rather on novelty value and greed.

That greed extended to those government ministers who were prepared to accept bribes to help keep share prices unrealistically high. Sunderland himself had allegedly received £50,000 worth of new stock, before the South Sea Bubble spectacularly burst, in 1720. Harried by his political enemies, who insisted on a full enquiry into the allegations against him, Sunderland reawakened his contacts with the Jacobites, so he could be sure of a bolthole somewhere, should a prison sentence be looming. By dint of a private understanding with his successor, Robert Walpole, Sunderland left his ministry the following winter, without facing justice.

There was to be no further resurrection of Sunderland's career. He fell ill in April 1722 and died within a few days, only in his mid-forties. His death had a different significance for different interest groups. William Bowyer, a contemporary printer, recorded in his memoirs:

19 April 1722. This day, about three in the afternoon, died Charles Spencer, Earl of Sunderland, which I note here, because I believe that by reason of his decease some benefit may accrue to this Library, even in case his Relations will part with none of his books, I mean, by his raising the price of books the higher now; so that, in probability, this commodity may fall in the market, and any gentleman be permitted to buy an uncommon old book for less than forty or fifty pounds.

The effect of Charles Sunderland's death on the political world of early Hanoverian England was somewhat more dramatic than these scholarly and mercenary musings. Lord Cardigan wrote to Lord Gower:

The death of my Lord Sunderland has very much disconcerted the measures of the court, and puts their affairs into some confusion. As soon as he was dead, the Executors and the Duchess of Marlborough sealed up his scrutore till his son returned from his Travels. But the Lord President of the Council [Lord Carleton], the Lord Privy Seal [the Duke of Kingston], and the two secretaries of State [Lord Carteret and Lord Townshend] came and tore off the seals, seiz'd what papers related to Publick Affairs, and carried them away, which all the world says, has put the Duchess into a very great passion, and she threatens them with a law suit. He has died in much better [financial] circumstances than his friends expected.

Now that her favourite daughter's family was no longer under the control of the man whom she and her husband had come to dislike increasingly, Sarah Marlborough decided to become the de facto head of the Spencer family, formally adopting Lady Diana, and taking firm control of the school careers of Charles and John, moving them from Eton to her lodgings in Windsor Great Park, with a tutor of her choosing.

When the Duke of Marlborough died in 1722, aged seventy-two, there was no son to carry on the Churchill name into the next generation. John, Marquess of Blandford, fourth of the duke and duchess's seven children and the eldest boy, had died of smallpox at the age of sixteen, in 1703. Charles, the youngest of the seven, lived only from 1690 to 1692.

Usually English hereditary titles can pass only through the male line. However, given Marlborough's extraordinary military achievements, Parliament agreed that the dukedom could be perpetuated through the direct female line if no male alternative existed, in an effort to keep the new creation alive. This meant that the second Churchill daughter, Henrietta, was now effectively the Second Duke of Marlborough and her son, William, the Marquess of Blandford, her heir.

However, the real power in the Marlborough family still resided with Sarah, thanks to her husband's will. She effectively controlled his £1 million estate, receiving a massive £20,000 per year pension and had the right to occupy Blenheim Palace, near Woodstock, and Marlborough House, in London, for life. On top of this, she had her own enormous wealth. She decided to use this power base to control her family; the twenty-two years of her widowhood were largely spent manipulating her children and grandchildren to her own ends. Given that her relations with her two surviving daughters, Henrietta, the Duchess of Marlborough, and Mary, the Duchess of Montagu, were frequently fraught, there seemed to be only one branch of her family on which she could focus particular attention with the prospect of minimal external interference: her orphaned Spencer grandchildren.

Sarah's main hope lay with Lady Diana Spencer. In 1723, Sarah praised the thirteen-year-old girl by claiming that she already possessed 'more sense than anybody that I know of my sex'. Certainly, Lady Diana appears to have been an exceptional girl. Blessed with looks and a fine temperament, she was even more attractive to prospective suitors because of her known closeness to the fantastically rich, and increasingly elderly and infirm, Duchess of Marlborough.

Sarah watched as the most eligible young men in the kingdom were pushed forward as potential husbands for Diana. The Duke of Somerset suggested his grandson, Master Wyndham. Lord Orkney's great-nephew, Lord Weymouth, was another contender; as was Lord Shaftesbury. But Sarah wanted somebody who combined wealth, title and political clout. Holding out for the right suitor was a risky tactic, a point brought home when Diana developed scrofula, an unsightly disease which disfigured her neck. But Sarah paid a top surgeon to reduce the effect of the condition and, in 1730, it was decided that the twenty-year-old girl was ripe for a proper launch on to the marital market. A £50,000 dowry was known to go with Diana, and this on top of contemporary reports which described her as 'amiable and graceful in her person, in her temper generous and affable, compassionate to the poor, by all beloved . . .' Sarah herself boasted that Diana Spencer was 'a treasure in herself besides what I shall give her'.

Outside the peerage, there was one contender who met all of Sarah's criteria for the perfect match with Diana: the Prince of Wales. Still deeply critical of the Hanoverian kings, Sarah was hardly any more enamoured of George II than she had been of his father. In 1737, John Percival, First Earl of Egremont, recorded a story in his diary which underlines the exasperating haughtiness Sarah reserved for her monarch:

Mr Capel Moore dined with me. He told me that the last time the old Duchess was at Court, which is long ago, the King spoke to her in English, but she replied she begged his pardon for not understanding him, because she knew nothing of French, giving him to understand he was too much of a German. Upon this he in a passion turned on his heel, and said so loud that all the room heard him, 'Why, I have been speaking English to you all this while'.

Sarah was more accepting of Frederick, Prince of Wales. Importantly, the Prince was the enemy of the Prime Minister, Sir Robert Walpole, the political figure most at odds with Sarah, and for whom she had reserved all her most bitter hatred. As William Eckhart Hartpole Lecky said of Frederick, 'He made his Court the special centre of opposition to the government, and he exerted all his influence for the ruin of Walpole.' This, allied with his social eminence, made the Prince an intriguing potential match for Diana.

Although exact details of this scheme are scanty, Horace Walpole recorded that marriage negotiations between Frederick and Sarah reached an advanced stage, a dowry of £100,000, and a date for the wedding apparently being agreed between the parties. However, Robert Walpole allegedly got to hear of the secret plans, and stymied them. The Prime Minister encouraged the King to find someone less politically threatening as a daughter-in-law, and so Frederick, aged twenty-eight, found himself tamely marrying the seventeen-year-old Princess Augusta of Saxe-Coburg.

On 5 February 1731 Sarah renewed the impetus behind the marriage campaign by giving a ball at Marlborough House for Diana. At last Sarah was successful for, later in the same year, Diana made a worthy if not spectacular match, when she married the Duke of Bedford's younger brother, Lord John Russell. Their married life together got off to a tragic start when, in 1732, Diana was thrown from a carriage when pregnant, the shock of the fall inducing the premature birth of a son, who did not live long.

Soon after this dreadful mishap, the Duke of Bedford died, without an heir, making Lord John the Fourth Duke and Diana his duchess. The new duke now focused obsessively on the need for an heir to his name and to Woburn, and he became deeply agitated when Diana had another miscarriage – this time through not looking after herself properly during the pregnancy.

In the spring of 1735 Diana felt changes in her body which she optimistically assumed to be her third conception. In fact the stirrings within her proved to be the harbingers of death, not life. What she had thought to be morning sickness was a malady of a more menacing kind, and she started to fade away. When Sarah visited Diana at Woburn, she looked at her favourite granddaughter and found 'Death in her Face'. On 27 September Diana died of consumption.

The obituary in *The Gentleman's Magazine* recorded Diana's qualities, and made particular reference to the fact that she was loved 'most tenderly by her Grandmother the Duchess of Marlborough', before even mentioning that she was also loved by her husband. Unbalanced by grief, Sarah acted with her customary aggression by accusing Bedford of being party to Diana's death – at which accusation the duke fainted – and then retired to her house at Wimbledon, where she had spent so many happy days with her favourite grandchild, rereading all the girl's letters to her, then tearfully burning them one after the other on a fire.

The septuagenarian Sarah was to become accustomed to seeing her grandchildren predecease her, in an age of poor medicine and sudden death. Diana's eldest brother, Robert Spencer, Fourth Earl of Sunderland, had died six years earlier, in Paris. The *Northampton Mercury* recorded mournfully on 6 October 1729:

Yesterday at two o'clock in the afternoon the corpse of the late Earl of Sunderland was landed at the Tower-Wharf from on board Capt. Taylor's sloop; the body was in a leaden coffin, the heart in a leaden case, and the bowels in a leaden urn. In the evening it was brought in a hearse, followed by a mourning coach, to his late dwelling house in Piccadilly.

From there, he was later removed to the family vault in Brington, near Althorp, his coffin 'faced with velvet'.

Sarah had adored Robert, once telling him, 'I hope I shall find in you all the comforts I have lost in your dear mother, whose picture you were once, and as I believe from what you write that you will act like a son, I shall have all the pleasure in the world in making you mine.' Indeed, as a boy, his likeness to his mother had been so great that Sarah had found it difficult to look at him after Anne Sunderland's death.

Sarah was fiercely protective of her grandson, when he succeeded to the Spencer titles on Charles Sunderland's death. The young man had an intriguing heritage. His father and paternal grandfather had been dominant figures in England for half a century, so much was expected of him in the political sphere, while his Marlborough blood and money marked him down for further attention from those who would use him for their own ends. Sarah warned him, as he returned to take up his inheritance from abroad, to treat with scepticism the ministers who would move to welcome him back in the country, 'who I know will court you very much in order to deceive you, and make you as they have done many noble men a tool of theirs to carry on their dirty work for mean pensions, and the hopes of preferment, as they call it in some places . . .'

Robert, the third successive head of the Spencer family to be addicted to gambling, was a willing pawn in his wealthy grandmother's scheming, relying on her munificence in return for accepting her directions as to how he should conduct his life. The old lady's wish that Robert should steer clear of a court position was yielded to when Sarah offered him a generous annual allowance instead of becoming a Gentleman of the Bedchamber. She had earlier arranged for Robert to be free of his father, and the Spencer purse strings, by ensuring that he had been included in Marlborough's will.

In truth, Robert Spencer, Fourth Earl of Sunderland, showed little promise or talent during his brief life. Even Sarah, in her more candid moments, knew that he was only good to her out of an overweening interest in her will, writing that, despite that,

I must be contented and make the best of those comforts I have left, and I do believe that whole branch [the Spencers] and Lady Anne Egerton [daughter of Sarah's fifth child, Elizabeth, the Duchess of Bridgwater] will be good to me, not only because I hope they are so in their natures, but most of them will want me, and my fortune is in my own power.

So Robert, as the head of the Spencers, 'the only branch that I can ever hope to receive any comfort from, in my own family', was the heir apparent to Sarah Marlborough's estate. His premature death, brought about by Parisian doctors bleeding him excessively when he was suffering from a fever, forced her to reconsider her options. The picture was further complicated two years later, in 1731, when she lost another titled grandson, William, Marquess of Blandford, heir to the dukedom of Marlborough. His death meant that the importance of the remaining Spencer family in Sarah's dynastic plans increased, as Charles Spencer, the Fifth Earl of Sunderland, Robert's younger brother, was now in line to be the Third Duke of Marlborough.

When the Third Earl of Sunderland had married Lady Anne Churchill, it had been settled that, if their eldest son ever became Duke of Marlborough, the second son would inherit the traditional Spencer estates in Northamptonshire and Warwickshire. While Blandford had lived, this had not been an issue. Now he was dead, and Henrietta, the Duchess of Marlborough, was fifty, it was time to sort out the division of Spencer and Churchill riches and titles that would follow Henrietta's death.

However, before that death occurred, an unforeseen set of circumstances took place. Charles, Fifth Earl of Sunderland, inherited the Spencer estate, living at Althorp, secure in the knowledge that this was a mere stepping stone to the even more impressive inheritance of Blenheim Palace. He also took possession of the Spencer home in London, Sunderland House, described in *A Journey Through England*, an anonymous gentleman-traveller's reminiscences, written in 1732, as the Palace of Charles, Earl of Sunderland . . . separated from the street of Piccadilly by a wall, with large grown trees before the gate . . . The greatest beauty of this palace is the library, running from the house into the garden; and, I must say, is the finest in Europe, both for the disposition of the apartments, and of the books . . . No nobleman of any nation hath taken greater care to make his collection complete, nor does he spare any cost for the most valuable and rare books.

This gives an idea of the extravagance and style that were part of the Fifth Earl of Sunderland's make-up. Further evidence of the same can be seen at Althorp where, during his four years in charge, many great and lasting alterations were made, most obviously to the Stables, which were pulled down, and replaced by a Tuscan-style Palladian building to accommodate the many hunters and grooms that the Fifth Earl needed for his favourite pastime, foxhunting.

Sarah Marlborough had an uneasy relationship with Charles Spencer, Fifth Earl of Sunderland. He reminded her of his father, the Third Earl, both in looks and stubborn temperament; she preferred her grandchildren good-looking and malleable. Sarah had tried to bring him under her control, hoping to divert him from the Spencer penchant for gambling, and she had attempted to instil in him a sense of the value of money, stressing the need as a student to study accounts and mathematics, rather than theology and the Classics. Sarah wrote to Charles's tutor in 1727: 'If a young man would make his fortune in this country he must make himself useful, and consequently some time or other, such a one as may be fear'd by ministers. Otherwise, there is nothing to be got here, but by such vile means as I would not receive life upon.'

However, Charles was too much of a wastrel to have time for his grandmother's advice on how to better himself. When Sarah packed him off to finish his education in an academy in Geneva, he concentrated on high living, rather than on academia. The bills that he amassed were substantially in excess of the £500 per year allowance given him in his father's will. Sarah wrote disapprovingly that Charles was 'much too expensive for a younger brother'. By the time Charles left Althorp in 1733, he had accumulated debts of

£30,000, and was spending more annually than the First Duke of Marlborough had managed to at the height of his pomp.

But, until that climax of extravagance was reached, the problem for Sarah lay in the fact that after Blandford's death the Fifth Earl had sufficient income to become the first Spencer grandchild not to be dependent financially on the controlling old lady's diktats; or, as the Fifth Earl himself put it, he was fortunate to 'be no longer obliged to manage that unloving, capricious, extravagant old Fury of a Grandmother'. During a not infrequent drunken episode, he claimed he wanted 'to kick her arse and bid her kiss his own'.

The relationship reached a trough after Sarah had encouraged him to marry in order to produce an heir. Monogamy was not something that appealed to him, for he claimed to be bored by any woman after only a few months. However, he eventually succumbed to Sarah's wishes, marrying in May 1732. The difficulty was, his wife was a daughter of Lord Trevor, who was an old enemy of the Marlboroughs from the days of the War of the Spanish Succession. Sarah had not been consulted about the match and in retaliation she rewrote her will; removing Charles's name from the list of beneficiaries, and taking pleasure in telling him of her actions.

Charles, feeling free for the first time in his adult life to tell his grandmother what he truly thought of her, sent Sarah a sizzling reply:

I received Your Grace's extraordinary letter last night, and I own my discerning won't let me see any reason in what Your Grace is pleased to say against my marrying; unless invectives are to be looked on as arguments ... In the passion Your Grace must be, when you wrote such a letter, all arguments would be of very little use. As for putting me out of your Will, it is some time since I neither expected or desired to be in it. I have nothing more to add but to assure Your Grace, that this is the last time I shall ever trouble you by letter or conversation.
I am Your Grace's grandson,
Sunderland.

Sarah was determined to have the final word. 'You end that you are my grandson,' she retorted, 'which is indeed a very melancholy truth; but very lucky for you. For all the world except yourself is sensible, that had you not been my grandson you would have been in as bad a condition as you deserve to be.'

In the last decade of her life, Sarah would have the satisfaction of seeing Charles Marlborough (as Sunderland now was) struggle, without her financial might to keep him afloat. He became increasingly dependent on moneylenders, and it looked to contemporaries as though he would end up penniless.

Sarah might have forgiven her prodigal grandson, if the difference between them had been caused merely by his indolence, and his wish to be independent of her influence; however, the Duchess never forgave treachery. Thus when, out of a wish for increased income, rather than because of any military or court ambitions, Charles Marlborough agreed to become the colonel of a West India regiment and a lord of the bedchamber, Sarah recognized that her own flesh and blood had been bought off by her arch enemy, Sir Robert Walpole, in whose gift both positions effectively were.

Through this great betrayal Charles Spencer, Duke of Marlborough, ensured that his grandmother's and his grandfather's great wealth would remain parted for ever. From that point onwards there was to be no hope of reconciliation with Sarah.

With Robert and Diana no more, and Charles as good as dead in her eyes, Sarah was left with two Spencer grandchildren. The elder one was Anne, born in 1702, who had married the banking heir that George I had so enjoyed creating Viscount Bateman. Anne was as strong in character and as clever in manipulation as her grandmother, the result being a toxic relationship between the two which caused both women tremendous hurt and damage.

Sarah suspected Anne of being prepared to stop at almost nothing in her efforts to control her brothers and sister – including, allegedly, procuring women for Charles and Robert. Anne also meddled dangerously in the sphere which Sarah believed to be very much her own preserve – the Spencer men's choice of brides. Sarah decided the only way to end this sort of interference was to ostracize Anne from her siblings. However, this tactic had markedly different results: whereas Diana was compliant with Sarah's wishes, Charles and John took a more independent line. Sarah received an anonymous letter on the subject, most probably written at Anne's behest; certainly it smacks of her characteristic forthrightness:

I know your Grace is mad, but if you ever have an interval do but consider what you are doing now in a family that you pretend to espouse, instead of making them considerable by being united which is of more consequence than all your ill gotten money, you are endeavouring to bring them in to as many quarrels as you have your self, brothers and sisters and all you would have quarrel, I think there is now of those that are in your power, but the Duke of Bedford and the Duchess of Manchester that you have not made infamous by quitting Lady Bateman's friendship only because you have taken a fancy against her. Is it not enough for you to exercise your pretty temper your self and for some atonement to your family, entail our money without your wickedness, and die as soon as you can.

Sarah could match Anne, spiteful sentiment for spiteful sentiment, calling her granddaughter 'the vilest woman I ever knew in my life; and deserves to be burnt'.

The result was that, at the end of her life, Sarah was effectively left with one Spencer grandchild on whom to pin her hopes: John. To be fair there was not much obvious potential in him. Like Charles, he had squandered his schooldays in Geneva by living well beyond his means and studying barely at all. Contemporaries recall the thirteen-year-old boy's excitement at setting off for the foreign academy, longing to be free of his grandmother's influence. The thought that this travel was based around a wish to improve his mind was a notion that seems never to have occurred to him.

Sarah was deeply dissatisfied with her Geneva initiative, and she decided to entrust John to a tutor, Humphrey Fish. It is through a letter she wrote to Fish that we catch sight of how important John now was to her: 'I am sure [I] wish him better, and love him more, than anybody that is now in the world.'

In the summer of 1728, master and pupil moved to Dijon, where they both became dangerously ill. Fish eventually died from a fever.

Sarah, although reassured that her 'Johnny' was not in the same danger, wrote to him: 'No words can express how dear you are to me, and I shall be in torture till I see you, therefore pray let it be as soon as you can come with safety.'

In the mid eighteenth century, political power was greatly influenced by the landowners in each locality. Woodstock, the constituency in which Blenheim Palace was built, was virtually a private fiefdom for Sarah, and in 1732 she effectively gave the parliamentary seat there to Johnny. But this was a Spencer with little interest in politics. Self-gratification was of more importance to him than public service; indeed, he was never actually to speak in the House of Commons, while a Member.

His vices were the usual ones for rich young aristocrats of the time – women, gambling, drinking – and did not attract much comment. However, his penchant for taking baths was a subject of amused derision among his social peers, because it was thought a decidedly odd thing to want to do for pleasure. The First Earl of Egmont's diary for 2 June 1732 records of Johnny:

It seems this young gentleman is fond of frequent bathing and has a bath in his house. By mistake a gentleman who came to see him was admitted while he was in the tub, whereupon making a short visit, he took his leave that he might not keep Mr Spencer too long in the water; but Mr Spencer out of a sprightly and frolicsome humour, leaped out of the bath, naked as he was, and waited on him down to the very street door. The Queen at her levee talking of this action as a very extraordinary one, my Lord Peterborough replied that Mr Spencer was a man of extraordinary breeding to acknowledge the favour of a common visit in his birthday clothes.

This perceived eccentricity aside, Johnny earned the respect of his contemporaries for standing by his brother, the Fifth Earl of Sunderland, when Sarah Marlborough fell out with Charles over his wedding to Elizabeth Trevor. Sarah offered Johnny the extraordinary sum of £400,000, if he would undertake never to see, or communicate with, his brother again. Johnny replied that he had always loved his brother, and that no sum existed which could make him desert him, 'breaking this friendship and the ties of nature'.

Before we assume that John was a man of the strongest moral fibre, he was to show considerably less resilience when Sarah insisted that he not see his sister Anne, Lady Bateman. He eventually yielded, because Sarah told him that refusal to do so would result in him being forced to quit his apartments in Marlborough House. This panicked Johnny, who said he could not possibly be expected to leave, since he was in the middle of long and painful treatment for venereal disease, and did not want to be seen in public. But Sarah was not bluffing, and Johnny agreed not to see his sister again, rather than be cast out of the comfort – and the privacy – of his lodgings.

Sarah was determined to overlook Johnny's shortcomings in her determination to create out of him the founder of a branch of the family in which she could invest her ambitions and riches. Her plan was to see Johnny raised to the peerage as Lord Churchill, with her fortune allowing him to live in a style appropriate to his new status. Johnny soon learned that such aspirations from his grandmother were not without reciprocal demands. The most pressing of these was Sarah's insistence that he marry. Although this was not a step that he had ever considered before, after some thought Johnny judged it wiser to obey his grandmother, rather than risk forfeiting his inheritance. As for who the bride should be, that hardly seemed important to him.

Charles Greville, writing a century later, tells us how Johnny Spencer chose his wife, with more than a little help from Sarah:

He expressed his readiness to marry anybody she pleased and at last she sent him a list, alphabetically arranged, of suitable matches. He said he might as well take the first on the list, which happened to be letter C, a Carteret, daughter of Lord Granville's, and her he accordingly married.

The Carterets, a Bedfordshire family, were thought a suitable bloodline for Johnny to marry into. Sarah had immense regard for the head of the family, Granville, who had been a close political ally of John Spencer's father, the Third Earl of Sunderland. For his troubles, Granville had been banished to Ireland by Sir Robert Walpole, as Lord Lieutenant. Walpole knew that Granville was a capable enough politician to be considered a potential future Prime Minister – a Whig one, of course. He did not want him on the British mainland.

The match found favour with the Granvilles because of its political expediency, rather than because they had any enthusiasm for Johnny himself. Struggling to find an aspect of her new son-in-law to admire, Lady Granville wrote to a friend, 'My daughter tells me Mrs Spencer will improve her music with learning, for Mr Spencer loves it extremely, and plays himself very well on the German flute . . .'

Despite the absence of romance in the selection of his bride, Johnny Spencer chose St Valentine's Day 1734 for the marriage. His wedding present from Sarah Marlborough was a large house she had just had built in Wimbledon. Three weeks before the wedding, the division of Spencer and Churchill assets was finally agreed, as the *Daily Courant* reported:

On Tuesday last the estates of his Grace Charles Duke of Marlborough in Northamptonshire and Bedfordshire, together with Sunderland House in Piccadilly, were in due form conveyed to the Honble John Spencer, his Grace's only brother, pursuant to the last will and testament of the late Duke of Marlborough to settle such estates he was before in possession of on his younger brothers or brother, or give him an equivalent in lieu thereof, within three months after the acquisition of those honours. We hear the Duchess Dowager of Marlborough hath settled £5,000 per annum on the Honble John Spencer, her grandson, and his heirs forever.

The financial affairs of the Carterets were slightly less ordered, and considerably less substantial, than those of the dynasty into which they had married. Lord Granville himself was 'more careless than extravagant', according to his contemporary, the Earl of Shelburne. As the father of the bride, he was expected to provide a large monetary settlement; this, despite all the wealth that had already been directed towards the couple via the groom's family. However, his family knew he could not possibly meet the obligation. They repeatedly asked Granville to address the problem, but he showed no inclination to face up to the potential embarrassment of the situation, and became a master of benign procrastination.

Eventually, the day before the settlement was to be formalized, Granville's father-in-law, Sir Robert Worsley, asked for a private word with him. Worsley managed to turn the conversation round to the matter of the wedding, and said that he hoped that everything was in order with regard to the finances, because otherwise Sarah Marlborough might prove to be more than a little peeved. Worsley went on to say that, of course, he did not assume Granville was unprepared, 'But if you are, I have £5,000 at my bankers, with which I can accommodate you.' At this news, Granville brightened considerably, saying, 'Can you really! If so, I shall be much obliged to you, for, to say the truth, I have not a hundred pounds towards it.'

At the wedding service at St George's, Hanover Square, Georgina Carteret wore white satin embroidered with silver, set off with very fine lace. Her jewels were given to her by Sarah Marlborough. After the wedding ceremony, the couple joined their guests at the gaming tables, dined at ten in the evening, and went to bed between twelve and one, before heading to Sarah Marlborough's house at Windsor.

It was customary, soon after the marriage of an aristocrat, for the couple to be presented to the monarch at St James's Palace, in what was termed the drawing room. The convention was for this to be a formal but happy occasion, one which the newlyweds would have looked forward to as a blessing on their union from the highest in the land. But this was to be a meeting that would hold no happy memories for the Spencer–Carteret party, who had turned out in force for the prestigious event. The First Earl of Egmont captured the drama of it all in his diary:

The Lord Carteret and his Lady, the Earl of Sunderland and his Countess and several others attended on the occasion and as is usual expected the honour to kiss hands, but the King turned his back to them all, nor did the Queen (who usually makes amends for the King's reservedness) say anything to them, only after a considerable neglect of them all, at last came up to Mr Spencer and only said to him, 'I think, Mr Spencer, I have not seen you since you was a child'; to which he answered as coldly, 'No, Madam, I believe not', and so they all came away displeased. It were to be wished the King had more affability . . . there are conjunctions of time when Kings should take some pains to please. These Lords Carteret and Sunderland have affections for his Majesty's family, but are no friends to Sir Robert Walpole, but it appears whoever are not friends to him are not to be countenanced at Court.

The result of this graceless snub was Johnny's decision to join his brother and brother-in-law, the Dukes of Marlborough and Bedford, in 'the Rumpsteak Club'. This was made up of aristocrats who had suffered from George II's unfortunate rudeness, the name having been suggested by one of the members after he complained that George had 'turned his rump to him'.

The marriage of John and Georgina was a happy one. She adored her husband, who carried on as though nothing had really changed in his life – the perpetual bachelor. Georgina was known for her charm and ease of manner, having inspired an admirer to write of her when she was a mere child in Ireland:

> Little charm of placid mien,
> Miniature of beauty's queen,
> Numbering years a scanty nine,
> Stealing hearts without design,
> Young inveigler, fond of wiles,
> Prone to mirth, profuse in smiles,
> Yet a novice in disdain,
> Pleasure giving, without pain;
> Still caressing, still carest,
> Thou and all thy lovers blest;
> Never teaz'd, and never teazing,
> O, for ever pleas'd, and pleasing . . .

Georgina needed limitless patience to put up with John's behaviour. True, their union got off to a successful start, with a son – also called John – being born in December 1734. Sarah Marlborough was delighted that there was an heir in the Spencer line, although disappointed that the baby resembled his mother more than his father: 'If he makes a good man and is healthy,' Sarah conceded, 'I do not much care whom he is like.' A second pregnancy followed towards the end of 1735. However, a month before its culmination, Lord Egmont reported that John was back to his old ways:

Snowball, our beadle, told us at the Vestry that five o'clock in the morning one day this week the Duke of Bedford, Mr Spencer . . . and Lord Beaumont, the Duke of Roxburgh's son, together with two others he knew not, came from a tavern in Pall Mall with three ladies (as he called them) to the watch house and stayed there till seven, drinking wine they brought with them, after which the gentlemen went away, leaving the ladies.

Johnny also kept a mistress, Fanny Murray. She was treated honourably by the family after his death, being given a pension of £160 per year, provided she stop being a courtesan, and marry an actor called David Ross. Georgina knew about her during the marriage, and put up with her erring husband's ways without public comment.

Apart from his sexual peccadilloes and his heavy drinking, Johnny's other physical vice was chewing tobacco, to which he became addicted. The combined effect of John's excesses on his health was such that his doctors, whom he shared with Sarah Marlborough – forty-eight years his senior – were convinced that grandson would predecease grandmother. However, the old matriarch finally died, aged eighty-three, in 1744. Her estranged daughter, the Duchess of Montagu, betrayed her lack of emotion at her mother's passing, merely remarking that dying was not in her mother's style.

Writing on the life of Pitt in 1910, Lord Rosebery referred to

Sarah as a 'vigorous old termagant', and went on to justify this character judgement:

All through her life she had been more bellicose, though with less success, than her illustrious husband, and of late years had devoted her peculiar powers of hatred to Walpole. This bitterness extended even beyond the grave, for by a codicil dated two months before her death she bequeathed legacies to the two men who had most distinguished themselves by their attacks on that Minister. One was Chesterfield, to whom she left £20,000; the other was Pitt, to whom she left £10,000 – 'for the noble defence he made for the support of the laws of England, and to prevent the ruin of his country'.

Pitt, although no doubt delighted by this unexpected windfall, made it clear that he had some reservations about its source, when he wrote to Sarah's executor, Marchmont,

Give me leave to return your Lordship my thanks for the obliging manner in which you do me the honour to inform me of the Duchess of Marlborough's great goodness to me. The sort of regard I feel for her memory I leave to your Lordship's heart to suggest to you.

Pitt and Chesterfield were also to share Wimbledon, if Johnny Spencer and his sickly young son failed to produce a surviving heir between them; and Pitt, thanks to Sarah Marlborough's influence, was to succeed to the Spencer estates, too, in the same circumstances. As Rosebery recorded, though:

Fortunately the splendid contingency did not take effect. For Chesterfield died without legitimate issue, and the Pitts have long been extinct; but the descendants of John Spencer's only son have been men of a purity of character and honour which have sweetened and exalted the traditions of English public life.

There was one overriding condition, though, if Sarah's wealth was to pass in its entirety to Johnny and his son. In her will, she wrote: 'I have settled all the estates in this Paper upon John Spencer and his son; but if either of them take any employment or Pension from the Crown they are to forfeit the whole and they are to go to others as if they were dead.' The only honours they were allowed to receive were a peerage and the Rangership of Windsor Park. Control of her family, and hatred of the royal family, were not to be diminished by the small matter of mortality.

There was no question of Johnny Spencer risking his huge inheritance by going against his benefactor's instructions. He now became the possessor of twenty-seven landed estates in twelve counties, the majority in Northamptonshire, Buckinghamshire and Bedfordshire, but as far afield as Kent and Staffordshire. Dr Frances Harris of the British Library has estimated that the capital value of this land was £400,000, with an annual rent roll of £17,000 per year after outgoings. A gentleman at this time could live on £300 per year. There was also in excess of £250,000 not tied up in land, together with paintings by Stubbs, Rubens and Hondecoeter, and the fabulous Marlborough silver. All this on top of his paternal inheritance of Althorp and Wormleighton. He was fantastically wealthy – way beyond his expectations as a young man, when he was resigned to being only a relatively well-off third son of an aristocratic family.

However, Johnny did not have long to enjoy his Marlborough possessions. His drinking, tobacco-chewing and other indulgences finally proved his doctors right, and he died in June 1746, only twenty months after Sarah. Charles Marlborough now expected to be reconnected with his Spencer possessions, and was amazed to discover that this was not to be the case. Horace Walpole wrote to George Montagu:

The great business of the town is Jack Spencer's will, who has left Althrop [sic] and the Sunderland estates in reversion to Pitt; after more obligations and more pretended friendship for his brother, the Duke, than is conceivable. The Duke is in the utmost uneasiness about it, having left the drawing of the writings for the estate to his brother and his grandmother, and without having any idea that himself was cut out of the entail.

# 10. A Secret Marriage, a Public Love Affair

The eleven-year-old boy who was now possessor of such fabulous wealth was Master John Spencer. He had not been expected to survive his first few years, and poor health was to be the theme of his life, ultimately shortening it substantially. He was shy and awkward throughout his life, and Viscount Palmerston evaluated him thus:

He seems to be a man whose value few people know. The bright side of his character appears in private and the dark side in public ... it is only those who live in intimacy with him who know that he has an understanding heart that might do credit to any man.

Certainly, he was a man of contradictions.

John's mother, Georgina, subsequently married the Second Earl Cowper. She did not feel the necessity to bring up her son from her first marriage in a strict or disciplined way, and it would be fair to deduce that his later profligacy stemmed – at least in part – from the lack of parental control during his formative years. A tale from the boy's childhood illustrates how he became used to getting his own way – and how cavalierly he treated his money.

Part of the inheritance from Sarah Marlborough had been the house where she herself had grown up, Holywell, on the outskirts of St Albans. It became a regular stopping-off point for the family on their travels between London and Althorp. As a boy, John Spencer used to visit an inn near by. One day, noting that the innkeeper was looking unhappy, the richest schoolboy in the kingdom asked him what was the matter, to which the reply was given that business was going badly, with creditors closing in. The subsequent conversation apparently went like this:

JOHN: That is pity; how much money will be required to reinstate you?

INNKEEPER: Oh! Your honour, a great sum: not less than a thousand pounds.

JOHN: And would that sum perfectly answer the purpose?

INNKEEPER: It would, Sir, and I could honestly repay any gentleman who would be generous enough to advance it.

On reaching London, John went to his guardian and asked for £1,000 to be immediately made over to him. The guardian was perplexed by the request: 'A thousand pounds, Sir, it is a large sum; may I ask to what purpose it is to be applied?' John's reply was, 'No purpose of extravagance, upon my honour; but I will not tell you to what use it is to be destined.' Understandably, the guardian declined to advance the cash to his charge.

John then went to his mother, and consulted other senior relatives, complaining that it was effectively his money, and he should therefore be allowed to have it. A family meeting followed, and it was agreed that John should be given the money, with no questions asked as to its proposed purpose. John then took it to the innkeeper who, according to the tale, subsequently made a great success of his business.

John lived like a prince all his life, with a huge retinue of servants in his five main residences, and no concept at any stage that his wealth might be finite. All his tastes were expensive: he inherited the gambling addiction of his forefathers in full; he had also the family penchant for the very finest artistic acquisitions, regardless of cost; and he had an appetite for politics, without the personal attributes to forge a way forward for himself in that field – which left him funding ruinous election campaigns on the behalf of others.

The side of John Spencer's character of which I was most aware when I was growing up was his romantic streak. From his late teens, he had been very much in love with Georgiana Poyntz, youngest daughter of the Right Honourable Stephen Poyntz, who had been governor to the Duke of Cumberland – who was later in charge of the English army when it destroyed Bonnie Prince

Charlie's Scots at Culloden – and of Anna Maria Mordaunt, a former maid of honour to Queen Caroline.

There was no question of marriage for the young couple until John had reached his twenty-first birthday. There were to be lavish entertainments at Althorp in December 1755 to mark this personal landmark, and John secretly decided to combine his birthday and his marriage celebrations.

Before setting off from London, John went to take his leave from Lord Granville, his grandfather, and told him in confidence that the next time they would meet, it would be with John as a married man. Lord Granville, angry that he was being presented with a *fait accompli*, said tersely, 'I am very glad of it; I never interfere with what so nearly concerns anybody; one of the benefits of a great fortune is to be able to please oneself.' The twenty-year-old John was expecting such prickliness, and refused to rise to the bait, replying, 'So I always thought, my Lord, and I have done so. When I come back, I hope you will give me leave to bring Mrs Spencer to wait on your Lordship.' Granville effected a bow, and said, 'Most certainly, Sir.' However, as John made to walk out of the room, Granville's stiffness eased, and he called after him: 'Johnny, goodbye, nobody wishes you happier than I do.'

The journey to Althorp was not uneventful. John's carriage fell into a river, the horses and servants were only just saved, but the majority of the family's finest clothes was soaked through, and the best silver had to be retrieved from the mud. It was also noted that John's health was suffering from the excitement and the exertion of the trip, and members of the family began to question why the celebrations could not have been held at the Spencer home in Wimbledon, thus sparing everybody the inconvenience of a trek to Northamptonshire.

Meanwhile, on arriving at Althorp, Mrs Poyntz, Georgiana's mother, set about establishing precisely how big the fortune was into which her beloved 'Don' – as she and her husband called their favourite child – was marrying. Triumphantly, on 15 December 1755, she relayed the following to Lady Sarah Cowper: 'L.C. [John's mother, Lady Cowper] told me that Mr S. has two thousand pounds a year that is personal estate, and three hundred thousand pounds besides, which she says, and I daresay rightly, that his personal estate is greater than any man's in England.'

Four days later, John beckoned Georgiana away from the party for his twenty-first birthday, and kissed his future mother-in-law's hand, before saying: 'Madam, I always resolved to marry my dear Miss P. the first moment it was in my power and I beg you will not let the ceremony be delayed one hour.' The two of them then slipped upstairs into the Oak Bedroom with Georgiana, Lady Cowper, and other immediate members of the families, as well as John's tutor, the Reverend Holloway. Mrs Poyntz continues the story, her report written immediately after its conclusion:

Holloway read so slow and prayed with such devotion that the ceremony lasted three quarters of an hour. Mr S. and Don behaved as well as possible with the greatest seriousness and spoke distinct though low. As soon as it was done he kissed her and they both knelt quite down to Lady Cowper and I, and almost to my Lord . . . William [Georgiana's brother] cried a little; we all cried a little; we all hugged and kissed and dispersed as soon as possible. They are all dancing. I must go down and see them.

Georgiana was now expected to dress and behave in a manner suited to her new wealth and status. Contemporary gossips noted approvingly the sumptuousness of her clothes. The first dress she was seen in in London was 'white and silver, as fine as brocade and trimming could make it'. The second was blue and silver. After that, white, gold, with a colour design that cost £6 per yard. Then, a dress of plain pink-coloured satin.

And there were the jewels, inherited by her husband from Sarah Marlborough: the diamonds alone were worth £12,000; the earrings were 'three drops all diamonds, not paltry scrolls of silver'; also a necklace, 'most perfect brilliants, the middle stone worth £1,000, set at the edge with small brilliants . . .' Jealousy there most certainly was, but this was lessened by Georgiana's obvious lack of interest in the material worth of all that now surrounded her. It was noted that even at this time, when she might be forgiven for being totally

*Above* Robert, First Baron Spencer, by Marcus Gheeraerts the Younger, 1602. Reputed to possess more ready money than anyone else in England, Robert was created a baron by James I the year after posing for this portrait, which was also the first year of the Stuart dynasty.

*Above right* William, Second Baron Spencer, by Sir Anthony van Dyck, *c.* 1633. Although he is dressed in armour, William's early death spared him from fighting in the English Civil War, where his love of both King and of Parliament would have placed him in an invidious position.

*Right* Penelope, wife of William, Second Baron Spencer, the painting attributed to William Larkin, *c.* 1635. The daughter of Shakespeare's patron, the Earl of Southampton, Penelope transformed the domestic arrangements at Althorp to ensure a minimum of waste and a maximum of gracious hospitality.

Henry Spencer, First Earl of Sunderland, by the circle of Pieter Nason, *c.* 1642. He has the pale face of a man of promise, surrounded by darkness; a harbinger of the untimely doom awaiting him on the battlefields of the Civil War, where he died for a cause he abhorred.

Robert Spencer, Second Earl of Sunderland, by Sir Peter Lely, *c.* 1670. Driven by his lust for power and money, Robert always allowed his conscience to take second place to his ambition, making him one of the most influential but unpopular politicians of the seventeenth century.

Sarah Jennings, wife of John, First Duke of Marlborough, by Sir Godfrey Kneller, *c.* 1689. Sarah remains one of the most controversial and fascinating female figures in British history, controlling Queen Anne until their spectacular falling out, while amassing a huge fortune which she left to her Spencer descendants.

'Johnny' Spencer, standing with his son, John – later First Earl Spencer – on horseback, attended by their servant, Caesar Shaw, painted by George Knapton, c. 1744. Sarah Marlborough made it a condition of her will that neither John Spencer accept any position from the Crown, if they wished to remain principal beneficiaries.

Georgiana Poyntz, wife of John, First Earl Spencer, by Pompeo Batoni, c. 1765. Batoni was a favourite artist for young noblemen completing the Grand Tour of the Continent. This portrait shows Georgiana, always keen to be seen as something of an intellect, surrounded by symbols of culture and learning.

View of Green Park, with Spencer House centre left, English School, c. 1770. Built as a love token by John, First Earl Spencer, for his wife, Georgiana, Spencer House was to become a bastion of Whig politics in London until the end of the nineteenth century. The red-brick mansion on the right is the precursor to Buckingham Palace.

Lady Georgiana Spencer, later Duchess of Devonshire, with a lyre, by Robert Edge Pine, *c.* 1772. Georgiana's fresh good looks radiate from this rarely seen painting of the girl who was to become a fashion icon and society leader of eighteenth-century Europe.

Lady Georgiana and Lady Henrietta Spencer with their brother, George John, later Second Earl Spencer, by Angelica Kauffmann, *c.* 1778. The three surviving children of the First Earl and Countess Spencer all left their mark: Georgiana as the celebrated Duchess of Devonshire, Harriet as mother to Lady Caroline Lamb, and George John as the patron and commander of Nelson.

George John, Second Earl Spencer, by John Hoppner, *c.* 1800. By the end of his life, George John had turned eight rooms at Althorp into libraries, in an attempt to house his 43,000 books. In the process of establishing perhaps the greatest private library in Europe, George John all but bankrupted the Spencer family.

*Right* Lavinia Bingham, wife of George John, Second Earl Spencer, by Sir Martin Archer Shee, *c.* 1810. An awkward woman, Lavinia was highly influential in her children's lives, ensuring that all her sons were God-fearing Christians. Her pretensions and affectations made her deeply unpopular with her family, although she was a famously attentive society hostess.

*Below* Wimbledon Villa, by T. H. Shepherd, *c.* 1805. The lordship of the manor of Wimbledon was part of the great inheritance from Sarah Marlborough. A generation after her death her house at Wimbledon was destroyed by fire, being replaced by this more manageable villa, built by Henry Holland at the behest of George John, Second Earl Spencer.

John Charles, Viscount Althorp, later Third Earl Spencer, by Sir Joshua Reynolds, 1787. In old age 'Jack' Spencer was to claim he was the only man to have sat for Reynolds and to have had his image captured for posterity by that modern invention, the camera.

Frederick, later Fourth Earl Spencer, by Charles Allingham, c. 1820. This portrait betrays the sternness of manner that made Frederick such a successful naval officer but somewhat lacking as a father. Queen Victoria once told him, much to his delight, that he had the finest legs she had ever seen.

The Hon. and Rev. George Spencer, later Father Ignatius of St Paul, artist unknown, c. 1850. George eschewed the easy existence of an Anglican gentleman-preacher for the rigorous demands of life as a mendicant friar. He believed it was the duty of all Roman Catholics to pray for England's return to the papal fold.

*Right* Captain Sir Robert Cavendish Spencer, by Charles Allingham, *c.* 1820. 'Bob' is captured in an uncharacteristically relaxed pose, bearing an uncanny resemblance to his cousin twice removed, Sir Winston Spencer-Churchill. He remains the only Spencer to have seen active service against the United States.

*Below* John Poyntz, Fifth Earl Spencer, with his wife Charlotte, rifle-shooting on Wimbledon Common, by Sir Henry Tamworth Wells, 1864. 'The Red Earl' was to receive the gratitude of the nation when he gave Wimbledon Common to the people in perpetuity. He was a co-founder of the National Rifle Association, a welcome diversion from his duties as a cabinet minister throughout the majority of Gladstone's four premierships.

Albert Edward John, Seventh Earl Spencer, by Juliet Pannett, 1966. Known as 'The Curator Earl' and 'Jolly Jack', he had a deep knowledge of the history and contents of Althorp and Spencer House, allied with an unfortunate disdain for those who could not match his enthusiasm for things cultural.

Edward John, Viscount Althorp, later Eighth Earl Spencer, by Sir William Nicholson, 1934. Growing up at Althorp between the wars was a lonely time in Johnnie Spencer's life: the family had to adapt to existence in a virtual palace with a negligible income, with his father's strong character frequently dominating proceedings.

immersed in enjoying her husband's wealth for her own ends, she was deeply affected by the pathetic pleas of a begging letter, 'which brought tears into her eyes, and made her appear with much more lustre than the diamonds'. As one contemporary, Elizabeth Montagu, noted warmly: 'I like Mrs Spencer, she is a natural good young woman, no airs, no affectations, but seemed to enjoy her good fortune by making others partakers, and happy with herself.'

Attention was soon centred on John and Georgiana's fertility, since the dearth of Spencer males was a matter of concern to the wider family. Indeed, it became a topic that attracted attention throughout London society, as an entry in the betting book at White's, a gentlemen's club in St James's, makes clear. Dated 20 January 1756, it reads: 'Lord Middleton wagers Mr O'Brien Twenty Guineas that Lady Robt Manners has a child born alive before Mrs Spencer.'

In time there would be five children – one son and four daughters. Two of the girls died in infancy; the surviving pair, Georgiana and Henrietta, known as Harriet, were destined to become two of the most celebrated figures in late eighteenth-century society. The son, though born prematurely, in 1758, was a celebrated addition to the family. Elizabeth Montagu reported on the boy, George John's, arrival:

I went yesterday 'pour égayer' a little to see Mrs Spencer after her lying in, and there is nothing but joy and magnificence; the child is likely to live though it came, they reckon, six weeks before its time. Mrs Poinne showed me all the fineries; the papboat is pure gold . . .

The health of the baby may have been sound, but that of his father was not. John Spencer's continual physical frailty made him seek warmer climates, away from the English winter. He had completed the Grand Tour as a young man, and had acquired a taste for European travel. He was also an enthusiast of the fad, among the European aristocracy, of spending time in health spas on the Continent. The winter after his marriage he went with his wife, her sister and two brothers, her mother, a chaplain, a cousin, and Major Barton — who had been John's governor — to Spa itself. The Spencers took with them such a retinue of servants that they needed two boats across the Channel: one for the family party and one for their attendants. They bought so many objects on their travels — John's mother-in-law buying fourteen gowns for herself and her daughters in Antwerp alone — that they chartered a third boat on their return to bring their purchases home.

The Spencer–Poyntz party was embarrassingly loud in its behaviour, according to other English travellers. Georgiana's mother was regarded as responsible for the boisterous mood of the party, and her lack of grace was put down to excitement at the fabulous wealth her daughter now possessed, and a belief that, having been a figure at court herself, she was somehow superior to the people she met on her travels. In particular it was noted that she would have very little to do with the English people she met abroad, claiming they were either Jacobites, or in political opposition to the court. However, she did not reserve such negative sentiment exclusively for her compatriots. She made no secret that she had only contempt for the French and Flemish, as well.

A later expedition to Spa resulted in uncalled for excitement. In September 1779, the Spencers and their daughter Georgiana were returning to England from Ostend after a recuperative visit to the Continent when their two packet boats were chased by French cutters, crewed by privateers. Fortunately John Spencer had arranged an escort for his party — a sloop called *The Fly*, captained by Captain Garner. The sloop had only fourteen guns, but it fought for two hours with the French, losing several of its crew in the fight while inflicting casualties on the two French ships. Eventually the privateers withdrew. At this juncture, John Spencer appeared from the hold of his boat, and was taken over to *The Fly*, where he thanked Garner, while adding that there had really been no need to fight, as he would have gladly paid whatever ransom the Frenchmen demanded! There is no record of how the captain responded to this statement, although no doubt he was grateful for the silver pieces his wealthy passenger gave him as a token of thanks for the safe delivery of his party.

Forbidden by the terms of his inheritance from actively serving the Crown – something that his ancestral traditions would otherwise have marked him out for – and weighed down with wealth, John needed to find appropriate ways of spending his money and his energies, while enhancing his status.

A priority was to secure a hereditary title, suitable to his financial and social standing. In 1760, the King let it be known that he was considering raising his 24-year-old millionaire subject to the peerage. This encouraged John to write on the subject to his cousin, Thomas Pelham, First Duke of Newcastle, with what appear now highly presumptuous recommendations as to how he would like to be styled, should the promotion proceed. 'As I am now the representative of the Sunderland family,' he wrote on 27 November 1760,

and as my particular circumstances are such (from the Duchess of Marlborough's will) that I cannot receive any favour from the King except a title, I should hope that if his Majesty thinks me worthy of a peerage, he will not confer upon me a less dignity than that of a viscount, and it is for that honour I must beg your Grace to lay me at his Majesty's feet. I am very cautious of not desiring to assume any of the titles, which have been in the Sunderland family – some of which are now vested in the Duke of Marlborough, but confine myself to the title of Althorp which has never been made use of . . .

Newcastle obliged his cousin, and John became Viscount Althorp in 1761. Further elevation followed, four years later. Lady Cowper was able to write to her confidante, Miss Dewes: 'My son is to be Earl Spencer, offered in the most gracious manner by his Majesty, unasked, which greatly enhances the value of the dignity.'

Of equal importance to the issue of social status was the question of a suitable London residence. By the mid eighteenth century, the Spencer family's annual tour of their various properties was beginning to fit a pattern, whereby they would be based in London from Easter till September, except when the heat and squalor of life in the city made a retreat to the house at Wimbledon desirable.

Then there would be a trip to the Continent – Montpellier and Nice were both popular with the family – followed by autumn trips based around country sports – foxhunting from the lodge in Pytchley, near Althorp, or shooting on the Norfolk part of the estate, in North Creake – before spending the bulk of the period from November to March back at Althorp.

In London itself, Sarah Marlborough had left John and his father a house in Grosvenor Street, which was all she had to offer at the time, since Charles Marlborough had first claim to the grander family residences in the capital. John decided that the best option was to build something entirely new, both as a fitting reflection of his own importance and also as a love token for his wife. Out of these aims was born Spencer House.

The design for Spencer House was the work of an amateur, Colonel – afterwards Sir – George Gray, a friend of John's from his dining club, the Society of Dilettantes. Traditionally, and incorrectly, much of the credit for the beauty of this private palace has gone to John Vardy, who, in fact, merely executed and superintended Gray's designs. He incorporated the fashionable Greek styles of architecture, with statues in front, at the apex and at the base of the pediment. All things classical were enjoying huge popularity among the social élite at this stage – a taste that had been fostered by the recent rediscovery of the petrified remains of the city of Pompeii.

James 'Athenian' Stuart was chosen to decorate the interior of the first floor, including the most decorative and memorable room in the whole house: the ornate Painted Room. The Library was also important, given John's keenness to build on the collection of books he had inherited. He had recently acquired 5,000 volumes from the late headmaster of Eton College, William George. As a result, the Spencer House Library was given the generous proportions, for a town house, of thirty feet in length and twenty-five feet in width, with a polished white marble chimney-piece. The drawing room, at twenty-four feet by twenty-one feet, was smaller, but no less impressive: the ceiling and ornaments were of white, gold and green, the chimney-piece bordered by Sienna marble. Then there was the saloon, forty-five feet by thirty feet, with its coved ceiling, adorned with compartments of mosaic, 'green, white, gold, interspersed with gilt medallions'.

The basic structure of the house cost 50,000 guineas, the contents many times that sum. In Georgiana's own handwriting, there is a record of the pictures which hung in her Spencer House dressing room. Among the twenty-four Old Masters she enjoyed in this most private of rooms were a landscape by Poussin over the chimney-piece, and great works by Titian, Leonardo da Vinci, Rubens and Guercino. The more public rooms were similarly bedecked with masterpieces from the finest painters in Europe.

In the Great Room, the theme of love that John wanted to celebrate in the creation of Spencer House was most graphically depicted through the designs of the pair of long mirrors, which can be seen today upstairs in Althorp's own Great Room. Either side of the tops of the mirrors, John had a chariot carved, each driven by Cupid. On one side of each mirror, Cupid is in full flow, the chariot charging ahead, pulled by a galloping griffin, the mythical animal the Spencers had incorporated into their coat of arms. On the other side, the chariot is stationary, the griffin equally immobile, the Cupid hunched with sadness. The message was clear to eighteenth-century onlookers, well versed as they were in classical tradition and clever symbolism: when Spencer's love life was buoyant, then all was well with the world, and he could push forward with confidence and happiness; but if there was a problem in this sphere of his life, he was reduced to impotent slackness, dead in his tracks for as long as the unhappy state persisted.

These were two items among many that John Spencer bought for his London home, regardless of cost. In a letter to Sir Horace Mann, dated 9 February 1758, Horace Walpole wrote disapprovingly of this trend for ridiculous prices being achieved in the art world because of aristocratic spendthrifts like John:

But our glaring extravagance is the constant high price given for pictures: the other day at Mr Furnese's Selection a very small Gaspar sold for 76 guineas; and a Carlo Marratti, which I am persuaded is a Giuseppe Chiari, Lord Egremont bought at the rate of 260 pounds. Mr Spencer gave no less than £2,200 for the Andrea Sacchi and the Guido from the same collection. The latter is of very dubious originality.

Even when Spencer House was completed, a decade after its inception, the trawling for great works of art to adorn its interiors continued. The Spencers employed Gavin Hamilton to hunt out suitable treasures in Italy. His brief was not solely connected with quality, though. John and Georgiana were once advised that one of the rooms required a pair of paintings that needed to be seven feet three inches by five feet six inches, in order to match the proportions of the other works of art there. It was because of this design requirement that the two great Guercinos – of King David, and of the Samian Sybil – came into the possession of my family. They now hang in the Marlborough Room at Althorp, and it is hard to believe that such exquisite paintings were bought primarily to fill a pair of walls in Spencer House.

It had taken Hamilton's agent over a year to find the Guercinos, Hamilton reporting the find to Georgiana, while decrying the endless small bribes he had had to pay in order to get to the position of being able to buy them from the Marchese Loccatelli for 1,000 crowns. 'Your ladyship by experience will be satisfied that nothing can be done in this country without money,' he reassured his client.

Reading the correspondence surrounding this purchase, it is clear that the actual transaction was a less complicated business than getting such large works of art back to their new owners in Britain. Hamilton explained the procedure he felt forced to adopt:

As the pictures are in perfect preservation I have ordered a large roller to be made with a case in which they will remain suspended, after they are well secured with wax-cloth, canvass, etc. I propose to send them to Pesaro upon a stracino made with a network of cords to prevent any damage by jolting; from Pesaro I shall see them set out in the same manner for Civita Vecchia by the Furlo, so that by avoiding Rome, we shall save time, trouble and expense.

Gavin Hamilton was part of a network of art experts established across Europe for the continued embellishment of the interior of Spencer House. Even on holidays, the obsession with finding precisely the right type of chattel for each room continued, as this letter to Sir William Hamilton, a British minister in Naples, written on Christmas Day 1765, demonstrates:

I have not lost the taste I acquired in Italy for Vertu. I have been bidding through the means of your namesake at Rome, for a very fine picture there, but in vain; he has, however, succeeded in purchasing for me, some little marbles that are very clever. I shall be very glad if you can get the Mercury's head. My house in Town is at last near being finished, and I believe will be fit to open next spring. As I have an aversion to China and Japan [i.e., china and porcelain], I shall endeavour to furnish it as much as possible with this sort of thing.

Building, decorating and furnishing his London palace was a very effective way of making huge inroads into the Sarah Marlborough inheritance. John was similarly extravagant with the house at Wimbledon, which his grandmother had completely rebuilt earlier in the century, altering the formal avenues and terraces laid out for the duchess by Bridgeman, with the help of 'Capability' Brown, and making a 'great sheet of water', known to all who have been to the lawn tennis championships.

Similarly expensive overhauls to the Park at Althorp were fortunately avoided when 'Capability' Brown was satisfied that he could not improve on the layout of the land. The mansion of Althorp itself was relatively neglected in the first twenty years of John's tenure, showing the results of a lack of even the most basic care when the library ceiling caved in during the early 1770s. A major programme of restoration was implemented, in 1772, with the usual lack of attention to cost or value for money. To avoid the inconvenience, noise and dirt of the builders, the Spencers spent the winter of that year abroad, again haemorrhaging money wherever they went. However, at least there was something to show for such expense, both in terms of architecture and treasures.

This was not to be the case in the world of politics, where John lost huge sums of money, with only slight temporary advantages of an altogether less tangible nature. As his grandson, Jack, Third Earl Spencer, recorded, 'He spent extravagantly large sums in contested elections, and endeavoured to obtain great parliamentary influence, without as far as I am aware, ever having been at all eager as a politician.' He certainly showed no aptitude for public speaking. Lady Mary Coke remarked, after listening to him in the Lords: 'As much as could be heard was very pretty, but he was extremely frightened and spoke very low.'

It seems that John's involvement in elections was directly connected to his addiction to gambling. There was also the feeling that his gargantuan wealth should entitle him to a say in the running of the country, even though his grandmother's will made a direct hand in such affairs impossible.

In the latter part of the eighteenth century only the propertied classes were entitled to a vote. Those voters not over-interested in politics were available for persuasion, be it through generous entertainment or outright bribery. Either course was expensive; but the Northampton election of 1768 was to prove to be downright ruinous.

It was a contest of three lords, as much as of their favoured candidates. They were Spencer, Northampton and Halifax, and each built up a strong band of supporters to assist in their electioneering. The upshot of this was a fierce fight in the streets of Northampton, which resulted in some serious injuries to the brawlers, while their three lordships looked on.

Back at Althorp, John was using his money to back up the muscle of his mob. A footman was posted either side of the front door of the house, holding small cakes and sandwiches on silver salvers. Rather than having a conventional filling, each piece of food contained two golden guineas, as an inducement to vote for the Spencer candidate. News of this spread very quickly round the neighbourhood, resulting in an unprecedented stream of visitors to the house, eager to partake of the First Earl's 'hospitality'.

The cost of the election was enormous. Lord Halifax was ruined, and had to sell all his possessions. Lord Northampton was forced to dispose of all his timber in Warwickshire and Northamptonshire, and to sell a large proportion of the contents of his two main country residences, Compton Wynyates and Castle Ashby. He then retired to Switzerland for the rest of his life.

As for John, his losses were estimated at £120,000. He was not affected as dramatically as his opponents, but this was a hugely expensive trial of strength, which demonstrated a fundamental lack of judgement and a regrettable inability to control himself – both traits of someone who, according to his grandson,

was a man of generous and amiable disposition, spoiled by having been placed, at too early a period of his life, in possession of what then appeared to him inexhaustible wealth; and irritable in his temper, partly from the pride which this circumstance had produced, and partly from almost continued bad health.

The irresponsible erosion of the Spencer estate was overwhelmingly John's fault. However, he also had to contend with the fact that, unbeknown to him, his chief 'man of business', Thomas Parker, stole extensively from his employer. This was not discovered until three years after John's death, by his heir. Parker was brought to account on a couple of easily detectable matters, but there was doubtless much more that never came to light. The crook died in penury in February 1792. When Parker's widow, Frances, died, in January 1804, many deeds and papers belonging to John were discovered, hidden among her possessions.

Extravagances and misappropriation of family funds aside, there were also the normal demands upon its money that any eighteenth-century aristocratic family would be expected to meet, one of which was that of acting charitably to the needy. John was known as a man of great generosity, a 1768 notice in Wimbledon's local newspaper recording one of many acts that led to this reputation: 'We hear that the Rt Hon The Earl Spencer has given Orders for 200 guineas to the poor of Wimbledon and Roehampton in Surrey.'

It was not only the underprivileged who hoped for a share of the

Spencer wealth, there was also the unwritten obligation of entertaining fellow aristocrats and aspiring gentry, richly and originally. For this role, John and Georgiana Spencer were perfectly suited, luring people into the hedonistic world they enjoyed inhabiting, and making guests relax, particularly in the more homely setting of Althorp – Spencer House could only ever be grand – where their genuine affection for one another was most readily on show. Georgiana's happiness in the country was so evident that the Earl of Bristol stated, 'Nothing could tempt Lady Spencer to London but the restlessness of her poor husband and I heard her say before him she hated even the sight of Town.' Georgiana herself referred to Althorp as 'this place, which I always must love preferably to any other'.

Another nobleman, the Earl of March, a guest at Althorp in December 1767, wrote of the mansion:

I like everything here so much, that I have no inclination to leave the place. I wish you were here. It is just the house you would wish to be in. There is an excellent library; a good parson; the best English and French cookery you ever tasted; strong coffee, and half-crown whist. The more I see of the mistress of the House, the more I admire her, and our landlord improves very much upon acquaintance. They are really the happiest people I think I ever saw in the marriage system.

March continued, before signing off this correspondence, 'We are now all going to the ice, which is quite like a fair. There is a tent, with strong beer, cold meat, etc.; where Lady Spencer and our other ladies go on airing.'

Georgiana's life-enhancing qualities never deserted her. Even as an old woman, she was written about with genuine appreciation by Susan, Marchioness of Stafford, in a letter of November 1801 to her son, Lord Granville Leveson Gower:

I do not wonder at your liking Lady Spencer; all men formerly liked her, and she was most captivating and pleasing. But the beauty of it was that she managed them ALL without their knowing it. Even the late Lord Bath never sat after dinner or supper at Wimbledon; he was among the

first at skittles, cards or whatever Lady Spencer liked to have done . . .
She, somehow or another, has the art of leading, drawing or seducing
people into right ways.

Despite John's health being a constant worry throughout the
marriage, Georgiana kept up the role of the enthusiastic and imaginative hostess, beguiling her guests with her entertainments. In
October 1766, she managed to persuade a Mr Wildman, of Ply-
mouth, to come up to the villa at Wimbledon with his performing
bees, to entertain the Spencers' guests. A variety of performances
began with Mr Wildman hanging a beehive from his hat, and an
empty second hive from his hand, before transferring the bees from
one to the other. He then demonstrated how he could take honey
and wax from the first hive, without destroying the bees.

To the delight of the guests, Wildman proceeded to go inside
the house, only to return with the bees draped around his chin and
cheeks, like 'a very venerable beard'. He gathered the excited
onlookers around him, then made a full hive of bees swarm busily
around them, without anybody being stung. For his fourth trick,
he took handfuls of bees and hurled them up and down, 'like so
many peas', again without being hurt in any way. When he had
done this several times, he gave a command which sent the bees
flying back into their hive.

Because the First Earl was ill in bed, Wildman gave him a private
performance in the earl's bedroom, in which the bee-keeper was
covered by three swarms of bees – one on his breast, one on his
head and one on his arm. This manoeuvre involved Wildman being
blindfolded, riding backwards and forwards on one of the Spencers'
horses in front of the house, himself still covered in live bees, before
he dismounted, stood next to the hives and a table, and apparently
made the bees march down on to the table and, 'at his word of
command, retire to their hive'.

Such original diversions made Georgiana one of the most popular
and successful hostesses of her time. Her gifts worked even on
visiting foreigners, as an anonymous French gentleman attested in
his *Memoirs of a Traveller.*

La Bruyère has said that a pretty woman who has all the good qualities of a gentleman, is the most delightful companion in the world. The merit of the two sexes is then united.

This phenomenon, rare enough in these times, is to be seen in Lady Spencer; she has an easy and open manner; her physiognomy takes, in conversation, the air best suited to the subject, with a facility that makes her extremely interesting: she has a lively understanding and an elegant discernment and comprehends everything in an instant. A well cultivated mind renders her conversation varied, sensible and almost inexhaustible, without being at all studied; but appearing as if she were listening to your discourse.

Such gifts of personality and intellect resulted in a varied and talented group of people becoming regular guests at Spencer House and Althorp. David Garrick, the actor, was a special friend of Georgiana and John's, spending Christmas at Althorp in 1778 as an honorary family member, less than a month prior to his death.

John Spencer and Garrick shared a close friendship with the Reverend William Arden, an Eton and Cambridge scholar whom the first Earl had involved in the early education of his son and heir, George John. Arden was as much a companion and friend as he was a country parson, accompanying the Spencers on their foreign travels in 1763 and 1764 – which was when the priest met Garrick. Subsequently John made Arden the vicar of Brampton Ash, a part of the Spencer estate situated on the Northamptonshire–Leicestershire border. On his appointment, Arden received at the vicarage the free services of Lord Spencer's own head gardener, to make it more pleasant for the new incumbent to live there.

The Garricks spent part of their summers every year at Althorp. J. Cradock, a fellow thespian of Garrick's, in his *Literary and Miscellaneous Memoirs* recalled that his eminent colleague enjoyed these visits enormously: 'The mansion was always highly spoken of from the elegance of the society and the great attention that was paid to all the friends who had the honour to be admitted into it.' As a token of his appreciation for being included in these house parties, Garrick gave a bust of himself to the Spencers.

There were frequent visits to and from William Arden. The vicar was a keen amateur actor, who used to enjoy reading parts with Garrick, the finest performer of his day. Cradock noted that, 'When we were reciting parts [at Althorp], Garrick said that Mr Arden had the most genuine comic humour of any man he knew and particularly praised his Falstaff.' Comedy may have been Arden's forte, but it was tragedy that was to mark his end.

After an active bachelorhood, the time had come for Arden to contemplate marriage. It was a development he had sought to avoid for some time, but respectability demanded he settle down into a life of worthy domesticity. Eventually a wealthy young lady from Northampton was produced as a match for the vicar, and he speedily married her in July 1768. Cradock and Garrick went to pay their respects to the newly married couple, and Cradock was taken aback at the change in Arden's demeanour:

I do not know that any blame could attach to the lady, but a lurking melancholy had overtaken Mr Arden. He had been accustomed to the highest company and certainly was a most finished scholar and gentleman, but I fear had not duly weighed that humble domestic life was not immediately adapted to a man who till then had only been connected with the excitements of society at the most splendid tables . . .

It signalled the brutal end of a friendship that had given equal pleasure to the earl, the actor and the priest. Three months after the marriage, Cradock was having dinner with guests one evening when there was a violent rap at the door, and a messenger from Drury Lane Theatre told him he must come quickly, as Mr Garrick needed to speak with him at once. Cradock made his excuses, and rushed across London to find Garrick standing in the wings, dressed to go on stage as Felix, holding a letter in his hand, which he passed to Cradock. It reported that Arden had been found on his lawn at Brampton Ash, after blowing his brains out with a shotgun.

The intensity of the friendship of the three men was shown by Garrick's reaction to the news of Arden's suicide:

All was confusion at the theatre and the orchestra continued to play. The audience became quite clamorous; the play commenced; and Garrick absolutely rushed on with eyes swollen with tears and somehow or other dashed through the character of Felix. He was attended home and had a serious illness afterwards.

The Spencers were similarly stunned by the death of their dear friend.

By 1780, it was clear that the First Earl was not going to see old age. When his mother, the former Georgina Carteret, died in August of that year, after a long and painful battle against cancer, John's demise was also believed to be imminent. Horace Walpole wrote to friends: 'The Countess Cowper is at last delivered from her misery. She died with consummate courage and, at the same time, with the weakness of trying to conceal the cause of death.' As a postscript, he added: 'Her own son, Lord Spencer, is in a bad state of health.'

The following year, John became permanently disabled, losing his hearing and suffering what appears to have been a severe stroke, which left him partially paralysed. No longer able to travel abroad, he spent time in Bath, trying to gain whatever healing goodness he could from taking the waters there. It was on such a visit, in October 1783, that he died. Georgiana, despite having known for years that such an event was increasingly likely, was dismayed when the blow actually fell, writing in her diary on the day after his death: 'I have passed another day half-stunned with affliction and stupefied with laudanum.' The following day's entry expands further on her overwhelming grief:

I felt as if every nerve about my head and heart would break. I never can describe or forget what I felt when they came to fetch me – my reason almost forsook me, I was left frantic and wanted to go into his room – I had not power to pass by his door, and my brother and George [her son] were forced to drag me down the stairs and lift me into the coach.

She went back to her beloved Althorp, to await the arrival of her husband's body. It was carried from Bath to Northamptonshire with the pomp reserved for a man of Spencer's legendary wealth and power. Robert Hawdon, under-steward to the Spencers at their Holywell residence in St Albans, reported to his mistress on the progress of the coffin over the last few miles of its journey:

My Lady,

All your Ladyship's servants met the corpse at Huntsbury [now Hunsbury] Hill yesterday morning at eleven o'clock, and joined the procession, which was nearly as follows: all the charity boys two and two first; about thirty tenants two and two, Doctor and Mr James Preedy in a mourning coach and six; next to the state horse with a man uncovered, carrying before him the coronet on a crimson velvet cushion; after a man on foot carrying the plume of feathers; after him eight mutes on foot two and two; after the hearse, richly ornamented; after, all the servants in order two and two; after, two mourning coaches, etc.; and the gentlemen and tradesmen about sixty in number, all in deep mourning, closed the procession, riding in order two and two; they went in this order through the town to Dallington Gate, where the procession ended, until they came to the Atterbury Gate, when it begun as before except the boys. There were the greatest concourse of people ever known on the like occasion, and I believe there were full three thousand people walked through Northampton streets with the procession and at Harlestone the whole or major part of the people came with the procession to the gate. I believe it was the most solemn, the most numerous, and most respectful procession that has ever been seen in this kingdom. The body lies in state in the great dining room, and will proceed to church in the same order it came here.

Georgiana's life changed dramatically with the onset of widowhood. She announced that she would observe a period of mourning of two years, and that she would retire to Holywell, the Duchess of Marlborough's childhood home, leaving Althorp for her son, George John, his wife, Lavinia, and their baby heir, Jack, born a year before the First Earl's death.

The Spencer family took stock of its possessions, on the death of the First Earl, and it was stunned to find that a life of unremitting extravagance had, in under forty years, reduced the entire estate to less than a quarter of its assumed size. The elections, the books, Spencer House, the gambling, the art collection, the high living, had each taken a hand in reducing the once fabulous wealth to an altogether more modest level. The resentment felt by John's immediate descendants at this irresponsibility can be detected in Jack, the Third Earl Spencer's, pious observation of his grandfather that: 'Whether he [John] was a religious man or not, I do not know; but it is clear, from the total absence of all self-command which was exhibited in his conduct, that the true principles of Christianity could not have entered fully into his mind.'

Georgiana, on the other hand, demonstrated in her widowhood a side of her character that had previously been obscured by material concerns: a devout Christianity, which led her to dedicate her remaining years to good works.

By the terms of her husband's will, she had been left as sole guardian to the three children of the marriage, as well as the only executor of the will. George John, now Second Earl Spencer, was left the furniture of Althorp and Spencer House, as well as the Duchess of Marlborough's stunning silver. But Georgiana, who had always hankered after a simple life, agreed to hand everything over to her son, in exchange for his agreeing to pay off all her husband's debts and allowing her to take whatever furniture she might need for her modest St Albans home.

During her husband's youth, the couple had spent tens of thousands of pounds every year on themselves and their pleasures. Now, Georgiana was left with an allowance of £3,000, which George John insisted on increasing to £4,000 annually. Georgiana was touched by this gesture, knowing that there was not that sort of money to spare from the overstretched resources of the estate: 'As I had fully made up my mind to live upon this £3,000, the additional £1,000 makes me quite rich,' she gamely wrote, 'and I cannot but receive with pleasure an obligation from such a son . . . All I am anxious about is to have my Lord's kindness to me known to those who care about me.'

Holywell was nothing like Althorp in terms of scale or style, but it had two attractions for the dowager countess: it was manageable, and it was perfectly situated, half-way between Althorp and London, to guarantee visits on a regular basis from her family and friends. It was regarded by her contemporaries as an eccentric choice of home for a lady of title to live in, *The Topographer* periodical carrying an article in October 1789 describing 'A Tour through the Midlands', which read:

Early in the morning on opening our windows we were pleased with looking down upon the trees and white house of the Countess Spencer, at the bottom of the street which descends very rapidly. The name of it is Holywell House. It was built by old Sarah, the famous Duchess of Marlborough, whose family we presume by an inscription we saw in the abbey church were natives of this place. It is now Lady Spencer's jointure house. On strolling out before breakfast, we found that the back part of this house and each side looked entirely into the countryside, incommoded by the town. The garden is, however, small, and surrounded after the old fashion with brick walls. Altogether it had not the appearance of the house of nobility.

And yet it was exactly what Georgiana wanted. She had moved into Holywell when it had not been a home, merely a stopping-off point for changing horses or staying the occasional night, functions the house had served for two generations. Despite its twenty fire-places, visitors found it a cold place. This Georgiana was determined to change, bringing her love of informality to her dower house, and transmitting it to her guests. A friend, Hannah More, reported in March 1784, just a few months into Georgiana's widowhood, 'Lady Spencer is very composed and cheerful, [and] lives with great regularity . . . There is no ceremony or form of any kind, as you will believe, when I tell you that I have not changed my dress till today, though we have many noble visitors . . .'

Georgiana, Countess of Carlisle, Georgiana Spencer's granddaughter, recalled her childhood visits to Holywell with enormous affection – entering the double courtyard in front of the white house, past 'fat old Joe' the porter, into the hall with its old clock, noting how extremely clean everything was, and how the living arrangements were grand, but somehow homely – even the full-length Gainsborough of Georgiana Spencer's brother, William Poyntz, appearing more family portrait than imposing masterpiece.

Outside, the garden was laid out with a simplicity that was ideal for a middle-aged, then elderly, woman to oversee and enjoy. There was a bowling green, where the family would take their coffee. To the right of that a canal, where Georgiana kept a boat, and from which John Ward, the butler, would catch carp and tench for the table. Opposite the house was an open grove, bordered by a high wall. The terrace beside the grove had a greenhouse in the middle of it, and a small plant nursery alongside that.

Georgiana Carlisle's memories were of a place – as her grand-mother intended – entirely suited to the needs and appetites of the children of the house, except for the regimented timing of meals in the dining room.

Oh! The good dinners in this room at half past three o'clock! I remember I was so hungry – the time appeared to be very late. The true English cookery of Jenny Matthews . . . How good were the breakfasts and teas in this room, and the brown bread and butter with sage leaves sometimes stuck thereupon; the honey in the honeycomb . . . My grandmother coming in tired sometimes with the business of the day . . . in a peculiar sort of dress something between a riding habit and a Joseph, particularly not young looking, as my mother said of her in her verses on Holywell, written many years before:

> For though she tries her face to hide
> In covered cap and bonnet wide,
> And more one's judgement to surprise,
> With spectacles conceals her eyes,
> Yet still all bounteous and serene
> The every look the Fairy's seen;

And were she not, in every word
Her powerful sense and worth is heard,
And every hour her deeds impart
The stamp of a superior heart.

The last two lines of this verse refer to the first Lady Spencer's life of good works. She had turned to Christianity after the death of her daughters Charlotte, in 1766 – shortly after her first birthday – and Louise, three years later. Frederick, Fourth Earl of Bristol, had noticed Georgiana Spencer's concern for the less privileged during a visit he paid to Althorp in 1779:

Lady Spencer you know is my model of women, and having seen her in retirement and in all her domestic employments, my admiration and respect of her increase: she has so decided a character that nothing can warp it, and then such a simplicity of manner one would think she had never lived in it – Her charitable institutions are worthy of her, both for their object and their direction. She has reclaimed the manners of a most vicious parish [Brington, next to Althorp], merely by her charitable institutions in it and is so bent upon having the parishioners neat as well as religious and virtuous that she is paving every path through it – not ostentatiously but with a single flag-stone, just to give the inhabitants a taste for cleanliness.

In her widowhood, such charitable impulses only increased. After Sunday schools were introduced in England, she was an early champion of the initiative to bring children into the Christian faith in a gentle but structured way. At first, she funded one such school in Brentford, under the care of a Mr Trimmer, before setting up another in St Albans. She took a full and active role in this school, teaching in it herself, and often following her poorest pupils back to their homes, to see that they were being properly cared for, and were observing the respect and obedience for God and their parents that she had been teaching the children earlier in the day.

Her kindness and concern were not limited to children, though. Sarah Marlborough had endowed an institution in St Albans with funds to look after up to thirty-six elderly folk, people who had 'known better days, but who were happy to find, in this asylum, a refuge from the vicissitudes of fortune, and to enjoy there that quiet and repose so essential to those who are far advanced in life', as a contemporary admiringly wrote. Georgiana oversaw the institution personally, often spending time with the aged occupants to alleviate their loneliness.

Georgiana also became known around St Albans for her care of the sick of all ages, as well as for her willingness to visit prisons – the latter considered by many of her own social background a quite extraordinary thing to choose to do. Tales of her feeding the hungry and clothing the poor abounded. Mrs Trimmer, wife of the Sunday school teacher in Brentford, and helper to Georgiana in her work in St Albans, was a great admirer of the charitable countess:

. . . comforting the afflicted, consoling the dying, and pouring into all the balm of kindness and sympathy . . . Though blessed with an excellent understanding, and adorned with every advantage that exalted rank, splendid connections, riches and great personal accomplishments could bestow, all sunk beneath the virtues of the meek and pious Christian.

As well as having them to stay, Georgiana also frequently visited her growing family – particularly enjoying spending time at Althorp, and also calling on her daughter, Georgiana Devonshire, at Chatsworth, or Devonshire House. As she wrote to her third surviving child, Harriet Duncannon, in 1792: 'The happiness of my children I think I do not deceive myself by saying, is that on which mine entirely depends.'

She unostentatiously assumed the role of matriarch, trying hard to impart some of her Christian values to her two increasingly wayward daughters. Her son, George John, was altogether less of a disappointment to her. In fact, the only rebuke I have ever found from mother to son is an oblique one, dated September 1786:

Many thanks for the invitation to Althorp, indeed I have great pleasure in the thoughts of going to see you there and elsewhere sometime or other, but I always resolved not to visit that place till your father's monument should be put up – as I hate to have (what has so often happened) those sort of things talked of and not done.

Georgiana then cleverly insinuated her own specifications for such a monument – again without any outward appearance of bossiness:

By the by, I have been very careless in not consulting you about an inscription; I do not like much, but something I think should be said to mark his being a worthy character and so far to explain the design of the monument as to point out that among many virtues Liberality claimed the right to preserve his memory.

Because of her longevity, Georgiana Spencer lived to see several of her grandchildren reach adulthood, and she found the time to go to see them, as she had her children, in the various mansions that were their homes. Aged seventy-three, in 1810 she went to visit her granddaughter, Harriet, who was by then Countess Granville. Harriet wrote,

My grandmother arrived here yesterday morning. She has been quite delightful and it is to me to see her so much pleased and at her ease with Granville . . . I should imagine that she had passed half her life here, and her perfectly good and 'sans son assiette' manner in whatever society she falls into always excites my surprise and admiration. Very early hours, very good books and most unwearied chess-playing are just what suit her. She is all kindness to me and I think, pleased with our having wished to have her here so intimately.

But wherever Georgiana went, her own customs and conditions accompanied her, as Lady Granville's valedictory sentence in the letter explained: 'I must leave you for we breakfast an hour earlier than usual for my grandmother.'

The one relation she experienced difficulty with was her daughter-in-law, Lavinia, married to George John, and herself the daughter of the Earl of Lucan. At first, Georgiana had been impressed by

Lavinia, telling Georgiana Devonshire, in a letter of December 1782:

Lavinia has made some very good alterations in the hanging of the pictures and has turned a bit of a dirty littered orchard near the Kitchen Garden and Nursery into a sort of pleasure ground with, I think, a good deal of taste – in short she has a great many pretty ideas and seems really fond of Althorp, which delights me as I know it gives your Father pleasure.

However, after the First Earl's death the following year, the relationship between the two very strong, but totally different, women quickly unravelled. When he came to write his memoirs, John Charles, Lavinia's son, alluded directly to the *froideur* between the two Ladies Spencer: 'I knew my grandmother [Georgiana] . . . very well, and I think I can form the estimate of her character; but I am aware that, from the circumstance of my mother never having liked her, my estimate will probably be more unfavourable than it ought.' That was the case, for this grandson's assessment of Georgiana is perhaps the least generous that can be found to survive from a first-hand source.

The tension between the two ladies was obvious to all. At the end of 1811 Harriet Granville wrote: 'Lady Spencer [Lavinia] is certainly better without my grandmother [Georgiana], for they irritate and fidget each other from morning till night. My grandmother cannot tolerate Lady Spencer's intolerance and they have no taste or pursuit in common.'

Poor George John was caught in the middle of all this, both the key women in his life looking to him for support against the other. On 17 October 1801, he received the following from his mother, about the gardens at his Wimbledon home, and the landscape designer, Lapidge, of Hampton Court:

The flat surface from the mulberry tree on the east is the only bad point as it is more seen than it used to be. I would give my ears that Lapidge had the management of it but I think neither of you like him, so I have promised Lavinia I will say no more about him though I do think him invaluable both in point of taste and expense, for he is perfectly honest and from long habit knows how to do things in the most reasonable way.

Lavinia's letter to George John, two days later, gives a contrary view of the same set of circumstances:

Your mother left me on Friday . . . She put me very near into a passion once or twice about different things she observed about Wimbledon and teased me so about having Lapwich or Lappage, whatever is his name, that you see I am not yet quite cool. She told me that you would always have continued employing him if I had not prevented you – I am sure this is the most unfounded charge of hers, for I don't remember ever saying anything against the man to you . . .

But, fourteen years earlier, after he had been asked to quote for alterations to the grounds at Althorp – including filling in the dry moat around the house itself – Lavinia had made sure that Lapidge was not employed by her husband – a fact she chose to forget with the same guile that made her pretend she could not remember the man's name properly.

George John constantly tried to reconcile his wife and his mother, but without success. In 1807, for her seventieth birthday, he gave Georgiana a white cornelian seal, magnificently set in gold, with an inscription from the Proverbs of Solomon: 'Her children shall arise up and call her blessed.' These words, in Roman letters, were surrounded by the names of the four families which she had contributed to as mother and grandmother: Spencers, Cavendishes, Ponsonbys and Howards. Georgiana loved the present, but she treated with complete disbelief her son's claim that the design was as much Lavinia's as his own.

It is hard not to believe that Lavinia was more at fault in the relationship between the two ladies: she was a more brittle and domineering character than her affable and charming mother-in-law, and being made to feel somehow inferior to Georgiana was more than she could bear.

Georgiana's last years, however, were less concerned with her matriarchal role in the Spencer family, than with the life beyond. She openly prepared herself for death, frequently reassuring those around her that she had no fear of what was to come, since God had spared her such anxieties, out of his great kindness.

Her last few months were spent in great illness, before a recovery that proved to be as illusory as it was temporary. Georgiana spent her last evening deep in happy conversation with her beloved grandson, the young Duke of Devonshire. When she retired to bed, she seemed well and in good spirits, as she did when she got up on the morning of 18 March 1814. However, while dressing, she was seized by a violent stomach cramp. She had only time to tell her maid, who was assisting her with her clothes, not to be alarmed. She then fell, dead, to the floor.

On her death her obituarist summed up the achievements of Georgiana's long, two-paced life thus:

It may be said of her with sober truth, that during the prosperity and splendour of her early life, and the retirement and regret of her widow-hood, she fulfilled exemplarily and exactly the duties of each situation. Amidst the pleasures and occupations of the world she never had forgotten the offices of benevolence and piety, nor did sorrow and seclusion, and advancing years, tinge either her thoughts or her deportment with the slightest degree of harshness or austerity.

# 11. Duchess of Devonshire, Empress of Style

The first Countess Spencer gave her Christian name to her eldest daughter. Born in June 1757, young Georgiana was destined to become one of the most famous figures of late eighteenth-century English society, being noted for her style, charm and magnetism. Horace Walpole encapsulated her special gifts, when he wrote: 'She effaces all without being a beauty; but her youthful figure, flowing good nature, sense and lively modesty, and modest familiarity, make her a phenomenon.'

Georgiana's life was governed by the conflicting tensions of glamour, addiction, controversy and tragedy. Infectious in her enthusiasm for life, driven in her political beliefs, she was also prey to weaknesses which she proved incapable of overcoming, even when she recognized them in herself. Having enough self-knowledge to identify her faults, but insufficient resolve to correct or eliminate them, she found deep unhappiness in her own state – unhappiness that she consistently transmitted to those around her.

At Althorp there is a beautiful portrait of the three adult children of the First Earl and Countess Spencer by Angelica Kauffmann. To the right stands George John, the middle in age, his bright red hair swept back, looking down at his two pretty sisters, seated together, in sumptuous dresses, their hands clasped devotedly. The central figure is Lady Harriet Spencer, the youngest of the three, her left arm gently placed around Georgiana's shoulders; and it is to Georgiana that the eye is inextricably drawn. She sits there so arrestingly, without actually being beautiful, toying with a string of pearls, and looking out of the canvas with an expression of freshness, intelligence and extreme vulnerability.

Other portraits of her at Althorp are similarly captivating. Both Reynolds and Gainsborough painted her as a little girl, and I have placed the pictures next to one another in the South Drawing

Room, because they show how the two great portrait painters of the time viewed their sitter: Reynolds has her as a slightly chubby, deeply angelic, sweet and unthreatening child presence, standing on a table, eyes level with those of her doting mother; whereas Gainsborough, with sharper lines all round, shows a highly intuitive old soul, captured in a girl's body, knowledge beyond her years blazing from feline eyes.

I believe Reynolds's and Kauffmann's portraits have proved to be the most accurate projections of Georgiana's essential spirit. There was something deeply childlike about her; and also something fundamentally fragile. It was the outward attractiveness of Georgiana, her physical appeal, combined with the refreshing energy of her character, which marked her out for singular attention both from her contemporaries and from the burgeoning press of her time. It also lay at the root of the unhappiness that would be the dominant theme of her life.

As Georgiana was the daughter of one of the wealthiest men in the kingdom, her hand in marriage was among the most highly prized in the country. However, recognizing their daughter's impetuosity and relative immaturity of character, the Spencers were keen to spare Georgiana from too early a marriage. But she was wilful enough to ignore their advice.

As early as January 1772, there was speculation linking her to one of the richest young men in the land. Mrs Delaney, who always liked to be up to date on such matters, wrote to the Reverend John Dewes:

Many weddings are talked of, but so often contradicted, I am afraid of naming them; it is 'thought there is a future scheme under consideration for a union between the Duke of Devonshire and Lady Georgiana Spencer.' I think that paragraph would make a figure in a newspaper, and just in that style!

Two years later, Mrs Delaney's prediction came true, Georgiana's mother writing to Viscount Nuneham, in April 1774:

Nothing but the incessant hurry I have lived in for several weeks could have prevented my writing sooner to inform you of Georgiana's intended marriage with the Duke of Devonshire. You will have heard of it from others, but what you cannot hear so well as from myself, is that it is really a match of inclination, which makes it infinitely more satisfactory to us than his riches or rank could have done . . . She had several very great offers, but gave the preference without hesitation to the Duke of Devonshire, and seems perfectly satisfied with the choice she has made, which indeed we have great reason to believe is a very good one.

A month later, perhaps with more honesty, Countess Spencer wrote to Mrs Henry:

I had flattered myself I should have had more time to have improved her understanding and, with God's assistance to have strengthened her principles, and enabled her to avoid the many snares that vice and folly will throw in her way. She is amiable, innocent and benevolent, but she is giddy, idle and fond of dissipation.

Public interest in the match was so intense that, rather than marrying on the appointed day – Georgiana's seventeenth birthday – the couple secretly brought matters forward by forty-eight hours. Perhaps partially inspired by the romance of her own parents' secret wedding, as well as by fear that the ceremony would lose dignity through the curiosity of so many, Georgiana agreed to the change of plan. Her cousin, Charles Poyntz, officiated at the ceremony.

Mrs Delaney had seen too many such unions, not to be able to detect underlying difficulties:

It was as great a secret to Lady Ga. Spencer as to the world. Sunday morning she was told her doom; she went out of town (to Wimbledon) early on Sunday, and they were married at Wimbledon church . . . as quietly and uncrowded as if John and Joan had tied the Gordian Knot. Don't think because I have made use of the word 'doom' that it was a melancholy sentence (though a surprise) to the young lady; for she is so peculiarly happy as to think his Grace very agreeable, and had not the least regret – a bliss which I most sincerely hope will prove a lasting one.

She then gave a grave hint as to why that might not be possible:

The Duke's intimate friends say he has sense and does not want merit –
to be sure the jewel has not been well polished: had he fallen under the
tuition of the late Lord Chesterfield, he might have possessed 'les graces',
but at present only that of his dukedom belongs to him.

Despite all this, Mrs Delaney ended up by imploring, 'I heartily
wish they may be as happy as they are great!'

It did not take long for Georgiana to see her marriage as others
viewed it: with pessimism. Within a year of the ceremony, she had
miscarried and nearly died. The duke had proved less attentive than
she would have expected, and tensions were increased by her
growing gambling problems. Despite an allowance of £4,000 per
year, she was already in debt to the sum of £3,000. Georgiana's
parents agreed to pay this off, on condition that she confess the
extent of her folly to her husband. When she obeyed them, the
duke reimbursed his parents-in-law for the full amount, without
comment. However, others were openly talking about the profligacy of the young duchess, and Devonshire's growing sense of
humiliation was reinforced when Sheridan's play *School For Scandal*
debuted in 1777; it was evident that Georgiana's reputation was
the inspiration for the dizzy character of Lady Teazle.

From an early stage, the elderly relations on each side could see
that all was not well with the marriage. Countess Cowper, the First
Earl Spencer's mother and Georgiana Devonshire's grandmother,
alluded to the problem in a letter to a Mrs Port, dated February
1778: 'The Duchess of Devonshire is much quieter than she was,
and is always at home before the Duke . . .'

Gradual acceptance that the marriage was not a success led
Georgiana to take an increasingly independent stance, socially,
politically and romantically. These three strands constantly overlapped, but Georgiana's undoubted pre-eminence in social status,
allied with her increasingly intense desire to partake in the sphere
of politics, combined with her vulnerability to passionate attach-
ments to members of both sexes, formed a heady cocktail which

certainly assured her of the attentions of the masses. Long intrigued by the goings-on of the aristocracy, they were now served by a newspaper industry of unprecedented sophistication and influence. By the end of the 1770s, the decade in which Georgiana was launched into the public consciousness, there were nine daily newspapers competing with one another in London alone.

With her distinctive style, Georgiana was a godsend to circulation figures, attracting huge attention for every new nuance of fashion that she initiated. It was largely thanks to her that the hoop, with its rigidity and formality, became a thing of the past; and yet her championing of the equally ludicrous hair tower, which was a yard high, was slavishly imitated by any lady who had the leisure time and the money to employ hairdressers to build up such a showy statement of vanity and indolence. Similarly, the French hair powder she favoured gained enormous popularity, and her liking for muslin gowns made them the height of fashion. It would be no exaggeration to state that Georgiana was the epicentre of all that was modish and desirable.

There is no doubt that, although bemused by the attention she received, the young Georgiana also revelled in the shallow excitement of it all; a point not missed by her increasingly prim mother, who scolded Georgiana on her twenty-fifth birthday: 'In your dangerous path of life you have almost unavoidably amassed a great deal of useless trash – gathered weeds instead of flowers. You live so constantly in public you cannot live for your own soul.'

However, she was prepared to sacrifice some of her privacy for those causes closest to her heart – and none was closer than that of the Whig politicians. The Spencers and the Devonshires were two of the leading Whig families, but this can only explain Georgiana's inclination to support them – not the fervour she expended in the cause.

In all she did, Georgiana betrayed the characteristics of an addictive personality: her relationships were indicative of this, as were her uncontrollable vices. Indeed, this mindset extended to the way in which she threw herself so wholeheartedly into politics. Even when she was severely damaged by public and private criticism for getting involved in what was viewed predominantly as a man's game, she could not resist the thrill of the unpredictability of it all, the agony and ecstasy of defeat and victory.

It was Charles James Fox who ignited Georgiana's passion for politics. He stayed with Georgiana at Chatsworth in 1777, although they would have met prior to that at Althorp, where he was a frequent guest of the Spencers. During his Chatsworth visit, he gave the twenty-year-old duchess confidence that she could be more than merely the fashion icon wife of one of the most wealthy and influential men in the country. She could, through her direct interest and involvement, exercise power of her own, by helping to persuade people to support the Whig party.

Georgiana was eternally grateful that a figure she respected so greatly could see value in her own contribution to the party they both espoused. Later, she would repay Fox's confidence in her with a poem, which she had placed with his bust at Chatsworth:

> Here amidst the friends he loved, the man behold
> In truth unshaken, and in virtue bold;
> Whose patriot zeal, and uncorrupted mind,
> Dared to assert the freedom of mankind:
> And whilst extending desolation far
> Ambition spread the baneful flames of war;
> Fearless of blame, and eloquent to save,
> Twas he – 'twas Fox the warning counsel gave,
> Midst jarring conflicts stemmed the tide of blood
> And to the menaced world a sea mark stood.
>
> Ah! Had his voice in Mercy's cause prevailed,
> What grateful millions had the statesman hailed
> Whose wisdom bade the broils of nations cease,
> And taught the world Humanity and Peace.
> But, though, he failed, succeeding ages here
> The vain, yet pious, effort shall revere;
> Boast in their annals his illustrious name,
> Behold his greatness, and confirm his fame.

Horace Walpole once said of one of Georgiana's poems that it was 'easy and prettily expressed, though it does not express much'. However, the above composition shows the intensity of her belief in Fox and the causes he represented. She believed – as did her brother, George John, then Viscount Althorp – that the American colonies should be granted their freedom from the unwelcome tyranny of the British Crown, and she adopted the blue and buff colours of the colonial soldiers to show her solidarity with their cause. In this way her position of 'empress of fashion' cross-pollinated her desire to be seen as a serious political figure in her own right.

Lord North's Tory ministry fell in 1782. Now Georgiana devoted all her energies and a considerable amount of money to helping the Whigs, who triumphed in the subsequent general election. So important was the support of the celebrated aristocrat seen to be by the Whigs at the time, that they even had fans made with images of Georgiana on them, which they sold by the hundred to help fund and publicize their aims.

Two years later, in 1784, Georgiana, with her devoted younger sister, Harriet, again pitched in to help the Whigs. This time the cause was directly that of Fox, who was seeking one of the two important parliamentary seats of Westminster. There were only 18,000 voters, since the right to enfranchisement in Britain, until 1832, was very strictly regulated, being based on qualifications of income and property. However, it seemed to those who watched the two Spencer girls canvassing that they intended personally to address each of those eligible to vote, in a bid to do their best for Fox. Indeed, the lengths to which these two noble ladies were prepared to go to grub up votes, struck many as unseemly. Cornwallis noted that Georgiana was prepared to visit 'some of the most blackguard houses in the Long Acre', while Horace Walpole remarked that she was 'coarsely received by some worse than tars', and that she 'made no scruple of visiting some of the humblest of electors, dazzling and enchanting them by the fascination of her manner, the power of her beauty and the influence of her high rank'.

Georgiana and Harriet were not the only ladies of title prepared to get their hands dirty in this most grubby and bitter of campaigns – Lady Salisbury was doing much the same for the Tories – but Georgiana's notoriety made her an easy target for critics of her party and herself. They said she exchanged her kisses for votes, something she always denied, but definitely a charge that has stuck for over two centuries – it was the first story about my great-great-great aunt that I can remember being told as a boy. And then there were insinuations at the time, particularly in the Tory press, that she was not stopping at kissing. The accusation that she was having an affair with Fox may have been more valid, but the picture of a depraved aristocrat hawking her body around the most unsavoury parts of Westminster, prepared to prostitute herself in return for votes, was a concerted attempt to belittle and undermine through vicious and persistent libels one of the Whigs' most potent electoral weapons.

The result was a vindication of Georgiana's stoicism in the face of vile abuse: Fox was elected in a victory that became a hallowed part of the Whig tradition. Furthermore, Georgiana had achieved her goal by becoming a recognized political figure in the country at large. However, this success was at a cost not just to her peace of mind – the press abuse continued well after the votes were counted – but also to the Devonshire finances. It was estimated that Georgiana spent over £30,000 in support of Fox in the 1784 Westminster campaign, much of it, according to her opponents, through inducements that bordered on outright bribery.

Georgiana Spencer was becoming increasingly concerned at the way in which her daughter's life was unravelling, and, as was her wont, the Dowager Countess Spencer looked to her own inadequacies as the reason for her favourite child's shortcomings. Young Georgiana rejected such assertions:

You talk of the bad example you have set me, you can mean but one thing – gaming, and there, I do assure you it is innate, for I remember playing from seven in the morning till eight at night at Lansquenet with old Mrs Newton when I was nine years old and sent to King's Road for the measles.

Young Georgiana was right: gambling coursed through her veins. We have already seen how the four preceding generations on her father's side were all addicted to the thrill of chance. Added to this her mother's family, the Poyntzes, for all their sincere Christian inclinations, was afflicted with the same predisposition. Lord Lansdowne's dry observation illustrated the contradiction perfectly: 'I have known the Poyntzes in the nursery, the Bible on the table, the cards in the drawer.'

It is perhaps not surprising, then, that Georgiana Spencer's advice on the whole subject of gambling should have something of the expert air about it. 'Play at whist, commerce, backgammon, trictrac or chess,' she said to her daughter, 'but never at quinze, lou, brag, faro, hazard or any games of chance, and if you are pressed to play always make the fashionable excuse of being tied up not to play at such and such a game. In short I must beg you, my dearest girl, if you value my happiness to send me in writing a serious answer to this.'

However, Georgiana Spencer was unable to control her own taste for gaming, let alone that of her daughter. George Selwyn reported in a letter of 1781 to the Earl of Carlisle:

The trade or amusement which engrosses everybody who lives in what is called the pleasurable world is Pharon, and poor Mr Grady is worn out in being kept up at one lady's house or another till six in the morning. Among these, Lady Spencer and her daughter the Duchess of D., and Lady Harcourt are his chief parties.

There were also widely believed rumours that, in her passion for gambling, Georgiana Spencer had even been seen to tear the rings from her hands to place on the gaming table as wagers.

The difference between the two ladies was that Lady Spencer could afford her losses, since her husband readily funded her gambling, while the duchess had to keep her losses secret for as long as it was possible from her altogether less sympathetic partner. However, when the younger Georgiana's losses were of a size that they could no longer be ignored, she had no alternative but to approach the duke for funds.

In early 1805 there was a rumour, reported in the *Morning Herald*, that Georgiana Devonshire had lost, chiefly at faro, and principally at the hands of fellow female gamblers, a quite phenomenal £176,000, of which a very close female friend of hers was supposed, individually, to have won £30,000.

Apparently Georgiana rushed into the duke's library, crying, and informed him that she would be a woman of no reputation if her debts were not discharged. Even though she had cashed in some of her own bonds, these had not realized more than a fraction of the outstanding sum. She was therefore looking to her husband to make good the enormous shortfall.

The duke was apparently stunned by two things: the size of the alleged loss, and also the identity of the supposed friends – five women and two men – who had clearly conspired to prey on his wife's uncontrollable weakness. He summoned two of his closest friends, and asked them what to do about both situations. They were unanimous in their advice: nothing should be paid.

It is likely that some money exchanged hands, but nothing like the vast fortune that had been mentioned. It is also clear that the public shame was dealt with as best it could be, with the *Morning Herald* being persuaded to recant its story a few days later. There were, the paper said, no gamblers of distinction involved in this story; neither was there a house, as they had erroneously stated, set up near St James's Street for such people to behave in a totally excessive manner; and, for sure, the Duchess of Devonshire had never partaken of any game of chance . . . By overstating the apparent correction, the newspaper was subtly able to reinforce the credibility of its original allegations.

It was not just her privileged friends who stood to benefit from Georgiana Devonshire's addiction. There was a famous gambler of the time, 'Old Nick', who took £100 off a man running an errand for her, although the money was meant to repay a debt elsewhere.

Georgiana thought it best to appeal to 'Old Nick's' gentlemanly instincts, and asked him – given the circumstances under which his opponent had been in possession of the £100 – to return all or most of the sum to her, its rightful owner.

It became evident instantly that 'Old Nick's' gentlemanly instincts were not as well developed as his money-making ones, and he retorted lustily: 'Well, Madam, the best thing you can do is to sit down with me at cards, and play for all you have about you; after I win your smock, so far from refunding, I'll send you home BARE – to your Duke, my dear.' This proved to be one gambling invitation the duchess turned down.

It was fortunate that Georgiana enjoyed the friendship of her banker, Thomas Coutts. However, being on good terms with him meant that she could be the recipient of his frankest advice. When informing her that her debts had risen to £6,000, he took it upon himself to administer a rebuke that was redolent with exasperation:

It shocks me to think that your Grace puts into Hazard by indulging a passion for play. There is nothing your Grace can acquire; you have already titles, character, friends, fortune, power, beauty, EVERY-THING superior to the rest of the world . . . all these to gratify this destructive passion. I should be happy beyond expression if I could think that I had even the smallest share in saving your Grace from the dreadful consequences I foresee.

But Coutts was telling her nothing that she did not know already. The deep self-loathing of the unreconstructed addict bleeds through this letter, written by Georgiana in 1797 to Selina Trimmer:

Surely you know the infirmity of my nature, that with a heart not bad (I humbly trust) I have an instability of nature that is sometimes madness. The only alleviation of this to my friends is that it is only to those I love I have ever shown these odious destructive paroxysms. A thousand little fancies, little suspicions and jealousies had long, perhaps, been brooding in my mind. A spark, I know not what, brought it out.

This admitted lack of self-control spilled over as dramatically into her love life as it did into her finances. There were extramarital affairs, with some of the most notable men in the kingdom, although whether this extended to the heir to the throne remains debatable. Wraxall, who wrote Georgiana's *Posthumous Memoirs*, stated that 'the Duchess of Devonshire succeeded Lady Melbourne in the attachment of the Prince of Wales', while adding, 'of what nature was that attachment and what limits were affixed to it by the duchess, must remain [a] matter of conjecture'.

Similar mystery surrounds the question as to whether or not she was bisexual. Certainly, she had especially close relationships with two very attractive women. The first was 'the beautiful Mrs Graham', Mary Graham, whom she met at the end of 1777. When Mary was sent abroad four years later to recover from consumption, Georgiana was left numb with sadness – to a greater extent than might be considered normal – at the physical absence of a mere friend.

More intense still was her relationship with Lady Elizabeth Hervey, the daughter of the Bishop of Derry, who was later Earl of Bristol. In an age when marital separation and divorce were still deeply unconventional, Lady Elizabeth had left her husband, John Thomas Foster, and had chosen to live by herself, despite the greatly reduced financial circumstances this left her in. However, she was confident of her own legendary irresistibility. 'No man could withstand her,' said the historian Edward Gibbon. 'If she chose to beckon the Lord Chancellor from his Woolsack in full sight of the world, he could not resist obedience.'

She managed to inveigle her way into the company of the Duke and Duchess of Devonshire, becoming a useful buffer to both in their troubled marriage. Georgiana's mother, Countess Spencer, did not like the unconventional arrangement at all, guessing that Elizabeth – also known as 'Bess' – was intimate at least with her son-in-law; and most likely with her daughter, too.

Georgiana was deeply protective of the burgeoning *ménage à trois*, telling her mother:

I have just been speaking to the Duke about your objection to Lady Eliz. He has often told me that (if we continue to live together, which my unfortunate conduct about money renders very doubtful) if I had a moment's uneasiness about her he would be far from wishing her to live with us . . . But good God, how far is this from being the case. I have, as well as him, the highest regard and respect and esteem for her as well as Love. In this case Dearest M. you must feel how impossible, how cruel, it would be to expose her to the malignant ill nature of the world and to expose ourselves to all the misery of parting with her, for what we know to be unjust and false . . .

How 'unjust and false' such suspicions were to remain, is open to question. It would appear from a letter that Bess wrote in 1784 that there was an element of romantic passion in the relationship:

Who has any right to know how long or how tenderly we love one another! Why are excuses to be made for its sharpness and its fervency? . . . Why is our union to be profaned by having a lie told about it? Can I ever forget the note that contained 'the first instant I saw you, my heart flew to your service'? No, my dearest love, let spite and envy and jealousy do its full, I am proof against its sharper arrows, it has done its worst, for I do not reckon among possible things its now hurting you.

If Bess and Georgiana were lovers, it seems clear that monogamy was not a condition of their relationship. In 1791 the duchess embarked on an affair with Charles Grey, the future Prime Minister, and quickly became pregnant by her young lover. The Duke of Devonshire knew that the pregnancy was not of his making, and despite having his own mistresses – one of whom, Charlotte Spencer (no relative of Georgiana's), had borne him a daughter in 1774 – was beside himself with fury when faced with his own humiliation. He pursued Georgiana, her sister Harriet and Elizabeth to Bath, where they were trying their hardest to shield the truth from the cuckolded husband, and sent Georgiana into exile overseas. Harriet reported the decision to her own mother-in-law: 'We must go abroad immediately – nothing else will do. Neither prayers nor entreaties will alter him. He says there is no choice between this, or public entire separation at home. Bess has very generously promised to go with us . . .'

Georgiana Spencer thought it best for her two daughters to go to France, on the pretence that such a trip was necessary for Harriet's health. She tried to stop Bess going, too, but Bess and Georgiana were by now inseparable.

The banishment lasted two years, and ended only when the French Revolution took a startling turn in 1793, with Louis XVI's execution. Conditions were now simply too dangerous for the duchess to remain in France any longer. In the meantime, Georgiana had given birth to Grey's daughter, known as Eliza Courtney, in Montpellier. Eliza later joined Grey's family, and was introduced to people as his younger sister.

Devonshire had offered Georgiana a stark choice, as the birth became imminent: either give her illegitimate child away and promise not to see its father again, or be divorced, and lose any right to see their mutual children again. She chose the former, since the prospect of further absence from her Cavendish children appalled her. During her time in France, away from her young, she had written to her nine-year-old daughter: 'This year has been the most painful of my life.'

For all her weaknesses, Georgiana was a very loving mother, turning her amateur writing skills to amusing them. She wrote a poem, 'Passage of the Mountain of St Gothard', dedicated to them – a work that was sufficiently highly regarded to be translated into French, Italian and German between 1802 and 1805. In 1816 it was reprinted by Bess, along with 'Journey through Switzerland', a work which led Coleridge to write:

> O Lady, nursed in pomp and pleasure,
> Whence learned you that heroic measure?

On her return in September 1793 from her enforced stay abroad, Georgiana was somewhat chastened. She honoured her word, and did not arrange to see Grey again, even though she was still in love with him. She also managed to channel some of her energies into worthy pursuits, turning a room in Devonshire House into a laboratory – where she conducted her own scientific experiments – and attending lectures at the Royal Academy.

Georgiana also devoted her attentions to those whom she had missed most during her time in France. Her sense of family was not confined to a deep care for her children, and she remained on good terms with her Spencer relatives – particularly her brother, George John, who had stayed loyal to her throughout her disgrace and exile. In April 1794, she wrote to him: 'We passed last week at Woburn Abbey . . . I had the pleasure of seeing Althorp again; and now to make me like it as much as it deserves, it only requires for me to see it with you and Lavinia.' She continued, in loving and flattering vein, 'Woburn is magnificent and comfortable but I assure Althorp lost nothing by comparison; and the D: of B: [Duke of Bedford], who went with us, was very much delighted with it – and quite jealous of the Library and Dairy . . .'

If the Georgiana who returned from France was an altogether more thoughtful person than the one who had set out for it, there was sadly to be no such happy transformation for her physically. From 1796, her health started to deteriorate, and in a way that was cruelly obvious for one so vain, ravaging her looks: her right eye, initially merely painful, became inflamed and then swelled up to a huge size. Georgiana Spencer commented that her daughter had 'little sight in her right eye and cannot yet lift up the eyelid except a very little way without assistance – it is . . . horrible to look at'.

The duchess who had once happily turned heads wherever she went, now longed for nobody to so much as look at her. As she herself acknowledged: 'I grow more shy every day, and hate going anywhere except to my own boxes at the play and opera.' The doctors had no idea how to treat her, subjecting their patient to appalling abuse, in the name of medicine. They strangled her, supposedly to increase the flow of blood to the affected area. Leeches were used, but to no avail. The eye became increasingly infected, and its sight started to fail.

The final years of Georgiana Devonshire were marked with

sadness; with her continued addiction to gambling, the resulting debts were a major source of concern for her and those around her. In 1799, Georgiana Spencer wrote to her son of Georgiana: 'She is and always will be imprudent in the highest degree, but I trust in God she is not intentionally dishonest.' However, the boundaries between intentional and unintentional dishonesty were by now as blurred as her sight, and Georgiana cheated her friend the Duke of Bedford out of a loan he had advanced her to meet some of her outstanding debts, leading to his refusing ever to have anything to do with her again.

Meanwhile, illness compounded her financial misery. 'I have been fretful and low,' she confided. 'Worries about money which return with quarter days, and the unwholesome life I lead, put me out of sorts.'

In 1806, her health took a final turn for the worse when she caught a chill. Confined to bed, it was soon discovered that she was far more seriously ill than had previously been supposed, with a liver abscess which proved to be fatal. Again, the doctors not only failed to diagnose her condition correctly; in their keenness to be seen to be doing something, they caused Georgiana unnecessary pain. While she drifted in and out of a coma, they shaved her head and applied scalding blisters to her scalp. The right eye having failed her, the left one started to dim, too.

And so the final days of one of the most glamorous figures of her era were spent in tortured confinement, surrounded by relatives and friends appalled by the suffering they were witnessing in one they deeply loved, despite all the disappointments and troubles her flawed character had visited upon them during her life.

At 3.30 a.m. on 30 March 1806, Georgiana died. Bess's journal reveals the desolation she felt at the loss of someone so dear, in such ghastly, agonizing circumstances: 'Saturday was a day of horror beyond all words to express . . . My heart feels broken . . . my angel friend – angel I am sure she is now – but can I live without her who was the life of my existence!'

Georgiana lay in state for five days, and attracted a steady line of mourners. Outside, in Piccadilly, thousands of Londoners came to

Devonshire House to pay their own respects to a lady far removed from the realities of their existence, whose privileged life they somehow identified with – or, at least, were intrigued by.

The Prince of Wales, on hearing the news of Georgiana's death, gave her troubled life a fittingly generous postscript: 'Then the best natured and best bred woman in England is gone.'

Among the family members in the group who witnessed Georgiana Devonshire's tortured end was Harriet, her loyal and devoted sister. She never recovered from the loss of the sibling who was also her dearest friend, whose follies and misjudgements she had sometimes matched and at other times tried to defuse or gloss over.

Harriet, too, had made an unfortunate marriage – to Frederick, Lord Duncannon – although at the time of it, in 1780, the society figure Mrs Delaney had felt quite upbeat about this Spencer wedding, hoping that it would give Georgiana, Countess Spencer,

great satisfaction; as besides rank and fortune this is a most worthy amiable man, and I believe by all accounts she is a very valuable young woman, and I hope will have the good sense not to fall into those giddy errors, which have hurt her sister, who I hope is now sensible of those errors.

Indeed, there were some who worried for Duncannon in his choice, including Horace Walpole, who professed surprise to his correspondent at the choice of bride: 'I know nothing to the prejudice of the young lady; but I should not have selected for so amiable and so gentle a man, a sister of the empress of fashion, nor a daughter of the Goddess of wisdom.'

It appears that the common perception of Duncannon as a decent man did not tally with the cold bully that Harriet had to contend with at home. Those close to her noted that she appeared to be genuinely frightened of her husband, and did not like to be left alone with him. Moreover, he had not the money that people thought he had, leading the couple to live a life of further pretence, which resulted in them spending increasing time abroad, where the need to maintain a lavish lifestyle would not be so pressing, nor the failure to do so so obvious.

This partly explains the willingness of the couple to follow Georgiana into exile with their youngest child; that, and Harriet's unswerving loyalty to her sister. Their brother, George John, kindly paid for a doctor to accompany the party, mainly to look after Harriet, whose health was poor.

In 1793, Frederick's father died, at the age of eighty-nine, and Frederick succeeded him as the Earl of Bessborough. There was now the prospect of more money in the marriage, but it never truly materialized: the inheritance, such as it was, was almost completely swallowed up by long-term creditors of the couple. At the same time marital happiness remained every bit as hard to come by as it had ever been, leading Harriet to prefer the company of her children and her sister to that of her husband. She was with Georgiana as frequently as possible until the very end, despite her own feeble health.

Like Georgiana, Harriet was never short of admirers. Of these, the keenest was the Prince of Wales, who appears to have had a particular penchant for both the Spencer girls. Harriet was the lover of the playwright Sheridan and of Lord John Townshend. However, her most significant liaison was with Lord Granville Leveson Gower, whom she met on her travels in Naples. They subsequently had a child, given the name of Harriet Arundel Stewart. In what must have been a painful union for her, Leveson Gower later married Harriet Bessborough's niece, another Harriet, who in turn adopted her and Leveson Gower's love child.

Of more lasting fame was Harriet's eldest daughter, Caroline, better known as Lady Caroline Lamb, and as Lord Byron's mistress. Endowed with a luscious beauty, Caroline was also afflicted with a troubled nature that both scandalized and intrigued contemporary society. The end of her passionate affair with the poet led her to write a thinly veiled account of Byron, *Glenarvon*, which resulted in Caroline's being ostracized by her social peers, while they simultaneously raced to buy their copies of the exposé.

Caroline married William Lamb, who was subsequently Prime

Minister as Lord Melbourne. He tolerated his wife's eccentric behaviour – which included stabbing herself at a society ball, and sending Lord Byron a sprig of her pubic hair – until, in the 1820s, Caroline appeared to overstep the line between tolerable and insane behaviour. They separated in 1825, and Caroline died – aged only forty-two – in 1828.

Harriet was spared from witnessing the final tormented years of her daughter. Up until her own death, she continued to spend a great deal of time abroad, maintaining the standards of style and grace that she and her sister Georgiana had always aspired to. Even when she was approaching old age, we catch a glimpse of Harriet's innate sense of decorum in a letter she wrote after attending a ball on the Continent.

I cannot tell you how sorry and ashamed I felt as an Englishwoman. The first thing I saw in the room was a short, very fat, elderly woman, with an extremely red face (owing, I suppose, to the heat) in a girl's white frock looking dress, but with shoulder, back, and neck, quite low, (disgustingly so) down to the middle of her stomach, very black hair and eyebrows, which gave her a fierce look, and a wreath of light pink roses on her head. She was dancing . . . I was staring at her from the oddity of her appearance, when suddenly she nodded and smiled at me, and not recollecting her, I was convinced she was mad, till William pushed me, saying, 'Do you not see the Princess of Wales nodding to you?'.

The handmaiden to the Empress of Fashion had no time for such vulgarity and lack of elegance.

Harriet herself died in Florence in 1821, of a bowel complaint that killed her quickly. She was mourned as 'much the cleverest and most agreeable woman I have ever known', by a friend, Mrs Arbuthnot, in her journal, who continued:

She was dotingly fond of her children, who were passionately attached to her. In her youth she had been 'très galante', and in her mature years she retained those charms of mind and manner which, in her earlier life, had rendered her irresistibly attractive. She was the kindest-hearted person that ever lived, her purse and her good offices were always at the disposal of any one in distress, and she used to laugh and say that no one ever got into a scrape without applying to her to help them out.

And then an observation that might equally have applied to Georgiana:

Her errors arose from a false education and the seductive examples of clever but unprincipled men, & were well redeemed by a warmth of heart and steadiness of friendship that rendered her dear to her family and friends, who, I am sure, will long deplore her loss.

These easily discernible qualities in both the Spencer girls make their subsequent sadness and failure to overcome their demons all the more poignant. In 1792, Georgiana, Countess Spencer, had written to a friend about her son, whose conduct and demeanour were a matter of pride for her; just as the lack of substance in her sons-in-law was something to be decried: 'What would not my daughters have been had their husbands been like him?', she asked.

# 12. From Nelson to Caxton

Since 1783, Georgiana and Harriet's brother, George John, had been head of the Spencer family. The second of the five children of the First Earl and Countess Spencer, he was their only son.

No longer encumbered by the terms of Sarah Marlborough's will, he was free to embark on any career he wanted. So it was that he reclaimed the family's pre-eminence in politics – an option that had been denied his grandfather and father. It was a world in which, through natural aptitude and his social position, he was to prove thoroughly successful.

John Spencer was determined that his son should receive the very best teaching available. From the age of seven George John's academic progress was the responsibility of William Jones, an eighteen-year-old who was one of the four scholars of the foundation of Sir Simon Bennett at Oxford. This early stage of George John's education took place predominantly at the family home in Wimbledon, but Jones accompanied his young charge to Harrow in 1769, where the Spencer heir lived like a prince with his retinue of servants, and – unheard of for a student, no matter how grand his lineage – his own carriage, complete with liveried staff.

A staunch Whig of extremely fervent views, Jones was as inspirational as he was unusual. He fought hard with the First Earl Spencer, to stop him interfering in his son's education, and he attracted quizzical curiosity from the other tutors at Harrow with his eccentric approach to imparting knowledge. He preferred 'learning fancies' to traditional classroom methods, and this included getting his colleagues, Dr Parr and Dr Bennett, to join him and young George John Althorp in the fields outside Harrow, dividing the land up into different states and kingdoms. The three men and the boy would then each choose a dominion for themselves, and, each assuming classical titles, they 'enacted the wars, negotiations and conquests of antiquity'.

William Jones thought an enormous amount of wisdom could be gleaned from the learning of the classics. As a philosophy, he cherished the resistance of tyranny above all others; indeed, he was an ardent republican. It was in the classics that he found many worthy and proud examples to reinforce his creed, and he was keen to transmit them to his aristocratic charge, who repaid Jones's dedication and care by becoming his lifelong friend and correspondent. Indeed, it was to the adult George John – still Viscount Althorp at that time – that Jones addressed a poem that stated his 'system of government and of morality too':

> Althorp, what forms a State?
> Not high-rais'd battlement or labour'd mound,
> Thick walls and moated gate;
> Not cities proud with spires and turrests crown'd;
> Not bay and broad arm'd ports,
> Where, laughing at the storm, rich navies ride;
> Nor starr'd and spangled courts,
> Where low-brow'd baseness wafts perfume to pride;
> No, – Men, high-minded Men,
> With pow'rs as far above dull brutes endued
> In forest, brake, or den
> As beasts excel cold rocks and brambles rude;
> Men, who their duties know,
> But know their rights, and knowing dare maintain,
> Prevent the long-aim'd blow,
> And crush the tyrant, while they rend the chain.

Intrigued though the Spencer heir was by such thoughts, which underlined the Whig tendencies of his own heritage, the most lasting influence of Jones on the future Second Earl Spencer was to imbue him with a passion for books, a fact acknowledged by George John when, in 1776, he gave his tutor a twenty-volume edition of the works of Cicero, Jones's favourite writer. Way beyond the development of George John's ready intellect, this bibliomania would have far-reaching consequences for the Spencer family over the succeeding generations.

After leaving Harrow itself, George John was then tutored by the school's headmaster, Dr Heath, in preparation for going up to Cambridge University. In 1776, the young viscount was admitted to Trinity College, under the Reverend Charles Norris, prebendary of Canterbury. At that stage, undergraduates from aristocratic families were not obliged to take the ordinary exams at Oxford or Cambridge, since they were eligible for a 'nobleman's degree', which required little academic study or ability; but, on being awarded his MA, in 1778, George John was known to be an esteemed and accomplished classical scholar.

A Grand Tour of the Continent lasting two years followed, before George John returned to embark on his political career, standing successfully as a Whig candidate for the House of Commons, representing the borough of Northampton. He was bitterly opposed to Lord North's Tory government, and, when that administration fell, in the main because of its disastrous handling of the war in America, George John became a Lord of the Treasury, a junior post, but recognized as being the first step towards greater things. Along with his fellow Whig 'patriots', he resolved that a priority was the granting of independence to the American colonies. He was firmly against perpetuating what he saw as a morally unjustifiable, highly expensive and doomed campaign across the Atlantic.

A year earlier, in 1781, George John had married Lavinia Bingham, whose father had recently been elevated to the earldom of Lucan. Even before the official announcement of the match in 1780 – with George John admitting to being 'out of his senses' over Lavinia – the marital intentions of such an eligible bachelor had become a matter of great interest in high society, and the Spencers found it hard to guard the privacy they sought over the forthcoming engagement announcement. Sir Horace Walpole wrote on the subject to the Countess of Upper Ossory:

I caught Lady S. [Spencer] t'other night in one of these mysteries; it was
two nights before Lord Althorp's match was owned; but I had supped at
Lord Lucan's with the whole court of Spencer, and Lord A. [Althorp]
had sat at a side-table with the two girls, [as well as] Miss Molesworth
and old Miss Shipley. I knew if I asked directly I should be answered:
'Upon my word, I know nothing of the matter'; so after supper, sitting
by Lady S. on a settee, I said: 'Pray, Lady S. is it owned that Lord A. is
to marry – Miss Shipley?' She burst out a-laughing, and could not
recompose her face again.

We have already seen how Lavinia reached a state of mutual
antagonism with Georgiana, Countess Spencer, George John's
mother. However, as Amanda Foreman has written in her biography
of Georgiana Devonshire, initially Lavinia seemed the ideal match:

She was pretty in a conventional way with blue eyes and fair hair, talkative,
intelligent and possessed of a strong sense of propriety which Lady Spencer
[Georgiana] applauded. Less obvious until later were her more unattractive
traits: she was highly strung, vindictive, hypocritical and a calm liar who
maintained a veneer of politeness to her in-laws while freely abusing
them in conversation elsewhere.

Mrs Delaney, contemporary gossip and busybody, approved of
early evidence of Lavinia's sense of style, writing to her friend, Mrs
Dewes, two weeks after the wedding: 'Lady Althorp appeared at
the Drawing Room last Thursday – a fine and happy Bride: silver
tissue trimmed with gold, many jewels, and very well dressed. Most
of the relations and attendants on the occasion were in plain or
striped satins.'

There were to be ten pregnancies during this marriage, three of
which ended in miscarriage or still birth. Five sons and two daughters
survived into adulthood – an extraordinarily diverse and interesting
group, worth examining in some depth later. And yet it is as
politician, rather than as patriarch, that George John's life was
primarily notable.

After his father's death in 1783, George John became Second

Earl Spencer, and from that point onwards sat in the House of Lords rather than the Commons. A Privy Councillor and one-time ambassador to Vienna, it was as First Lord of the Admiralty that he achieved the pinnacle of his success.

Although a Whig in the Spencer family tradition, George John was conservative enough by inclination to be scared that the deeply disturbing events going on across the Channel during the French Revolution might overtake his own country. The more extreme members of the Whig party were exhilarated by events in France, but George John – together with fellow moderates, the Duke of Portland, Lord Grenville and Mr Windham – felt he could best serve his country by joining William Pitt's Tory ministry, succeeding the Prime Minister's own brother, Lord Chatham, on 20 December 1794 as the cabinet minister in charge of the Royal Navy.

George John's first slice of luck was to succeed as First Lord of the Admiralty a man as unpopular as Chatham. Of longer-term importance to him and to the Royal Navy, he was also deeply fortunate to have at his disposal during his tenure of the post, some of the greatest sea commanders of British history. As the publication *Public Characters* recorded in 1803 – two years before Trafalgar – the by then former First Lord had a uniquely successful record during his period of office:

No epoch in our naval history has been more brilliant. It was during this period that Lord St Vincent overcame the Spanish fleet, consisting of twenty-seven sails of the line; that Lord Duncan conquered the Dutch squadron under Admiral de Winter; and that Lord Nelson achieved the memorable victory over the French at Aboukir: three naval conquests unrivalled, in point of consequence, of glory, and of reputation, by any equal number in our annals.

Lavinia Spencer, always happy to luxuriate in her husband's triumphs, justifiably claimed of the three victories of St Vincent, Camperdown and the Nile (which was also known as the battle of Aboukir Bay), 'England, Ireland and India were all saved by victories won during his term in office.'

Spencer's gift lay in his flair for man management. During his time at the Admiralty, he frequently entertained his officers, making it customary for captains and admirals to dine with him whenever they returned from a foreign voyage. Wives were not invited, since these were working affairs, although Lavinia herself often joined the meals. In this way the First Lord not only kept open direct communications with his senior men, but was also able to assess them personally. He proved to be a shrewd judge of character.

One young officer who particularly struck the Spencers was Horatio Nelson. Lavinia remembered her initial impressions of the man who was destined to become Britain's greatest naval hero:

The first time I ever saw Nelson was in the drawing room at the Admiralty; and a most uncouth creature I thought him. He was just returned from Tenerife, after having lost his arm. He looked so sickly, it was painful to see him; and his general appearance was that of an idiot; so much so that when he spoke, and his wonderful mind broke forth, it was a sort of surprise that riveted my whole attention. I desired him to call next day, and he continued to visit me daily, during his stay in England.

Nelson seems to have genuinely liked the Spencers, giving them gifts from his voyages and mementoes of his triumphs. He wrote to Lavinia in September 1797:

Madam,

As you told me that Lord Spencer was in possession of a Spanish flag on which your Ladyship seemed to set great value, I have taken the liberty of sending you the sword of Don Tomaso Geraldino, a Brigadier and Commander of the San Nicolas of 84 guns, which I request you will do me the honour of hanging up in your dressing room, and which will at least have the novelty of being the first sword ever presented to a lady as an ornamental piece of furniture for her dressing room.

. . . Believe me I shall never forget your and Lord Spencer's kind attention to me, and your expression that I have honour enough, is the incitement to more deeds of fame. I must now keep my good name and recollect the LAST action is the best, with my very best regards to Lord Spencer . . .

George John had been as immediately and profoundly struck by Nelson's qualities as his wife and, against the objections of the Admiralty Board, his fellow ministers and even Pitt himself, he appointed Nelson commander of the English fleet in the Mediterranean, over the heads of two senior officers; this at a time when the Navy was weighed down with a system of the strictest hierarchy, making such startling promotion unheard of.

The day before Nelson left for his new command, he came to pay his respects to Lavinia Spencer. During a solemn farewell he asked Lavinia, if he should be slain, to look after his wife, whom he professed to adore, calling her an angel who had saved his life after his horrific injuries by dressing his wounds. He acknowledged that officers' wives were not usually asked to dine with the Spencers, but asked Lavinia to make an exception, 'with an earnestness of which Nelson alone was capable'.

Lavinia duly yielded, and invited the couple to dine at the Admiralty. She noted that Nelson was 'as attentive as a lover' to his wife, insisting on sitting next to her during dinner, while apologizing for doing so, and explaining that he treasured every second he could spend with her when not at sea.

Lavinia was to contrast this behaviour with that he exhibited on returning from the Mediterranean, where he had fallen in love with Emma Hamilton while based at Naples:

After dinner, Lady Nelson, who sat opposite to her husband (by the way he never spoke during the dinner, and looked blacker than all the devils), perhaps injudiciously, but with a good intention, peeled some walnuts, and offered them to him in a glass. As she handed it across the table Nelson pushed it away from him so roughly that the glass broke against one of the dishes. There was an awkward pause; and then Lady Nelson burst into tears.

Lavinia, who affected great moral probity, was among the many who looked down on Nelson for his affair with Lady Hamilton.

There were those, however, who refused to believe that the relationship was actually an adulterous one, including Lavinia's mother, the Countess of Lucan, who said to her daughter:

Lavinia, I think you will now agree that you have been to blame in your opinion of Lady Hamilton. I have just assisted at a private Sacrament with them both, which Nelson has taken before he embarks. After the service was over, Nelson took Lady Hamilton's hand, and, facing the priest said: 'Emma, I have taken the sacrament with you this day, to prove to the world that our friendship is most pure and innocent, and of this I call God to witness.'

Lavinia remained unconvinced by Nelson's claims. Indeed, she concurred fully with the opinion of her friend, Lady Frances Shelley, when she said of Nelson: 'True his public life is worthy of our highest admiration. If only it were possible to draw a veil across the private life of that great hero. Alas! A veil is so often necessary, in the domestic history of the world's greatest men.'

Matters of marital fidelity aside, Nelson did deliver up Lord Spencer's finest moment, with his victory at the battle of the Nile. It was Britain's greatest military triumph over the French for half a dozen years, and left Napoleon's army stranded in Egypt. The setback to his ambition was so undeniable, so huge, that Bonaparte said in the wake of the defeat: 'To England is decreed the empire of the seas – to France that of the land.'

However, such were the appalling channels of communication at the time that the Spencers thought, for a long time, that the Royal Navy, although the victor of the encounter, had suffered very severe losses itself. This would have signalled the end of George John's First Lordship because, throughout the spring and summer of 1798, Nelson had repeatedly missed opportunities to intercept the French fleet, every time that it had sailed. Spencer had been receiving the blame for Nelson's lack of success. As Lavinia recorded: 'He was reproached for having appointed so young an officer, when two others of greater experience were passed over to make way for Nelson.'

With the first news of the French defeat came rumours that seven of Nelson's battleships had been lost. Lavinia continued:

All the captains in the fleet were our particular friends, and for some of them we felt the anxiety which we should have felt for a son.

Many weeks passed before the official account came. I was sitting in my drawing room talking to Mr Grenville over the pros and cons, when Mr Harrison, Lord Spencer's secretary, burst into the room, and cried: 'Such a victory has never been heard of – the Town is in an uproar – my Lord is in his office – the particulars have not transpired.' And away he went.

Half an hour later, George John sent for his wife. She found him prostrate on his bed, 'pale as death'. He squeezed Lavinia's hand reassuringly, and said: 'God be thanked.' He then asked his staff to tell her the detailed results of the engagement, including the fact that not a single British ship had been lost. When his secretaries had told the First Lord the same news earlier, he had turned round, headed for the door, then fainted – 'His joy had mastered him,' as Lavinia put it. The Spencers dined alone that night, Pitt interrupting them to congratulate George John personally on his triumph.

In his poem celebrating the battle, Southey dedicated a section to the First Lord of the Admiralty, acknowledging his role in the glorious achievement:

> Spencer! Were mine the pow'r, by lofty lays,
> Guerdon of high desert, to lift thy name
> On the proud column of recording fame,
> I, to bold notes, that swell the song of praise,
> Had tun'd the lyre . . .

If the Nile was the most dramatic achievement of George John's time in charge of the Navy, there were other events which he oversaw that had less obvious, but long-term, positive effects on the service. In general, Spencer was respected by his juniors for his attention to detail and his ability to get things done. He was always at his desk at the Admiralty by nine o'clock in the morning, and was available to all for an appointment at short notice.

His drive for efficiency extended to the dockyards, where officers were told to give regular reports on their everyday operations; and these were expected to be handed in on time. Accompanied only by a servant, George John surprised the workmen at the docks at Deptford one morning by riding down before they started work, in order to see for himself the operation of the store ships there.

The First Lord was also adept at spotting improvements that could be made to assist in the smooth running of the Navy. Indeed, it was through George John's patronage that the engineer Brunel was first brought to public attention.

Brunel was convinced that he had invented a system of 'block machinery' which would be of great help to the dockyards in sorting out the potential muddle of vessels coming in and out of a harbour, but nobody in the relevant naval departments was prepared to look at his work with an open mind. So Brunel resolved to side-step officialdom and go straight to Spencer, who had a reputation for encouraging scientific endeavour of all sorts. With this in mind, he presented Lavinia Spencer with a prototype of his machinery; a mechanical toy into which a pack of cards could be inserted, which obviated the need for shuffling; the cards were dealt out in whatever manner the countess required. Lavinia was captivated by the device's cleverness, and excitedly showed it to her husband. It was Spencer who ordered the system proper to be installed at Portsmouth. It was completed under his successor, St Vincent, in 1802.

George John also had to contend with two mutinies, which jeopardized the effectiveness of the Royal Navy as a military force. As one of his contempories noted in the 1790s:

The minds of men of all classes and descriptions had been more or less affected by the principles and successes of the French revolution, where the permanent efficiency of physical force was exemplified, and encouragement given at the same time to the adventurous exercise of talent. The leaven of insubordination set to work in France had insensibly spread, the ideas of what are termed national rights were disseminated in numerous cheap or gratuitous publications, the discussion of bold opinion became fashionable in public houses, and our honest and open hearted seamen were seized with the contagion.

Conditions in the Navy were extremely tough. Half of the crews were pressed into service, either seized off the streets, or forced to serve through being held in debtors' prisons. Few sailors volunteered to be subjected to an existence whereby ships could be away from home for months, if not years, and living standards rarely rose above being wretched.

Discipline was invariably harsh, with the cat o'nine tails a constant threat to the miscreant, along with other punishments that, although not designed to be capital, frequently resulted in death. One such was keel-hauling, whereby a wrongdoer was bound by his feet with one rope, and his hands with another, before being thrown over the bow of the ship and then dragged the length of the vessel underwater. Apart from the danger of drowning, or crushing, there were also such hazards as barnacles below the waterline, which could cut a man open.

By the 1790s, British crews were not prepared to put up with the prevailing conditions any longer. They insisted on better wages, and on such remuneration actually being paid when due. At Portsmouth, the first rising was quickly dealt with when George John agreed to the demanded raise, and gave them back pay that had been owing for as much as three years, in some instances. When the same problems started to surface in the Channel fleet at the Nore, Spencer removed the ships' buoys and stopped the sailors putting to sea, while cutting them off from all contact with the shore. An unconditional surrender by the sailors was the conclusion. At one stage 50,000 men in 113 Royal Navy vessels had been in open mutiny against their officers and the Admiralty.

A year later, in June 1800, the Pitt administration came to an end when the Prime Minister resigned, and the Addington premiership began. George John stepped down as First Lord, and returned to the Whig party, acknowledging that the threat of the French revolution overtaking Britain seemed to have passed. However, he was not convinced that the end to hostilities between France and Britain, formalized at the Peace of Amiens, could last, given that so many issues between the protagonists remained unresolved. Napoleon was to prove his scepticism well founded.

Almost a century later, the *Daily News* would remember George John as 'the ablest administrator in the Government of Mr Pitt'. The reason he has not received more attention from historians has been put down to the fact that, soon after his retirement from political life, a servant inadvertently destroyed the bulk of his personal correspondence from his years of influence, depriving subsequent generations of an insight into the Second Earl Spencer.

However, the fact is that politics were never George John's main interest, and he partook in them only because he felt he should do so, out of a belief that people of his status and privilege had a duty to serve their country to the best of their ability. It is clear that, in 1807, after a brief stint as Home Secretary, he was happy to slip away from the front line of public service. Faced with limitless time, he now embarked on what he believed to be the purpose of his life, and the occupation that gave him immeasurably more satisfaction than being a cabinet minister ever had.

At Althorp there are portraits of George John by Reynolds, Kauffmann, Copley, Hoppner, Shee and Clint. They all bear out the description of him as 'tall and athletic, if not robust', as *The Gentleman's Magazine* described him in his prime. With light-red hair and all-knowing eyes, there is a presence about him that his contemporaries noted with respect. Even at play, people reacted to George John's charisma. As a young man he was reputed to be one of the finest skaters on the Serpentine, where he would attract an audience keen to witness his effortless style.

The Second Earl was also to be the inventor of a style of coat, considered very elegant at the time. 'The Spencer' was essentially a morning coat, but devoid of the bottom section. My father told me that this was an unintentional invention: George John had fallen asleep in front of a fire at Althorp and some coals rolled out of the grate on to the coat he was wearing, burning off the tails. Awaking with a start, and dousing the flames, George John found he liked the cut of what he was left with, and had other coats of his adapted to the look.

At the same time the Earl of Sandwich, eager to find a way of feeding himself conveniently and frequently, so as to be able to gamble for twenty-four hours at a time without too many breaks for sustenance, invented the food that has ever since borne his name. The two novelties together led a contemporary wit to write:

> Two noble earls, whom, if I quote,
> Some folks might call me a sinner,
> The one invented half a coat,
> The other, half a dinner.
> The plan was good, as some will say,
> And fitted to console one,
> Because, in this poor starving day,
> Few can afford a whole one.

The fashionable George John also enjoyed adventure. He and Lavinia were known for their daring travels – including, in 1786, a visit to the rumbling Mount Vesuvius, which Horace Walpole noted in a letter, with a mixture of wonder and disapproval: 'Lord and Lady Spencer have ascended the mountain while the lava boiled over the opposite brim. I should have no thirst for such bumpers.'

Each of these snippets gives us an insight into the multi-faceted George John. However, soon after his death, this more general assessment of him was given in a memoir of his life, in *The Atlas*:

In person Lord Spencer was tall; in his deportment eminently courteous, affable, and kind. His countenance was thoughtful, and could be severe; but in the circle of his family and friends it was lighted up with a benignity of expression which truly bespoke the benevolence of his heart. His habitual temper was in the highest degree cheerful, enjoying every thing – eager in all his pursuits, and delighted with witnessing the happiness of others. His charity flowed from his sympathy with distress . . . He lived honoured and respected by all men, even in a country where the violence of [political] party too often embitters the intercourse of private life. His memory will be revered by those who value the union of public principle and private worth, and the poor, lowly, and unfortunate will mourn the loss of a kind and generous benefactor.

The above qualities would explain the immense respect Lavinia held for her husband, demonstrated in her correspondence with him. From this it is also clear that she found him extremely physically attractive, something which made her the scourge of his various portrait painters who, she consistently believed, failed to do George John justice in their representations of him. In 1783, she wrote:

I forget whether it was after or before dinner that you told me your picture was like you. I think it must have been after, as you do not drink in the morning, and when you said this you must have been at least elevated, if not dead drunk. Oh Mr Humphry, I wish I had you here to have you ducked in the horse ponds before my windows! Such a vulgar spiritless ugly creature as he has made you I never saw. You that are the direct contrary to these three things.

Five years later, with another portrait planned, she again transmitted her concerns to George John:

I wish I could think that Lawrence will paint you like. I fear it is impossible for anyone to hit off that dear delightful expression of countenance which I so well know. Ah no! I must not expect it! That angelic benignity, that manly spirit, that perpetual good humour, that admirable good sense, that gentleness of nature and that firmness of mind. Can he express all these? Poor, poor Lawrence, how surely wilt thou disappoint me!

George John needed all these diverse qualities to cope with the flaws in Lavinia's own character, which nobody ever sought to eulogize. The couple's daughter, Sarah, recalled after Lavinia's death:

My mother was very indolent, hated all inferior society, and had somehow a higher position than was quite properly hers, owing, I believe, to my father's very high character and rank, so that she was, or behaved as if she was a sort of queen – and popular she never was anywhere.

Lavinia's difficult nature was often a source of embarrassment for George John. She seems to have enjoyed creating problems, before setting her husband the trying task of championing her intolerable position. To his credit, George John unfailingly rallied to his wife's defence, but, in so doing, he had to become accustomed to the humiliations that frequently attended his loyal stance.

An example of this took place in 1804. The artist Archer Shee had agreed to paint George John, and create a copy of the portrait for a friend of the Spencers. With no evidence whatsoever, Lavinia claimed that Shee had originally promised to let the couple have a copy at a discount of five guineas, forcing the painter to take his case direct to Spencer, with whom his indignation had to be cloaked in politeness. However, he made his disgust at the countess's questionable honesty evident to his patron. 'I consider myself very unfortunate,' wrote Shee,

in having undesignedly given to Lady Spencer any grounds to misconceive my terms, for I very solemnly assure your Lordship that I never for a moment intended, directly or indirectly to impress her Ladyship with an idea that I should execute a copy on lower terms than the original picture, much less at a price which I should consider an humble recompense for the performance of the lowest student of the art; nor until the receipt of your Lordship's letter did I conceive that any conversation had passed on the subject.

George John quietly paid the amount in full, no doubt aware that the artist was telling him the truth, while his wife was wilfully creating trouble where none was either necessary or desirable.

In fact, this questioning of expenditure was an all too rare event in the spendthrift existence of the Second Earl and Countess. Brought up in an atmosphere where extreme extravagance was the norm, George John found it impossible throughout his life to economize. There were periodic evaluations of the estate, its worth and its debts, but they never resulted in any notable changes in attitudes as to how life should be lived, or lifestyle funded.

Soon after becoming the Second Earl Spencer, George John resolved to have Henry Holland, the favourite architect of the Whig grandees in the 1780s, make a few alterations at Althorp. The result was a complete overhaul of the Spencer ancestral seat in Northamptonshire, the whole building becoming encased in off-white 'mathematical' tiles, the red-brick structure beneath condemned to eternal imprisonment. At the same time, Holland added corridors to the inside sections of both sides of the front courtyard, and sealed the oak panelling of the Picture Gallery – the only room in the house that had been left unaltered from its early Tudor origins – with wallpaper. The Saloon, which had been the internal courtyard of the house before Dorothy Sunderland's widowhood, had its mighty staircase painted white, in order to augment the natural light that the ceiling's windows allowed into this central space.

There had been no budgeting for this work. To finance it, George John had to resort to the desperate measure of borrowing money from Holland himself, repaying him periodically with interest. This occurred at a time when he already had huge financial worries. However, he was used to things being done to the highest standard, regardless of affordability, and Holland guaranteed that his 'improvements' would be magnificent. The result was a bill for over £20,000.

Profligacy was the underlying theme throughout the half-century of George John's earldom. Two years on the Continent, after Cambridge, had left him susceptible to the desirability of the finest objects Europe had to offer. In 1785, he went alone to Rome to look at various sites that he was interested in from his classical studies. It was not long before he had a confession to make to Lavinia, back at Althorp:

I cannot release you till I have told you of a piece of folly I have committed today, which is the more ridiculous as I had determined in my own mind not to be drawn into it; however I was tempted and the influence of the air of Rome, which makes everybody almost do the same sort of thing, overpowered me and in short I bought an Intaglio.

Writing from the Barberini Palace on the same visit, he acknowledged his monetary problems even more candidly: 'I have but very little money to spare . . . my finances are in such a situation that nothing but some very tempting picture would induce me to deviate any more from my resolution.'

George John had inherited fifty estates and mortgages in 1783, the fruits of the Spencers' medieval farming prowess married to the accumulations of Sarah Marlborough. In the 1780s and 1790s, he sold several of the larger ones: Chippenham, in Buckinghamshire, for £22,000; Chilworth, in Surrey, for £25,000; Balking, Inkpen, Tulwick, Syndelsham and Shillingford, all in Berkshire, for around £100,000; as well as St Thomas, Bashwick, Drayton and Weston, in Staffordshire, for £60,000. By the end of his life, George John had disposed of two-thirds of the properties that had come to him by way of inheritance. Even the Bedfordshire patrimony of the First Baron Spencer – Dunton and Milhoe – and Sarah Marlborough's beloved Holywell House were sacrificed in the constant quest for funds.

The primary cause of George John's parlous finances was his ever-deepening obsession with his library. The roots of this can be found in his time as the pupil of William Jones. There had also been a tradition of book collecting in the Spencer family, which may have fostered the Second Earl's interest. Wormleighton had had a library of renown before the Civil War, and the First Earl of Sunderland's brother, Lord Teviot, had left his own fine collection to the senior branch of his family on his death, in the mid seventeenth century. The intervening generations – especially the Third Earl of Sunderland – had maintained such traditions, although the best of the books had gone with the Fifth Earl of Sunderland to Blenheim, when he inherited the Marlborough dukedom.

But the family had never known a book collector like George John. His unprecedented appetite for literature was unleashed in earnest in 1789 and, from that date till his death in 1834, he 'spared neither time, labour nor money' in compiling what was to become, reputedly, the finest private library in Europe. His first major acquisition was the entire library of a Hungarian nobleman, Count Karolyi Reviczky, which consisted of Greek and Latin classics. Various rare Bibles, and works from the presses of Aldus and the Elzevirs, were also secured with this purchase.

George John initially decided to concentrate on specific areas of literature: primarily on books from William Caxton's printing press. By the time of his death, there were fifty-seven original Caxtons at Althorp, three of them unique. He then cast his net wider, professing a wish to possess an example of any and every book printed before 1500. Two generations later, it was said that Spencer had been so successful in this that 'in this respect the library is rich beyond any other private collection that ever existed, or can now be expected to exist'. The jewels of the collection were the first Mainz Psalter, of 1457, and the Mazarin Bible by Gutenberg, of 1456 – the first printed Bible. In terms of the number of different editions of the Bible that it contained, the Spencer library was said to be without equal.

Other works of extreme rarity included ten 'block books' – tomes produced before the introduction of movable type – as well as letters of indulgence sold by Pope Nicholas V in 1452, when the Holy Father was desperate for funds to pay for the defence of Cyprus from the Ottoman empire.

George John's classical studies meant that works relating to the ancient world and the Renaissance were eagerly sought by him. He had the first edition of the very first book to be printed in Greek characters, as well as similarly rare works by Dante, Petrarch and Boccaccio. As the Second Earl's tastes widened, so the earliest examples of the first presses of Germany, Holland, France and Naples were acquired. Of the latter, he secured a rich infusion when he bought the entire library of the Neapolitan aristocrat, the Duke of Cassano Serra, in 1819. Back in England, the same year, he managed to return to Althorp many books that had gone to Blenheim in the 1730s, when he was one of the major purchasers at the disposal of the Marlborough library.

For advice and encouragement in his all-consuming hobby, George John had the services of his own personal librarian, the Reverend Thomas Dibdin. The knowledgeable cleric criss-crossed Europe looking for rarities to bring back to his master. Dibdin was also to write the definitive catalogue of the collection for posterity.

While he was First Lord of the Admiralty, George John's unquenchable thirst for books was acknowledged as a harmless eccentricity by his contemporaries. A *Translation in Verse of the Mottos of the English Nobility*, published in 1800 by Amicus, in London, poked gentle fun at Spencer:

> With active and incessant zeal,
> I labour for the public weal;
> And work at it both day and night:
> 'Almighty God defend the right!'
> My countrymen I fane would save ye,
> By means of a tremendous navy,
> If the French came with hungry looks,
> In search of rare and matchless books,
> I then shall be at tenter-hooks!
> For France as well as Grande Bretagne,
> Is now become a 'Bibliomane'!

However, after his retirement from politics, it was clear that what had started out as a pastime had become an obsession with dire results for the Spencer family finances. It was this unique single-mindedness in his cause, though, that attracted the applause of fellow bibliophiles. The Frenchman Jules Janin, in an article on Paris's great book collectors, mentioned the English earl as an example to them all:

He spent only a year in Rome, where he visited neither St Peter's, the Colosseum, nor the Vatican. He occupied himself only with dealers, and, having at last found the 'Martial', edited by Sweynheym and Paumarty in 1743, he returned instantly to England without giving the Eternal City another thought. In the course of time his library became the most famous in London. Don't laugh, the love of books is a charming eccentricity: it is respectable, it is innocent, it proves that you have an honest soul, a contented mind. To love books is to renounce games, good eating, useless luxury, horseracing, political ambition, the pains of love. In his library the bibliophile is king.

This particular bibliophile was more like an emperor, turning eight of the rooms at Althorp into libraries, where previously one had sufficed. He also transformed the original drawing room at Spencer House into a second library there, putting up a partition to divide the bulk of the room from the bow window, in order to accommodate a still greater number of volumes. In the process, he ruined the proportions of the space, but mere aesthetics were forced to take second place to the earl's beloved books.

It was reputed at the end of George John's life that he had assembled a collection which contained a copy of every book published during the preceding thirty years. The only criterion for inclusion in the Spencer Library had become perfect condition, both in terms of text and outward appearance, rather than consider- ations of subject matter, author or provenance. Even the agricultural depression which followed the Napoleonic Wars did not stop his ceaseless buying. By the time of his death, Althorp contained more than 43,000 books, the fruits of an addiction every bit as potent, and certainly as expensive, as that of his gambling forebears.

To George John and Lavinia, the concept of cutting back on their life of unremitting extravagance was something they increasingly discussed, but consistently failed to act upon. Indeed, pretty much the only economy that the couple effected was to let their Wimble- don home to the Duke of Somerset.

In 1996 I sold the lordship of the manor of Wimbledon at auction, for a sum that paid for the complete replumbing of Althorp. By so doing, I was bringing to an end 250 years of Spencer connections with one of London's best-known suburbs, an area of land with a rich history of its own.

The manor of Wimbledon belonged to the see of Canterbury

from the time of the Norman Conquest of 1066 until the reign of Henry VIII, when Henry himself took possession of it. From the King, it went briefly to one of his closest advisers, Thomas Cromwell, and from him to one of Henry's queens, Catherine Parr, for the remainder of her life.

Wimbledon continued in the gift of royal favour during Queen Mary's reign, being granted to her Catholic henchman, Cardinal Pole. In the following reign it was owned by Sir Christopher Hatton, the courtier who built Holdenby House, across the valley from Althorp Park. When Hatton went bankrupt, the next lord of the manor was Sir Thomas Cecil. On becoming Earl of Exeter, Cecil elected to have his eldest son receive the courtesy title of Viscount Wimbledon, indicating the special attachment he felt for his new home and its surrounding area.

In 1638, the Earl of Holland bought the manor. Then followed a quick turnover of owners, including General Lambert, a florist and painter, who had been cashiered by Oliver Cromwell. After the Stuart Restoration of 1660, Queen Henrietta-Maria acquired Wimbledon, selling it on to the trustees of George Digby, Earl of Bristol – Anne Sunderland's father. It was at this stage that John Evelyn, in his famous diaries, gave us a view of how the place appeared to contemporaries in 1662: 'I went with my Lord of Bristol to see his house at Wimbledon, newly bought of the Queen Mother, to help contrive the garden after the modern [style]. It is a delicious place for prospect and the thickets but the soil cold and weeping clay.'

Later Digby's widow, Lady Bristol, agreed to sell Wimbledon to the Duke of Leeds. It was generally acknowledged to be one of the finest private residences in the London area – a fact attested to by Swift in his correspondence. When Leeds died, it was sold to Sir Theodore Jansson, who was forced to dispose of it after becoming a major casualty of the South Sea Bubble.

Wimbledon was now added to the huge estate of Sarah Marlborough, at a cost of £15,000. As we have seen, the cantankerous duchess spent most of her middle and old age tampering with her children's lives and fortunes. She also developed the expensive habit of remodelling her many houses, frequently falling out with the architects she employed to undertake such works on her behalf; her quarrels with Vanbrugh over the building of Blenheim Palace were notorious.

The house at Wimbledon that Sarah Marlborough bought had been recently rebuilt, by Sir Theodore Jansson, on the site of Sir Thomas Cecil's original residence. Sarah did not like it, and so employed Lord Burlington to design a new edifice. She was far from satisfied with the result, saying that the mansion looked as though 'it was making a curtsey', for it appeared to be dipping down into the ground, rather than standing tall and elegant. However, even when the design was changed, Sarah was not at all happy with what she saw, judging by her own comments on the place, in 1737: 'Came yesterday from Wimbledon – though it stands high, it is upon clay, an ill sod, very damp, and I believe an unhealthy place, which I shall very seldom live in; and consequently I have thrown away a vast sum of money upon it to little purpose.'

Although she did visit it more than this sulky entry in her journal might suggest, it was not a house where Sarah was to leave much of a mark. Indeed, perhaps the most striking reminder of her years of ownership lies in the name familiar to anyone who drives around that part of south London today, Tibbet's Corner, after Mr Tibbet, her gatekeeper, whose lodge was at the top of Putney Hill.

After Sarah died in 1744, Wimbledon passed to her grandson, Johnny Spencer. His premature death left the house and 1,200–acre park in the hands of John, later First Earl Spencer. He proved more interested in remodelling Wimbledon and creating Spencer House than he initially was in preserving Althorp. 'Capability' Brown was brought in to improve the landscape, creating a large lake by draining the wet fields round about, and laying out the entrance drive that is now known as Victoria Drive. The house itself was extensively rebuilt in 1749 using Roger Morris's designs, twenty years after he had built his beautiful stables at Althorp. So attached was John to Wimbledon that he very nearly chose to celebrate his twenty-first birthday there in 1755, rather than going to Althorp on the journey that was to see him return a married man – this despite the fact that the Northamptonshire mansion was steeped in

his family's history, whereas Wimbledon had been a Spencer property for only eleven years.

Inside Wimbledon, John and Georgiana Spencer perpetuated
the theme of extravagant self-indulgence that marked their life
together. The envy this extreme display of wealth provoked can
be divined in the following letters, between a Miss Talbot and a
Mrs Carter, dating from 1760. Miss Talbot reported:

On Tuesday I rode to Wimbledon . . . we visited Mrs Poyntz [Georgiana's
mother], admired the very charming park, walked to the menagerie, and
all over the ground floor of the house, saw many curious and pretty birds,
some very good pictures, and Mrs Spencer's closet, which I fancy you
have heard her describe. It is not near finished; though small is very
elegant and pretty, and will be immensely costly. And yet a plain green
paper, white curtains, two or three Dutch chairs, and a deal table would
be quite as elegant and commodious as all that ornament, and more
suitable to the size; and as my mother well observed to me, much more
suitable for a grave good woman to say her prayers in, than amidst all
those Cupids and Hymens and Metamorphoses.

Mrs Carter's reply demonstrates how eager she was to join in her
friend's proffered disapproval:

. . . I have a strange savage taste and a most unconquerable aversion to
finery though in so gay and glittering an age it may not be always prudent
or polite to declare it. Persons of large fortune may, I suppose, very
allowably employ some part of it on things by no means strictly useful,
yet is a pity they should lavish it upon toys of which they must so soon
grow weary.

A more generous appraisal of Wimbledon in the First Earl and
Countess's time comes from Hannah More, who was a guest there
in 1780. She noted with something approaching awe:

I did not think there could have been so beautiful a place within seven miles
of London. The park has as much variety of ground, and is un-Londonish

as if it were an hundred miles out; and I enjoyed the violets and the birds
more than all the marechal powder and the music of this foolish town.

Two years before Hannah More wrote this panegyric passage,
the Spencer household at Wimbledon had been dragged into a
scandal, through the public's interest in a salacious attempted murder
that belied the estate's rural charms.

Jane Bannister was one of Georgiana Spencer's maids. She had
been courted by Thomas Empson, a footman to Dr Bell, who
was chaplain to the neighbouring Princess Amelia. When the
relationship ended at the maid's request, Empson refused to accept
his rebuttal, and arranged for wedding banns in both their names
to be read at St George's Church, Hanover Square, without telling
Jane. When she was informed, she was both embarrassed and
furious, and forbade them being read again.

Empson had been obsessive in his love, but now he felt humiliated
at this public rejection of his suit. He decided to make Jane pay for
the hurt he felt, arranging for another servant in his household to
write the following to her:

Dear Madam,

Pardon me for taking the liberty of writing these few lines to you, it
being the desire of my friend. I should be very glad if you would meet
me between the Porter's Lodge and the laundry, where I am desired to
tell you something which may be to your satisfaction, as likewise the
same to my friend. I am bound of point of word not to enter the house.
If you will favour me with your company at the place appointed, you
will greatly oblige.

Your sincere friend and wellwisher,

Thomas Jenkinson.

This is requested as a most great favour from you.

It is not known if Jane realized that Jenkinson's 'friend' was
Empson. Probably not; for she set off for the agreed rendezvous,
only to be ambushed by her former love, who grabbed her tight.

Jane saw that Empson was holding a pistol, and sank to her knees begging for mercy. As Empson dithered, she picked herself up and ran away, only to be hit by a bullet that ricocheted from a wall. The lovelorn footman thought he had killed Jane, and fled from Wimbledon to Ireland. There, he learned that he had merely wounded his erstwhile lover, who was now recovering from her injury. He sent a series of letters to her, saying he would 'compleat the work he began', leading to excited speculation in the newspapers that the would-be murderer was set to return and see through his crime of passion. However, the Spencers made sure that ships from Ireland were monitored, and when Empson set foot in Liverpool, he was arrested and imprisoned.

Within a decade, the human failings of the staff at Wimbledon were to have much more far-reaching consequences than this tale of a lover scorned.

George John, Second Earl Spencer, had been in possession of his estates and titles for only a little over a year when he decided to spend some time at Wimbledon after Easter 1785. The staff got the family's sheets out to be aired and then warmed – it being only March – in front of the fire, but the maid overseeing this everyday domestic task failed to carry out her responsibilities with proper attention, going downstairs for a cup of tea.

The result was the subject of George John's letter to his mother, sent the day of his arrival at Wimbledon: 'I take the opportunity of Mr Graham's going over to you to let you know that the house is entirely demolished, there not being (in Townsend's [the steward at Wimbledon] own words) a single bit of wood remaining in any part of it.'

Initial impressions were mixed. The house itself, as George John had remarked, was gutted. However, because the place was fully staffed in anticipation of George John's arrival, and the local inhabitants had rushed to help, a surprising proportion of the contents was saved: all of the Second Earl's books; the house and table linen; the bulk of the furniture, including the hefty billiard table; and nearly all the best pictures – among them a very valuable

Hondecoeter farmyard scene, now at Althorp, torn from its frame
by the staff, before being rolled up and thrown out of a window
to safety. The one picture of note to be lost was of the first Marquis
of Blandford.

Over the next few days, the full extent of the fire damage started
to emerge. On 4 April George John wrote to his mother again:

Nobody was hurt much – one man had a little melted lead fall upon him
and a few men were a little bruised but there was nothing to signify. The
mob towards the latter end of the time broke into the wine cellar and
many of them got excessively drunk; Soullavie [the butler] examined it
today and misses about twenty dozen of different sorts of wine.

Evidence of the fierceness of the fire fascinated the amateur scientist
in George John:

There was very little silver found and, what was, was almost burnt to a
coal. The violence of the fire must have been wonderful as they found
a great misshapen lump of bell-metal which was one of the bells melted
– an operation that would require a very strong furnace to perform.

Georgiana's initial reaction was one of typically Christian charity
towards the girl who was being blamed for the fire, since the insurers
– who had to pay £4,500 for the destroyed contents, let alone the
full cost of the rebuilding of the structure itself – were believed to
be eager to have her imprisoned. 'If, as I suppose by Lord Lucan's
letter,' Georgiana wrote, 'this horrid business was owing to the
carelessness of the Nursery Maid, I shall wish to know what becomes
of the poor girl, who, however blameable, is much to be pitied,
for I cannot conceive a more terrible sensation than a consciousness
of neglect in such a case . . .'

The maid in question had apparently shown tremendous courage
during the dangerous salvage operation, having to be pulled out by
her legs from under a collapsed beam, which 'near demolished'
her.

Over the next sixteen years, the Spencers used the outbuildings at Wimbledon as their retreat from the heat and dirt of the London summer. In the meantime, Henry Holland was commissioned to design a smaller house of simple beauty. In 1801, Lavinia Spencer took occupation of the new family home, a villa, built slightly to the north of the mansion that had burnt down. She wrote to her husband: 'Here we are, my best beloved, so delighted and so comfortable; indeed I do think our establishment here will produce us as much satisfaction as we ought reasonably to expect from anything of the kind . . .' She was proud to relate that Holland had been to visit her at Wimbledon, and 'extremely pleased was he to see me already settled and happy in the villa which I see he thinks the best thing he has done in the building way . . .'

The enjoyment Lavinia had hoped to derive from her new Wimbledon residence lasted twenty-six years. It became a setting for the same lavish hospitality that she and George John provided for their guests at Spencer House and Althorp, adding to the seemingly endless strain on the family finances. We catch a glimpse of the scale of entertaining they indulged in, through the journal of the Hon. Mrs Calvert, written in July 1808: 'We all went yesterday morning to a breakfast, or rather, cold dinner at Lord Spencer's at Wimbledon . . . It is really a beautiful place, and the day being very fine, and an immense concourse of people all walking about gaily dressed in groups was very pretty.'

However, such scenes of privileged pleasure at Wimbledon were not to last into the next generation. In 1827, when the Duke of Somerset took on a lease for the Wimbledon villa, it marked the end of the Spencer occupation of the property. Within twenty years, it was sold altogether.

We have seen from her demanding relationship with her husband, and her fraught one with her mother-in-law and children, that Lavinia Spencer was not an easy person to live with or be related to. However, to be a guest in one of her homes was a joy.

In *Tour of a German Artist in England*, of 1836, M. Passavant recalled:

What, more than all contributed to render Althorp the favourite resort of all the rank and literati of England, was the all-enlivening genius of the late Lady Lavinia Spencer, who, by the urbanity of her manners, and the variety of her acquirements, inspired animation and cheerfulness to all around her.

The author may have had in mind the historian Gibbon, the sculptor Nollekens, or the political leaders Grenville and Grey. Gibbon is on record as having spent a memorable morning in the Library at Althorp, enjoying the seventy editions of Cicero collected by his host. George John was famous throughout Europe for his generosity in sharing his books with scholars of various disciplines.

At Spencer House, the salon consisted of all manner of learned men – Sir Humphry Davy, Sir Joseph Banks, William Wollaston and Thomas Young. The mixture reflected George John's broad interests, which included science. He was the first president, as well as being one of the founders, of the Royal Institution.

Once in 1821, the family was in residence in Spencer House when Sir Walter Scott came round for dinner. Young George Spencer, George John and Lavinia's youngest son, noted: 'We all stayed the evening listening to him telling Scottish stories.'

By this stage of their lives, their sixties, George John and Lavinia were satisfied with maintaining a less frantic social life than had marked their prime. It was not that they had turned against entertainment as such, rather that they preferred to do as much of it as possible at their homes, rather than being permanently on the move from one house party to another, in the houses of fellow grandees. George recorded his parents' dignified acceptance of their advancing years:

My father and mother were not like many aged veterans in dissipation . . . who to the last of their strength keep up what they can of youth, in pursuing still the round of the gay parties of one rising generation after another. They hardly ever went into society away from home. They kept a grand establishment, when in London, at Spencer House, as well as Althorp in the winter, when the first society, whether of the political or the literary and scientific were constantly received. It would, therefore, have been unreasonable in me to be fond of going out for the sake of society, when, perhaps, none was to be met with so interesting as at home; besides this, my father and mother were fond of being surrounded by their family circle; and if I or my brothers, when staying with them in London, went out from home several times in succession, or many times a week, they would generally express some disappointment or displeasure . . .

George John and Lavinia's last years were spent in increasingly intimate isolation, at their two primary residences. By now they had suffered the agony of outliving two of their adult children: Bob, a promising naval officer, who died at sea in 1830, and Georgiana, wife of Lord George Quin, whose life of unremitting illness ended in childbirth in 1827, aged just twenty-seven.

Lavinia's last act of any note with regard to the family's fortunes took place in 1830. She had set her heart on acquiring two portraits by Rubens, of Philip IV and Elizabeth of Bourbon, which were in the collection of Count Bentinck, in Flanders, where they had been since Rubens's time. George John told his wife that there was no money available to buy the pair of paintings for her. However, Lavinia was determined to get her own way, and wrote to her husband with her usual blend of cunning and persuasiveness:

Last night it was very hot and I tumbled and tossed, and many idle visions past and repast my brain, and one of them was this: What is the use, said I to myself, of those foolish pearls which lie like dirt in my strong box, and never will be worn again by me or ever be of use to anyone else? Why should they not be valued and if of sufficient value, why not lay out the money they are worth in purchasing those two Rubens's portraits? What think you of my waking dream?

'Those foolish pearls' were two of the most celebrated pieces of jewellery in England, having been owned by Elizabeth of Bohemia, Prince Rupert of the Rhine, and Sarah Marlborough. However, George John surrendered to his wife's demands, and they were sold. The proceeds secured Rubens's portraits, which hang today in the Great Room at Althorp. This proved to be the last piece of scheming manipulation that Lavinia inflicted on her long-suffering husband for, in 1831, she died.

George John was by now very infirm, and, in 1832, there were erroneous reports that he, too, was dead. Learning that this was happily not the case, John Taylor wrote a celebratory sonnet which shows the affection in which the old earl was held by many, after a life of diversity and accomplishment:

> Genius and Learning will delighted hear,
> Rumour said falsely SPENCER was no more;
> SPENCER distinguished for his classic love.
> A lib'ral patron, talents must revere,
> And, hence, to genius and to learning dear.
> Allied in blood to that great Bard of yore
> Ordain'd the heights of poesy to soar,
> And Fiction make with moral grace appear.
> Descended from a line of noblest breed,
> For martial and for patriot fame renown'd,
> Still to new honours may that line succeed,
> The prop and lustre of their natal ground,
> A nation's gratitude their rightful meed,
> A nation's praise to latest times resound.

In 1834, he was still to be seen making a weekly trek to the church at Brington, but he was so feeble by then that two of the Althorp footmen had to carry him to the altar for Communion, his head slumped on his chest, before returning him to his pew, his feet shuffling feebly as dotage took hold of his mind.

George John kept a journal of key events relating to his family and his country, written in his increasingly erratic hand: a small fire at Althorp, the sale of West Hill estate to the Duke of Sutherland, and the burning of the House of Commons and Lords being his three last entries. Beneath these was the following anonymous conclusion to the diary, and to George John's life: '1834. On 10TH November, Lord Spencer died at Althorp loved and lamented by all who knew him.'

# 13. Honest Jack Althorp

George John's will was left in the hands of a sole executor, his eldest son, John Charles, now Third Earl Spencer, but best-known to history as Lord Althorp, which was the courtesy title he held for over fifty of his sixty-three years.

It was fortunate for the succeeding generations of Spencers that such an able and decent man came to be head of the family at such a difficult time, for George John left behind him an estate valued for probate purposes at under £160,000, with mortgages of over £300,000. Out of this, £20,000 each had to be found for three of the younger children, and the Second Earl's house at Ryde, on the Isle of Wight, together with all its contents, was left to a younger son, Frederick.

A lesser man than Lord Althorp would have balked at the hopelessness of it all, but he had shown himself throughout his life to be a man of the strongest moral character for whom the concept of duty was the overriding consideration, whatever the consequences. Whether as a son, a politician or as a pillar of the community, Althorp was rock solid.

George John had been an attentive father, compared to many of his contemporary grandees. Throughout 'Jack' Althorp's childhood, he recorded the boy's small triumphs and progresses, keeping the ageing Georgiana Spencer up to date on the development of her eldest Spencer grandson. Althorp showed a fine practical intellect at an early age, and George John proudly reported in October 1788: 'Jack really improves in his reading and has got a very accurate notion of the general Geography of Europe – all the countries of which he can point out and call by their names on the great Globe in the Library.'

By then, Jack had already sat, dressed in a page boy's outfit, for the family friend, Sir Joshua Reynolds – he was, in old age, to claim that he was the only person to have been painted by Reynolds, and also to have been photographed – in one of the artist's most successful depictions of a child. Looking at the portrait today, dominating the Library at Althorp, the sky-blue sash cutting through the surrounding mellow tones of the book spines, it is possible to see that this is not a soul at ease with the finery into which it had been born; the sensitive face looks trapped between the dramatic sweep of an ostentatious hat and the fussy luxuriance of the silky clothes.

Jack Althorp was born and largely brought up at Spencer House, but was always at his happiest in the countryside. He came to hate the sophisticated urban living that his parents indulged in at their private London palace, but he understood that his father's political obligations necessitated long spells in the capital. Jack's education was started at Spencer House. He was taught to read there by a Swiss footman, and it was there that his tutor, Samuel Herrick, prepared him for boarding school.

At the age of eight, he was sent to Harrow. It was not a happy time for him, although he formed a lifelong friendship with his first cousin, Lord Duncannon, son of Jack's aunt Harriet. They were to remain allies during their respective distinguished public lives. Two of the great Whig politicians of the early to mid nineteenth century dominated Harrow's Public Speeches on 5 July 1798; Althorp declaiming 'The Earl of Arundel' by Lord Littleton, and Duncannon reciting Livy's 'Hanno ad Carthag.'.

Growing up as Lavinia Spencer's eldest son had not been easy. He did not conform to her ideal of a young nobleman. He was plain, lacked eloquence, and early showed a greater interest in country sports than in the refinements of her salons. And yet it was this very lack of flair, this absence of pretence, that was to mark him down as exceptional, in an age when trust and respect were words rarely attached to leading political figures. One of Lavinia's house guests commented on both sides of his character, the super-ficial and the internal, in 1805, before Jack entered the public life for which he was to prove so strangely suited: 'Lord Althorp, the eldest son, is just grown up. He is not handsome, and don't look like a man of fashion, but he seems very good-humoured and pleasing.' This affability would be an enduring attribute.

The Grand Tour which Jack Althorp was sent on was not a success. He returned in 1803, with no appreciable interest in the arts, missing his horses and his foxhounds back at Althorp.

Although his father was temporarily sidelined from mainstream political life, it was expected of Jack, as the Spencer heir, that he would follow in his father's footsteps by entering the fray himself. After being accepted as Member of Parliament for the Okehampton seat in 1804 – Okehampton was one of the estates acquired by Sarah Marlborough and passed down to the Spencers – two years later he stood for Northamptonshire, against Sir William Langham. The latter's supporters made it clear, in an electioneering ditty, that the twenty-four-year-old should think again, if he thought his father's eminence and political record would smooth his own path into public life:

A Peer's eldest son from Althorp has run,
To contend for a seat for the County;
The youth perhaps thought that our votes might be bought,
By the strength of the Treasury Bounty:
At the poll let him give his attendance;
We'll show him we like independence . . .

However, Althorp was elected; and was re-elected the following year. It was the start of a political career that was to go much further in terms of success and acclaim than the modest Jack ever sought, expected or wanted.

Although relieved that Jack was now launched on an acceptable career, Lavinia was concerned that her eldest son showed no interest in any of the things that she viewed as being important. She despaired that the next occupant of Spencer House and Althorp was happiest in the kennels or with the gamekeepers, rather than indulging in social niceties.

Turning Jack into a polished young nobleman was an ambition she knew to be doomed to failure from an early stage; a point she seems to acknowledge in a letter to her husband of June 1807, concerning the possibility of a party at Spencer House, which she hoped might at least force Jack into being seen at a high society event:

I have hitherto thought that it would not be necessary, but I find it is expected from us and so with your permission a little dance below stairs and an ambigu supper in the Great Room upstairs may be well contrived and we shall wipe off all scores and answer our acquaintances' expectation and Jack will once more appear in good company.

Jack was to show as little interest in settling down with a wife as he had done in socializing. However, his perceived wealth and undoubted status ensured that he ended up marrying one of the most desirable women in London.

Esther Acklom started attracting attention from the ladies who controlled high society in London in 1807. The Hon. Mrs Calvert recalled meeting the only child of Richard Acklom, a Nottingham-shire man, in that year, noting her wealth and beauty. Her own brother-in-law, Charles Calvert, was totally infatuated with the coquettish Miss Acklom at the time, and this was a potential match of which she thoroughly approved. However, it was not to be. Charles Calvert was told by young Esther that she would never contemplate marrying a man over thirty – which he was – leaving him both broken-hearted and angry, for he felt Esther had definitely egged him on with her flirtatiousness.

Within three months, two other potential suitors – Lord Lindsay and a Mr Wynne – had been similarly abruptly cast aside. Four years on, and it seemed that the flighty Esther had finally met the man she would wed – one Thomas Knox. Both of them were keen to marry, but the two fathers could not agree on the financial arrangements to be reached, and the couple broke off the engagement.

The last day of 1812 found Richard Acklom dead in his bed, leaving his daughter Esther independence in the form of a £10,000 annuity. Beyond that, her mother was given an annual pension of £16,000 which, it was assumed, would also be Esther's before too long. It was now believed that Esther would marry her latest admirer, a Mr Madocks. However, with her financial position secure, Esther decided against Madocks, paid him back all the money he had spent while courting her – which apparently amounted to thousands of pounds – and resolved to find a more eligible match.

When her eye alighted on Jack Althorp, there was no pretence of love on either side: Esther wanted a title, and Althorp was after money. Here, it seemed, was a match to answer both parties' material desires. However, the Spencer family did not like what they saw in their potential in-law. Indeed, Lavinia never warmed to Esther, and Jack's sister, Sarah, thought her 'a vulgar person and a spoilt child'.

Jack was no more enamoured than his relatives had revealed themselves to be. Faced with the prospect of marrying someone he barely knew, and certainly did not like, Jack decided to take a long walk in the Park at Althorp, to decide if he could go through with the match for the good of his finances. Two hours later he returned, his mind made up. He would wed the heiress.

From such unpromising beginnings sprang a marriage of unusual tenderness and sincerity. It would appear that, from the time that the engagement was announced, the betrothed began genuinely to appreciate one another's human qualities. The Spencer parents, disappointed though they were, put on a united front over their son's decision, the Hon. Mrs Calvert writing in her journal for 19 March 1814:

Miss Acklom is going to be married to Lord Althorp, Lord Spencer's eldest son, and they are delighted at the match, and Lady Spencer says she has been 'so well-educated – on the Continent'. Heaven preserve me from so well educated a daughter-in-law.

The marriage took place on 13 April 1814. Esther wrote to her mother of the beauty of the day, of the 2,000 people who were at the service in their honour, and of 'the feeling of real affection to dear Althorp which seemed to pervade through the heart of every person present . . .' The guests presented the bride with a nosegay, and shouted, 'Lady Althorp for ever', and, 'May she live long to enjoy it', followed by hurrahs. The bride was seen to smile, while shedding tears of gratitude at the warmth of her acclamation.

In June the newlyweds returned to Althorp after their honeymoon. A huge crowd welcomed them at the gates, on horseback, in carriages and on foot. There were wagons, garlanded with flowers and filled with women dressed in white. The Spencer flag was carried in front of the Althorps' carriage, while three huntsmen and four grooms rode on one side of them, and four of the Park and gamekeeping staff, dressed in their green and gold livery, on the other.

The following morning, after 'a very hearty breakfast', Esther gave her mother her initial impressions of the house at Althorp, which she supposed would one day be her and Jack's home. It was everything to which she had aspired:

This is a most comfortable and magnificent mansion, the library and picture gallery and staircase are very splendid indeed; the books and pictures are well worth coming to see, and I am perfectly enchanted with the house. My bed room and dressing room are very nice, and full of very fine pictures. My looking glass is set in richly worked silver, and I am quite grand. The Deer come close to the windows – there seem to be a vast number – the Park appears grand and extremely well-wooded, but not pretty, though I am not a good judge as I have only been to the stables as it pours with rain. There is a very nice chapel in the house – the old china jars and old cabinets here are very handsome.

She was equally enchanted by her husband, her postscript delighting in his simple rural pleasures: 'Notwithstanding the rain, Althorp is just going to see his "children" in the Kennel.'

Esther was taken on a tour of the villages by Mr Bailey, the Spencers' steward. As the future mistress of the estate, she was expected to take on a charitable role to alleviate the suffering of the less fortunate members of the community. Although this had not been a priority for Lavinia, the local people looked to the new Viscountess Althorp to fill the void left by the recent death of

Georgiana, the First Earl's widow, whose good works were greatly appreciated by all locally.

Esther was flattered by her welcome, but shocked by the deprivation she witnessed:

I gave fifteen pounds amongst the poor, and there is one poor girl, who is subject to fits to whom I intend allowing eighteen pence a week. As I paid fifty-two visits, you may suppose I was completely tired, having been out and on my legs from eleven o'clock till five . . . I went to see one old woman, who has been bedridden for some years . . . I also saw a woman who is confined to her bed being paralytic and having a cancer on her nose; I saw a child in the agonies of death, which was quite frightful, but every person else was comfortable enough though scarce one woman in the village did not complain of bad health. My popularity here is very great indeed, and I am called the charming Lady Althorp and the dear Dowager over again.

These were the happy days that Jack Althorp remembered till the end of his life: his new wife, loving and loved, happy with him and with his estate. They were a popular couple, and they looked after their staff and dependents with a care that was considered admirably enlightened by their contemporaries. A newspaper cutting of 1816 chronicles how,

On Saturday, Lord Viscount Althorp and family left their house in Pall Mall, on a four months' absence. His Lordship's conduct is truly noble, and we hope will be imitated at least by all who can afford it. He has not discharged a single servant, and has allowed them all board wages. He sent them to his estates in Yorkshire and Northamptonshire, where they were to be allowed milk, potatoes, etc. The stable boys and other menial servants, who cannot read or write, are to be sent to school to learn at his Lordship's expense, during his absence from England.

Happier than he had ever been, Jack also found in Esther's mother a figure far more loving and maternal towards him than Lavinia had ever been. In fact, to their embarrassment, other members of the Spencer family noticed that Jack addressed Mrs Acklom in a more affectionate way than he chose to treat either of his parents.

The perceived eccentricities of young Lord Althorp were of less interest to the Spencers than the need for him to produce an heir, something Esther was well aware was a priority for dynastic reasons, but also something she was eager to achieve, out of the genuine contentment she felt in the marriage. As Mrs Calvert noted in May 1816: 'I saw Lady Althorp yesterday. She is grown immensely fat. She says she is the happiest creature in the world – nothing wanting but a child.'

But childbirth was a very dangerous procedure in the early nineteenth century. Even the royal family was not immune from the high mortality associated with the process of giving life, the extremely popular Princess Charlotte dying in such a way at this time, to the public's dismay.

Conscious of the attendant risks, Esther fell pregnant at the end of 1817. By February 1818, she was openly talking about her fear of something going wrong with the birth. Tragically, that fear was to be fully justified.

On 8 June after a protracted labour, the child – a son – was born dead. There were deep concerns about the mother, but she recovered her senses, and the specialist doctors thought her better. They left her, and her family physician came in to find Esther eating a little bread and sipping some milk. However, when he felt her pulse, he realized that something was drastically wrong: it was far too weak.

The doctor went to Jack Althorp and told him that they were facing an emergency: if they could not get some brandy down his wife's throat, she would be dead within the hour. The two men mixed the brandy in arrowroot, so that it would not burn Esther's throat. However, she managed to take only a few drops, for she was having great difficulty in swallowing. Suddenly she passed out. Very soon afterwards, she was dead.

Jack Althorp, who had taken so long to find true love, was bereft. On 18 June 1818, he buried the caskets containing the bodies of his wife and tiny stillborn son in the family vault at

Great Brington. He wore black for the rest of his life, and never remarried.

Sarah Spencer, Jack's sister, had never liked Esther. However, on seeing the grief afflicting her brother, she was honest enough to admit that 'never was there a happier marriage – never more sincere and deep affection on both sides, and never deeper grief in any widowed heart'.

From the time of Esther's and his son's death, Jack Althorp devoted his life to God and to fulfilling that sense of duty that his Christianity underscored in him.

Jack Althorp's interests in life were farming, foxhunting and family. However, it is as a politician that his name is most readily remembered.

His early political life seemed to be little more than an intrusion on his other pleasures, his sister Sarah writing in 1809 to their brother, Bob: 'Althorp [is] chiefly on the high road between London and Northampton, flying from hunting to voting, and from voting to hunting again in his usual way . . .' However, politics dominated the next quarter century of his life. He remained a Member of Parliament for Northamptonshire from 1806 until his elevation to the House of Lords, on the death of George John in 1834.

For much of this period he was in opposition, Lord Liverpool's administration keeping the Whigs out of power for fifteen consecutive years. Throughout, Althorp consistently lent his name to the struggle against every measure which he believed to be a threat to the liberty of the subject. He was a champion of the move to allow Roman Catholics to have the same basic rights as their Protestant compatriots; similarly, he was an ardent supporter of the abolition of slavery; he backed the right of people accused of crimes to have legal advice before and during their trials; and, despite it impacting directly on his own agricultural income and interests, he never deviated from his belief in free trade, when others from his background advocated protective tariffs, during the debate over the Corn Laws.

If most of his beliefs were typically Whig, there was a sincerity and a decency about their proponent that was recognized as being admirable, respectable and unique. His sobriquet was 'Honest Jack' Althorp and, although he was short of charisma, a quite appalling public speaker, and the very antithesis of smooth charm, he proved to be precisely the right man to foster one of the most important reforms in Britain's political history.

However, before that, Althorp's first major political act was unintentionally and indirectly to bring down an administration. In 1827, George Canning had stated in his budget address the need for the whole financial condition of the nation to be subjected to a thorough investigation. The country was in an economic depression following a poor harvest the previous year, and Canning needed to show that something was being done to meet the people's concerns. He therefore announced his intention of forming a finance committee to head up the enquiry.

Canning's death soon afterwards led to one of the briefer, and certainly most insignificant, premierships of the nineteenth century; that of Lord Goderich, a highly emotional man ill-suited to the exercise of power.

On taking office, Goderich tamely reiterated Canning's pledge, and started to think about the composition of the proposed committee. George Tierney, Master of the Mint, suggested that Lord Althorp should be one of its members – an idea Goderich agreed to, provided George John, Second Earl Spencer, approved the move. This consent was readily given; at which point Jack was invited by Tierney to chair the committee.

Meanwhile Mr Herries, Chancellor of the Exchequer, knew nothing of Tierney's proposal, nor of Althorp's acceptance of the committee's chairmanship. When he did indirectly find out, he made it clear that Althorp was not somebody who could be accepted in such a sensitive position. He was seen by the Chancellor as too much of a party man, and – although Herries made it clear he had nothing but the highest regard for Jack's character and ability – this would inevitably lead to conflict between the chairman and the Chancellor, which would in turn undermine the entire process that the committee was meant to oversee.

The cabinet now found itself in an apparently irreconcilable position: Tierney and Huskisson, the Colonial Secretary, felt themselves honour-bound to see through the commitment they had made to Spencer and Althorp, whereas Herries remained unshakeable in his belief that Althorp was simply unacceptable in such a sensitive posting.

All of this might have been resolved, had a strong Prime Minister taken a firm grip of the situation, but there was only Goderich, and he had none of the qualities needed to appease the two sides. Furthermore, he found himself genuinely undecided as to what the best way forward was. In the end, unable to demonstrate any leadership qualities when they were needed, he decided to resign his premiership. Althorp, known to subsequent generations of historians as the man who helped hold administrations together under the most difficult of circumstances, made his first mark on the political landscape by inadvertently bringing one down.

In November 1830, the Whigs returned to power under Lord Grey, the man who had fathered Georgiana Devonshire's illegitimate daughter, a generation earlier. Althorp was entrusted with two key positions: Chancellor of the Exchequer and Leader of the House of Commons. For the former he showed little talent, but he was to show extraordinary suitability for the latter.

It is testament to the man's unerring lack of ambition that, even with two of the greatest offices of state entrusted to him, Althorp found his appointment as cabinet minister an unwelcome obligation, rather than a recognition of any abilities he might possess. Lord Broughton recalled, the month that Althorp assumed his new positions: 'I walked about some time with Lord Althorp, an excellent person, too good for a party man. He told me that he should retire from public life the moment he got into the "Hospital for Incurables".' And yet Jack knew that, while his father still lived, there was to be no escape to the House of Lords.

Althorp found the Chancellorship of the Exchequer an onerous office. His first budget, of 1831, was a fiddly affair, in which he tinkered with taxation on timber, newspapers and tobacco. Later, to general approval, he repealed taxes on sea-borne coal, as well as on tiles, candles and soap. However, such measures failed to convince his contemporaries that Althorp was anything other than a mediocre Chancellor, with little instinct for, or interest in, the economy and its efficient management. This explains the derision directed at him when he relieved some of the fiscal burden on the farmer by also repealing taxes on farm servants and farm dogs. A Tory cartoon of the time showed Jack, who was famed for his agrarian interests, dressed as an agricultural labourer, standing by a cow's rear end, with the caption: 'What a pleasure it is to get at something one does understand!'

Jack knew that his critics were correct, and that several others could have run the Exchequer with greater flair and success. However, the insistence of his cabinet colleagues that he carry on persuaded him that it was his duty to continue in a position he loathed. In 1833, he summed up his extreme distaste for the Chancellorship when he confessed to the Prime Minister, Lord Grey: 'I should certainly prefer anything, death not excepted, to sitting upon the Treasury bench in the House of Commons.'

There was a streak of melancholy in Jack verging on the suicidal, which grew in strength as his tenure of high office continued. In 1832, he dined with his trusted colleague Lord Broughton, who recalled:

Althorp talked very confidentially of his own repugnance to office, and said it destroyed all his happiness, adding that he 'removed his pistols from his bedroom for fear of shooting himself'. Such are the secrets of the human heart! Who would have imagined that such a notion ever entered into the head of the pure, the imperturbable, the virtuous Althorp? ... I took leave of this excellent man with greater admiration of him than ever.

This conversation took place at a time when Jack Althorp was helping to steer through Parliament one of the most forward-thinking pieces of legislation of its time. The great Reform Bill of 1832, which gave the vote to previously disenfranchised swathes of the British middle classes, was nicknamed in some places 'Althorp's

Act', so crucial was the Leader of the House of Commons' support for it seen to be.

The Reform Bill was extraordinarily contentious, throwing the opposing creeds of Whig and Tory into sharp relief. Given the intensity of feeling on both sides, its chances of success remained in doubt all the way through its parliamentary passage. Many were convinced that to extend the vote so dramatically was to invite revolution. Lord Broughton wrote in his diary:

Whatever may have been the cause of the alarm, there can be no doubt but that it was very general. Lady Shrewsbury told my wife that the Duchesse de Berri said to her, a day or two ago, that the people of England were mad; and that, if our Ministers did not resist all Reform, England would soon fall into the same wretched condition as France!

Althorp's contribution to the Bill's success lay in his ability to defuse such suspicions, and to reassure the nervous: charges of extremism and folly levelled against the Whigs foundered when answered by somebody as transparently cautious, wise and solid as Althorp. Once, in the midst of an extremely agitated debate about Reform, Althorp ended the chaotic scenes around him by getting to his feet and asking the Commons en masse: 'Has the House confidence in me?' Tensions immediately subsided, for there could be only one answer to the question – and nobody needed to voice it.

Jack Althorp's quiet calm, his undoubted patience and good humour all aided the radical Bill through to its successful adoption by Parliament. Far from plunging Britain into revolution, it is arguable that its timely acknowledgement of the need to extend democracy actually saved the country from the violent civil strife that overtook much of Continental Europe in the 1840s.

Yet universal respect for his integrity was not to spare Althorp from some extremely rough treatment from the Opposition Tories, and those sections of the press controlled by them or sympathetic to their cause. The *Morning Post* made much of his absent-mindedness when, in the general election following the passing of the Reform Bill, the Conservatives objected to Lord Althorp's vote, and sought for it to be struck off. He had entered himself as 'Viscount Althorp; residence, Althorp; qualification, renter of above £50 a year'.

Lord Althorp's steward assumed the objection was over the question of the rent, but the Tory queries were directed elsewhere, and they were valid. He might have had unquestionable ties to Althorp, but according to his tax returns, his residence was at Brampton, a nearby village where his Northamptonshire farming operations were based. And, in the Reform Bill that he had championed so effectively, it had been clearly stipulated that the Christian name and surname of the party claiming a vote had to be entered in full. His real name, for this purpose, was therefore not 'Viscount Althorp' – that was his courtesy title, borne as the eldest son of Earl Spencer – but 'John Charles Spencer'. One of the chief architects of Reform was thus left ineligible to vote – and entirely through his own lack of attention to detail.

The Tories found endless amusement in Althorp's unsophisticated nature, never sparing him from ridicule that was to hurt him deeply. The poem 'Rusticus, abnormis sapiens crassaque Minerva', which appeared anonymously in 1834, was typical of the genre, cruelly lampooning Jack's love for the rural life:

> Most rustic ALTHORP, honest, stupid, dull,
> Blunderer in thoughts, thy ev'ry act a bull;
> Poor erring man! Kind Nature's will forgot,
> For she had formed thee a happier lot;
> The grazier's oracle, the farmer's theme.
> Judge of the plough and well-directed team—
> Alas! That aught should mar designs so great,
> And make thee now a Farmer of the State.

However, the Whigs treasured their deeply unglamorous champion, fêting him and his cabinet colleagues for delivering the great prize that they had sought for years in the shape of Reform. Public collections were taken to buy suitable tributes for those who were perceived to be the defenders of democracy, and banquets were arranged to venerate their achievements.

In the George Hotel in Northampton, in 1832, 500 gentlemen met to dine in honour of Lord Althorp. The health of the King was drunk, followed by that of the Queen, then of the rest of the royal family. The fourth health was for 'the glorious triumph of Parliamentary Reform', and this was barely out of the proposer's mouth than the place erupted, the cheers lasting several minutes.

The chairman of the banquet got to his feet, and explained to those present:

For the achievement of that measure, to no person is the country more indebted than to my noble friend, Lord Althorp . . . the success of that measure was greatly accelerated by the ability, firmness, and integrity of Lord Althorp who, by his urbanity and good temper, had surmounted many difficulties in its way. Even his political enemies did not deny that no man but Lord Althorp could have so speedily and successfully brought that measure to a triumphant conclusion.

The speech was punctuated by huge cheers.

Despite their personal attacks on him, it was certainly true that Althorp's enemies were aware of his vital role in the Whig party's great triumphs. When asked what Althorp's contribution had been to the passing of the Reform Bill, a senior Tory replied, 'Oh, it was his damn good temper that did all the mischief.' But the most fulsome praise for his actions during this crucial stage in British politics came from his leader, Grey, who termed Althorp 'the leading member of government in the Commons, on whom my whole confidence rested, whom I considered as the right arm of the government, and without whom I felt it was impossible that the government could go on'.

Althorp was fully aware of his significance to the party's fortunes, although he found each day in office increasingly agonizing. There were consolations in continuing to wield influence, however, as he involved himself in issues close to his heart. In 1833, he had the great satisfaction of seeing the Abolition of Slavery Bill passed, and he was a strong advocate for another far-reaching change that year, when it was agreed to open up trade with China. The following year witnessed the Poor Law Amendment Act, which he had fought for with enormous vigour, and which greatly helped 'the moral and physical condition of the poor'.

Also in 1834, the whole issue of legislation in Ireland was under the spotlight. Lord Althorp made it clear that, if the more severe clauses then in force to control the Irish were renewed, he would feel obliged to resign from the government. When the majority of his cabinet colleagues decided to ignore Althorp's advice and perpetuate the repressive laws that he so despised, he carried through his threat. Grey resigned with Althorp, and the first Reform government was brought down by the departure of both these key men.

If Jack had hoped that he would now be free from the burden of ministerial responsibility, he was mistaken. The Tories were unable to form a government of their own, and William IV, against his own wishes, was forced to accept the Whig ministry of Lord Melbourne. Althorp, with no public protest but with huge private reservations, resumed his post as Chancellor of the Exchequer, having been persuaded that a Whig administration could not proceed without him.

Only his father's death was able to free Jack from the yoke of public office. It came late in 1834, and at last he now had the escape route out of the Commons into the 'Hospital for Incurables' that he had long talked about. He took it with alacrity and with no regrets. Sir Spencer Walpole mourned the passing of Althorp's career in the cabinet with the following assessment: 'He was trusted by the House of Commons and the country as no Minister has ever been trusted before, and as, perhaps, no Minister will ever be trusted again.'

The same devotion to duty that Jack Althorp showed in his public life was brought to bear in his private obligations as head of the Spencer family. He had long recognized that his parents' lifestyle, particularly his father's penchant for the most rare and expensive of books, would leave him with a greatly reduced inheritance. The fabulous wealth that his grandfather had received from Sarah Marlborough's generosity was now but a memory. There was

Althorp, there was Spencer House and there were still several landed estates, but of cash and liquidity there was none; and of mortgages and debts there was a seeming multitude.

In 1833, trying once again to face up to the consequences of his extravagance, George John had arranged mortgages on his lands of £356,500. There were further bond debts of £17,000. He earmarked various estates to be sold, but he died before his plans could be carried through.

How Jack coped with these inherited debts in the 1830s has since become something of a joke among succeeding generations of Spencers. It was admirable that he set about paying off the huge sum, in what he termed 'the Great Operation', with such earnestness. The regrettable part lies in his decision to sell off three outlying hamlets, which he thought of no importance to the core of the estate. The hamlets were Battersea, Putney and Wandsworth, and the Spencer share of them was disposed of for a mere £118,000. Within a generation, thanks to the advent of the railway, they had become parts of Greater London, worth millions.

Spencer House could also have been sold at this time since Jack had no need for anything so ostentatious and expensive in London, being happy with an apartment in Albany, the Piccadilly building that had once been the site of Sunderland House. In 1835 he seriously began to market Spencer House, some of the contents of the London mansion being moved to Althorp in anticipation of the sale, including the Second Earl's earliest printed books, which were placed in the old man's former bedroom on the ground floor of Althorp – an action of which the old bibliophile would doubtless have approved. However, despite some fleeting interest from other aristocrats, the sale of Spencer House was not to be. Nobody could be tempted to take on such a large and costly residence in a time of comparative economic weakness, and the property remains in Spencer ownership to this day.

The snapshots we get of Jack in his middle age are of a man living well within his means, concentrating on his farming, while keeping the family's two principal residences ticking over. He himself was happiest on his Wiseton farm, in Nottinghamshire, which had been left to him after Esther's death. Here he built up one of the most successful herds of shorthorn bulls that has ever existed, the Wiseton stock being noted for their huge strength and even temper.

I have dedicated a room at Althorp to Jack; it is, coincidentally, that same bedroom of his father's that he appropriated for the Spencer House books. On its walls I have placed two dozen portraits of his favourite bulls – huge beasts, with square bodies and tiny heads – which I found, flaking and battered, in the attics, when I took over at Althorp in 1992. I had the pictures restored, and now they hang together, in simple frames, the overdeveloped forms of the cattle looking quizzically down on the cases of medals that they won for their aristocratic owner at Smithfield shows.

There is one such picture, tucked behind the door, showing this least pretentious of men, his hands in the pockets of his yeoman's trousers, his dog Bruce beside him, discussing the merits of a favourite bull with his two land agents, a herdsman looking on. This was where Jack was happiest – in the fields, with people who shared his love of farming, far removed from the House of Commons and from London. He spent so many years in the capital, toiling away at political life, when all he wanted was to be with his animals. At least his final years were spent in the manner designed to give him greatest satisfaction.

Mrs Burditt, a resident of Church Brampton, a few miles from Althorp, was ninety-three in 1916, when she told my great-grandfather of her memories of 'Honest Jack Althorp' in the 1830s. He had, she said, 'a dread of getting stout', and she would often see him walking back over Kingsthorpe Mill bridge from North-ampton to his home, quite alone, after attending the meeting of the governors of the infirmary and the bench of magistrates. He sometimes spoke to the young girl as he passed. He was generally dressed as a well-to-do farmer and, Mrs Burditt recalled, 'He was always kind.'

# 14. Fourth Son, Fourth Earl

George John and Lavinia had five sons and two daughters that survived childbirth. A series of stillbirths and miscarriages between 1782, when Jack was born, and 1787, when the second child, Sarah, appeared, had left Jack very much the senior figure in his generation of the Spencer family. Further distance was placed between him and his siblings through the death of the next son, Richard, as an eighteen-month-old toddler in 1791.

It was just over nine months after Richard's death that Robert Cavendish Spencer was born at Althorp. He was given his second name as a mark of respect for his godfather, William Cavendish, Duke of Devonshire. His bust is in Painters' Passage at Althorp – the bald head and round face both highly reminiscent of his cousin, Sir Winston Spencer-Churchill, for whom he is often mistaken. In the Library there is a painting of him, in uniform, lying back reading a book, a mixture of chubby baby-facedness and keen intelligence, the unusually relaxed pose in direct contrast to the formal clothing of the officer-aristocrat.

He was first educated at Harrow. Then it was decided that he would enter the Navy, a standard career choice for the younger son of a nobleman, but almost inevitable when that nobleman had been First Lord of the Admiralty.

In 1804 he became a midshipman in the *Tigre*, and went straight into active service in the Mediterranean, before joining Nelson's force in pursuit of the combined French and Spanish fleets in the West Indies. He would have been with Nelson at Trafalgar the following year, but two days before the battle the *Tigre* was one of a handful of ships deployed away from the main body of the British fleet.

His elder sister, Sarah, recorded the family's relief at his safety, news of which reached them a full month after Trafalgar had been fought and won:

I cannot resist writing to you, to tell you how very happy we all are at the great blessing the Almighty has conferred on us – I mean the certainty of our dear Bob's safety – notwithstanding this great and glorious battle having happened so near him . . . What hurt . . . all of us most deeply, is the death of Lord Nelson. How is it ever to be repaired? I really almost dread Bob's next letter; he will be so very unhappy at the loss of so excellent a commander; he quite adored him . . .

Over the next five years, he was involved in various dangerous engagements, including two attacks on Rosetta in 1807, after which his immediate commanding officer, Sir John Duckworth, gave Lavinia Spencer 'a delightful account of Bob's character, of his popularity with everybody, and of the extreme fondness of the Captain for him, as well as of his remarkable diligence, activity, and attention to his duty, as was really pleasanter almost than a letter would have been'.

The British fleet's primary role after Trafalgar was the blockading of France's sea ports, stopping supplies being brought in from overseas, but also ready to strike if the French Navy made the mistake of sailing too far from shore, and fall prey to its superior force. Between 1807 and 1809, the *Tigre*, with Bob still on board, was detailed to watch the port of Toulon.

At the end of 1809, the British heard that the French might come out to fight in Rosas Bay. The *Tigre* captain, who always had his son, Ben, with him on the ship, took Bob aside, and said:

Well, I do think these people will at last put to sea, and then of course we shall have an action: and, if anything should happen to me in it, Spencer, I shall leave you my little boy here as a legacy; he will want protection and care, and I know you will have the will, and I hope you will have the power to give him both, and to bring him forward in the profession.

However, it was Bob's life that was to be the more endangered in the ensuing clash. He was in the *Tigre*'s launch, under the command of a Lieutenant Boxer, which was able to penetrate under the boarding nets that the French had deployed to keep the British away. Believing that the Royal Navy would never be foolhardy enough to attempt such a manoeuvre so near to their gun batteries, the French had neglected to tie the nets down properly. The result of the British attack was total success: all the vessels in the enemy convoy were destroyed or captured.

Promotion for Bob followed the next year, and by October 1812 he had his first command – the brig *Pelorus*. Within three months, he was raised to the rank of commander and stationed in the fleet off Marseilles. At his suggestion, a daring attack was made on gun emplacements at Cassis, a small port between Marseilles and Toulon.

While the Napoleonic Wars were still raging, Britain found herself simultaneously at odds with the United States. Bob is the only Spencer to date to have been involved in direct armed conflict with America. His sphere of operations was in, and off the coast of, Florida and Louisiana. His ship was part of a small force under Captain the Hon. W.H. Percy which attacked the West Florida stronghold of Fort Bowyer, near Mobile, in September 1814.

Later in the same year Bob was chosen by Sir Alexander Cochrane to land near New Orleans. With his knowledge of French and Spanish, he was instructed to find out what he could about Louisiana, and to secure guides and pilots for the proposed British expeditionary force. However, he was very nearly captured by General Jackson's cavalry, he and his colleague only just getting away in their boat before the enemy arrived at their secret hiding place.

After several further adventures for Bob on American soil, the campaign petered out in 1815. Bob was then selected to deal with the Native Americans who had assisted the British in the fighting. He saw that they dispersed peacefully, with all claims against the British settled, as he dismissed them from active service. A later naval report said,

This was arranged to the entire satisfaction of His Majesty's Government, notwithstanding the prejudices and wild habits of the Indians, amongst whom Captain Spencer lived encamped at Prospect Bluff, far up the Apalachicola river, for more than a month.

The strangest event recorded about Bob's life is his supposed death. In 1820, the Spencers were overcome by grief on being told that Bob had been killed in a duel. The story was that he had ordered his officers not to work the men so hard. Apparently this had led to a quarrel with the first lieutenant, McDonald. Then, the family was told, Bob had ordered all the men down to the main deck guns, leaving himself and McDonald alone. At this point Bob was supposed to have drawn his sword and told McDonald to defend himself. McDonald was reported initially to have refused, pointing out that he was a superior swordsman to his captain, since he had practised so much while a prisoner of war in France. The first lieutenant said, so the report went, that he would fight Spencer, if he insisted, but that the duel would have to take place on shore.

The story then became even more unlikely, Bob reputedly calling McDonald 'a damned rascal', and striking him with the flat of his sword. There was a tussle, in which Bob was accidentally run through by the first lieutenant. It was all untrue, but it was widely reported, a naval bulletin in Brazil noting, 'This melancholy affair has thrown a great gloom over the countenances of all naval characters at Rio.'

When the Spencer family learned that the story was just a mysterious invention, they shared their relief with the people of the villages surrounding Althorp, organizing for the poor to be given extra provisions, and for oxen to be roasted on spits for everyone to eat.

The Royal Navy's wide sphere of duties at this time is demonstrated by Bob's subsequent postings: Tunisia, South America and Algeria. In the South American campaign, Bob, ever interested in scientific progress, just as his father was, paid out of his own pocket for the installation of Congreve's Lights on his frigate, the *Owen*

*Glendower*, novel navigation aides that were soon to be widely adopted by the fleet.

The Algerian situation that he encountered was an unusually delicate one. In 1824, the bey of Algiers had provoked the British by forcing an entry into the house of their consul, and kidnapping two of his servants, claiming they were from an enemy tribe. Bob was dispatched to tell the bey that this was an unacceptable way to treat His Majesty's representative, his frigate escorted by a heavy-hitting brig. He arrived to find a much more complicated situation than he had been led to expect: there were two Spanish ships in the harbour, which had just been captured, their crews about to be sold into slavery.

The bey was a signatory to an agreement which stated that he would not enslave Christians. When Robert reminded him of this and insisted that the Spaniards be released, the bey refused. Worried about the consul's safety, Bob asked him and his family to board his ship. As they were all departing, the bey's warship that had captured the Spanish made a break for the open seas. Bob called on it to surrender, but it sailed on until he opened fire, capturing it with no English losses. Inside were seventeen of the Spaniards, now saved by Bob from a life of slavery.

From 1826, his active service days were mixed with the desk duties that increasingly high rank necessitated. When his frigate, the *Naiad*, was paid off at Portsmouth in the autumn of that year, the gunnery and the discipline on the ship were said by the commanding officer 'never to have been exceeded'. Bob now became private secretary to the Lord High Admiral, who was later to become King William IV, until 1828, being knighted at the conclusion of his term of office.

It is clear that his time in this position was noted for its authoritarianism, his obituarist later trying to forgive Bob his disciplinarian excesses:

If by some it has been thought that, whilst in this arduous situation, Sir Robert Spencer drew the strings of authority too tight, it must be recollected that to such an accusation all public officers are liable; and,

where so much real worth is acknowledged, a little occasional bluntness
and shortness of manner, unfortunately incident to the profession of a
seaman and the habits of command, may surely be excused.

An intensely religious man, a trait common to all the Spencer
brothers of his generation, Bob greatly impressed the future King
with the way in which he led a church service on board the Royal
Yacht, while briefly commanding it in 1828. This, though, was the
last act of any note that he performed in British waters.

Later in the same year he was sent back to the Mediterranean
fleet, in command of the frigate *Madagascar*. By now it was evident
that Jack was unlikely ever to remarry, and that Bob was effectively
heir to the Spencer earldom and estates. On Jack's appointment to
the cabinet in 1830, Bob was selected to represent the Royal Navy
at the Ordnance Board, as surveyor-general. He was instructed to
return home to assume this new responsibility. However, he was
struck down with 'an inflammation of the bowels' in Alexandria,
and died two days later. The *Madagascar* sailed on to Malta, where
the life of the Honourable Sir Robert Cavendish Spencer is commemorated by a monument erected by the officers, seamen and
marines of his final command on the Coradino Heights, above the
harbour at Valletta.

A decade after the false alarm of Bob's death in a duel, the Spencer
family had to deal with the reality of the demise of a man who was
not only the next head of the family but one (George John still
being alive), but who was also much loved and respected by them
all. His younger brother, George, later recalled:

Never was a man more calculated than he to get on, as it is said, in the
world. He was brave and enterprising, and skilled in all that might make
him distinguished in his profession; at the same time he was most eager
in the pursuit of field sports and manly amusements; and in society was
one of the most agreeable and popular men of his day.

Their sister, Sarah, wrote to a friend, Mrs Pole Carew:

We have indeed suffered a painful trial! An affliction which, though unmixed with any of the feeling of shame and horror which aggravated the 'report' ten years ago, has been, and will be a heavy one – a great blow to my Father and Mother – and a sad change in our family state, and our future prospects – so dependent on him we have lost, for comfort and brightness! And just now you know we were expecting him.

As a little girl, the same Sarah Spencer had written to her father on a far happier theme:

Dear Papa,

We have just received the good news of the arrival of the new brother, and I am writing to wish you joy of it with all my heart. We are all very glad of it, for we have expected it the whole morning. I pray God that Mama may continue well; pray will you let us know how she is to-morrow, and give her our loves, as well as to the little boy.

I am, dear Papa,

Your affectionate and dutiful,

Sarah Spencer.

The date was April 1798, and the 'little boy' was Frederick, to be known by his family as 'Fritz'. The birth took place in the Admiralty and, although when he was a boy there was a plan for Fritz to become an army officer – Sarah reporting 'Fritz already fancies himself an epauletted, red-coated cavalry officer . . . for he is a very fine, spirited fellow, and does all he can to prove his courage in facing danger, and his toughness and fortitude in bearing pain and hardship . . .' – it was to be the Navy that was to benefit from his martial qualities.

A godson of Frederick, Duke of York, young Fritz was sent to Eton for his education at the age of ten. Four years later, he went away to sea as a young midshipman. We know more about Fritz's personal views during his early naval career than about those of his elder brother, Bob, because of the survival of his diary from 1819 to 1824. It reveals a serious-minded young man, certainly intelligent, but verging on the priggish. Passages which deal with his feelings are sadly understated. All of Lavinia's children, particularly her sons, seem to have been emotionally constipated. Thus we learn of his distress at being sent on Sir Thomas Hardy's expedition to South America in 1819, with the almost apologetic admission:

Whether it was the great distance to which I was going or that my family were in an unsettled state being just about to leave England I know not, but it was the most dreadful parting I ever had. I had hoped to have been in command of myself when bidding farewell to my mother but her tears set me off and when I came to the end of the corridor meeting dear Sarah it WAS too much for me. I never felt such anguish . . .

Similarly, the entry for 23 April 1823 seems to cry out for a need for more openness with his feelings: '"The Fly" arrived from England and brought me the melancholy news of the death of my poor sister Georgiana,' he wrote. It seems an unhealthily inadequate response to the death of a sister in childbirth.

The most enjoyable entries relate to items we take for granted today, which were total novelties for the grave junior officer, and which he treated either with suspicion or with unwise acceptance. On arriving at Madeira in mid-September 1819, he recorded,

We got some wine and fruit, the last of which was very indifferent such as pears, peaches and a few bananas. I tasted one of them [a banana] for the first time in my life and was as near sick as possible, for the richness of it is too much for fruit and the smell is stronger than the ripest melon, it is a good antiscorbutic and promotes digestion very much and I am told that it is an acquired taste entirely.

Two years later in Lima – which he described as an 'odious place', because the locals delighted in imprisoning Englishmen without charge – he found that everyone around him was falling seriously ill. However, Frederick was convinced he had found the secret to good health, even in this primitive city:

As to myself I never was better although so much more exposed by living in Lima, and with almost all my acquaintances among the merchants ailing more or less at times. I think that the precaution I took of never going out of doors without a cigar in my mouth had a good deal to do with it, by which the damp air that occasions the Tertian had not the means of getting to my lungs.

The Royal Navy at the time had many rituals, from which not even the younger sons of former First Lords of the Admiralty were excused. The ceremony that accompanied the crossing of the Equator seems to have severely tested young Fritz's sense of humour, for he records, with unconvincing reassurances that he took everything in good spirits:

I liked the fun very well as far as it went with me but I had rather been excused the shaving part of the business; for nothing can be more beastly. They were not allowed to put any dirt more than tar and slush for the lather but they made it up in the pills which were the dung they found in the sheep pen and when a fellow was not quiet they pushed one or two of these into his mouth which made him splutter and open his mouth upon which the tar brush was rammed in and he was shaved with an iron hoop made up into the shape of a razor, and then tumbled back into the waist where a sail was spread full of water and he got a most complete ducking, one man in falling into the sail broke his collar bone and another was in such a fright he fainted.

A striking figure, tall with reddish hair, Frederick became a successful naval officer. In 1822, he was promoted to the rank of post-captain, and, in 1827, he took part in the last ever sea battle fought entirely under sail, when he served against the Turks under Admiral Sir Edward Codrington at Navarino. Frederick distinguished himself that day through his bravery and leadership. He was made a Companion of the Order of the Bath by his own monarch, and received the cross of St Louis from France, as well as becoming a Knight of St Anne of Russia. Although he never put to sea again in a naval capacity after 1828, he had reached the rank of vice-admiral by the time of his death.

At Althorp, in the portico of the Stables overlooking the deer park, lie four of the cannon from his ship at Navarino, reminders of the time when he was truly happiest – at sea, rather than on land.

Frederick married twice. The first marriage took place in 1830, after only three weeks' engagement. The bride was Elizabeth Poyntz, from the same family as Georgiana, wife of John, First Earl Spencer.

The Poyntzes had an interesting history in their own right. Although the Spencers' Norman origins remain open to some question, those of the Poyntzes are beyond any doubt. Their forebear was Drago Fitz Pons, who accompanied William the Conqueror on his 1066 invasion.

In the Middle Ages, the Poyntzes settled at Iron Acton, in Gloucestershire. The first Poyntz of the modern age to attract attention was William, who married as his third wife Jane Monteagle. She was a close cousin of Major-General Richard Deane, a distinguished naval and military commander, who had been particularly outstanding at the Battle of Newbury, where Henry Sunderland was slain.

In 1685 William and Jane's second son was born: Stephen, later referred to as 'the great light and ornament of his family'. In 1724, Stephen became ambassador to Sweden. Six years later he was made steward to the household of, and governor and tutor to, William, Duke of Cumberland, the nine-year-old brother of George II, and, incidentally, Sarah Marlborough's favourite out of all the young royal children she encountered in her latter years. This was the same Duke of Cumberland who attracted such notoriety after the bloodbath of Culloden in 1746, when his army routed that of Bonnie Prince Charlie, slaughtering thousands of Jacobites during and after the battle.

Stephen was the father of five children by his wife Anna Maria Mordaunt, a maid of honour to Queen Caroline, and a beauty whose charms were written about by Samuel Croxall, in his poem 'Fair Circassian'. Stephen and Anna Maria's favourite child was the youngest, Georgiana, who was to become the secret bride of John, later first Earl, Spencer in 1755.

Scandal touched the Poyntz name in 1786, when Georgiana Ann – a niece of Georgiana Spencer and granddaughter of Stephen and Anna Maria – was found by her husband, William Falkner, the Postmaster General, to be having an affair with Lord John Townshend. Falkner challenged Townshend to a duel with pistols. He duly fired at Townshend, but the bullet missed him, striking only his hat. Townshend then showed pity for the cuckolded husband, and discharged his own weapon in the air. Falkner divorced Georgiana Ann soon afterwards, Townshend marrying her before the year was out.

Georgiana Spencer's eldest brother was William Stephen Poyntz. One of the three best portraits at Althorp is of this man, tall and handsome, leaning against a tree, his spaniel Amber at his feet. The portrait is by Gainsborough – reputedly one of his best – and Amber was included after saving his master's life, having found a murderous thief waiting under William's bed, dagger drawn.

In 1794 William married the Hon. Elizabeth Mary Browne, daughter of the Seventh Viscount Montagu, whose family home was Cowdray, in Sussex. Through his marriage, William was to gain control of that estate and other lands at Battle Abbey and around Midhurst. However, the supposed workings of an ancient family curse would overshadow William's life, bringing tragedy in their wake.

The root of the events that overtook the Poyntzes and the Brownes lay, according to the superstitious, in the provenance of their landed estates. For, like many aspiring people of new fortunes – the Washingtons, as we have seen, were the same – they had acquired church property after Henry VIII's dissolution of the monasteries. According to Sir Henry Spelman in his writings about sacrilege, there was 'a fearful curse which was pronounced generally upon those who were guilty of that crime'.

In 1538, Sir Anthony Browne, son of Henry VII's standard bearer, received 'a grant of the house and site of the late Monastery of Battle in Sussex, to him and his heirs for ever'. During a celebratory banquet in the Abbots' Hall to mark the appropriation of the monastic property, a monk came in and quietly but purposefully walked up to the dais where Sir Anthony was seated with his family and his friends. The monk then issued a curse on the descendants of the Browne family, in posterity, ending with a phrase that was to ring down the succeeding centuries: 'By fire and water thy line shall come to an end, and it shall perish out of the land.'

Two and a half centuries were to go by, during which generations of Brownes were told of this hex hanging over them. It was not until 1793 that it was seen to strike home; but, when it did, it did so with double the anticipated strength.

It was in that year that the Eighth Lord Montagu, 24-year-old head of the Browne family, was completing the Grand Tour with a friend, Charles Burdett. Both men were accompanied by an old retainer from Cowdray. Half-way between Basle and Schaffhausen, at Laufenberg, they came across some waterfalls, and the two younger men announced their desire to shoot the rapids there. Their servant tried to dissuade them from being so foolhardy, reminding them of the curse. Seeing that his pleas were being ignored, the old man arranged for guards to be placed along the river to stop the madcap adventure from taking place.

However, Montagu and Burdett were determined, and they arranged for a boat secretly to be built for them. Even when the servant tried physically to stop them from getting into the boat, they pushed him aside, and careered down the river. Burdett's body was never found. Montagu's eventually appeared, killed by water, in accordance with the curse.

The old retainer headed back to Cowdray to inform the rest of the family of the tragedy that had overtaken the young master. At Calais, before sailing for England, he recognized another one of the staff from Cowdray disembarking from a ship, and asked him what he was doing there. The second servant replied that he had come to look for Lord Montagu, to tell him that the mansion at Cowdray had been completely destroyed by fire.

In his will, Lord Montagu had left everything to his sister, Elizabeth Mary Browne, soon to marry William Poyntz. However, the art treasures of Cowdray had nearly all been destroyed, and, it is believed, the celebrated Roll of Battle Abbey was also consumed by the flames that fateful night in September 1793.

The curse next struck in July 1815, weeks after the Battle of Waterloo, when Elizabeth and William took their two sons and three daughters on holiday to Bognor Regis, where they stayed at the Pavilion House.

On 7 July, a warm day with a calm sea, William suggested taking the two boys out sailing, with a couple of friends who had come to visit them. Ever conscious of the hex, Elizabeth pleaded with her husband not to go ahead with this plan, but he insisted, and the boat headed off, leaving Elizabeth and her daughters watching anxiously from a window.

From nowhere, tragedy struck. *The Gentleman's Magazine* recorded the rest of the story:

In the afternoon, about four o'clock, Colonel Poyntz [William], his two sons and their tutor, Miss Parry and Miss Emily Parry, daughters of the late Admiral Parry, of Fareham, a fisherman and his son, were returning to Bognor in a pleasure boat, when the whole party, excepting Colonel Poyntz and the boatman were drowned; the latter saved the Colonel by swimming with him on his back, Mrs Poyntz looking from the drawing-room the moment the accident happened.

It transpired that, when the boat capsized, William Poyntz had grabbed on to its side, his two sons in turn clinging to his coat. However, William could not support them for long and, whether through exhaustion or cramp, both the boys let loose their grip and drowned.

My grandfather wrote down in a notebook that the boys' mother, Elizabeth, 'never recovered from the shock, and it is said she never smiled again'. Contemporaries of hers suggested that the double tragedy unhinged her, and that daily 'she wept the terrors of the fearful wave'.

Elizabeth was delivered from her incessant turmoil when she died, in 1830. William Poyntz lived on, seeing his daughter Elizabeth marry Frederick Spencer in the year of his wife's death. After that he lived in London, visiting his daughters – there were three, not two, contrary to the report of *The Gentleman's Magazine* – in their respective stately homes.

The trio were great heiresses, and had made 'good' marriages. However, they had been brought up in an eccentric way by their bereaved mother, with her sadness having an adverse effect on their personalities. My grandfather, again drawing on what he had heard from his own relatives, who had witnessed for themselves the results of the drowning tragedy, wrote that

The three daughters . . . were brought up to consider everything wrong and wicked, so much so that one of them (I do not recollect which) on her death bed extorted a promise from my Aunt Sarah that she would never go [to the theatre] during the rest of her life.

One of Elizabeth Poyntz's sisters, known to the Spencers as 'Aunt Fan', married Lord Clinton when very young, having nursed him at Cowdray after he had had a bad fall from a horse. After Clinton's death, Jack, Third Earl Spencer, offered to marry her, but she chose instead Sir Horace Seymour – whose daughter, by coincidence, was to be Frederick Spencer's second wife.

'Aunt Fan' was known for her looks and her lack of intelligence. Although she adored Sir Horace, he had married her only to pay off his debts. He never concealed that fact from her and, as soon as the wedding service was over, he retired to his gentleman's club to resume his bachelor existence. Sir Horace's sister, a Mrs Damer, was so appalled by this behaviour that she immediately went to a jeweller's and bought an emerald and diamond half-hoop ring, which she gave to her new sister-in-law, claiming it was from Seymour. 'Aunt Fan' never knew otherwise.

The other Poyntz sister, Isabella, was also a renowned beauty, and became Lady Exeter. She was known for the number of men who proposed to her, including the truly eccentric Fifth Duke of Portland, who ended up never getting married at all. Isabella became a pillar of the evangelical church, and, according to Grandfather, 'had many children, some of whom were quite hopeless!'

The widowed William remained a popular figure, but he had the Poyntz addiction to gambling in its most rampant form. After his wealthy wife's death, he used to go to his daughters in tears, and beg them to clear his debts.

In 1836, while riding in Althorp Park, his horse stumbled in a rabbit hole, and he fell, landing on his head. For four years he survived, in constant pain. In April 1840, he sneezed violently, and died, apparently the jolt of the sneeze severing the last remaining piece of vertebra that had kept him alive for those last, agonized years. It was an end more ignominious than the monk of Battle Abbey could ever have prayed for.

William left the estate at Cowdray to his three daughters as co-heirs and tenants in common. They were not allowed the opportunity of buying one another's shares, so, in 1843, they sold the estate to the Sixth Earl of Egmont for £330,000. Various objects from Cowdray were left directly to Frederick and Elizabeth Spencer, the most important being the Reynolds double portrait of Georgiana, First Countess Spencer, and her daughter, later Georgiana Devonshire, which today dominates the South Drawing Room at Althorp, having once been a Poyntz heirloom.

Frederick, Fourth Earl Spencer, who married into the Poyntz family, found everyday domestic life a taxing business. He was accused of running his children as if they were part of his crew, and occasionally he resorted to the sort of cruelty that might have been thought appropriate when disciplining press-ganged sailors but was unacceptable in his role as father. He would lock his children in a cramped and unlit room under the main staircase in the Saloon at Althorp, when they were naughty. I can recall reading a journal that Georgiana, the eldest of the three Spencer offspring, kept of her childhood. In it she complained at how well her brother was treated, in comparison to her and her sister, Sarah, to the extent that he ate different food from them, and received all manner of favours that were denied the two girls. All three children found this sort of regime deeply difficult to accept.

Both parents justified their strictness by stressing their devotion to God, Frederick sometimes taking church services in the Chapel at Althorp. It was a severe and cold upbringing for the three children. His daughter, Sarah, told my grandfather that Frederick had a 'terrifying manner, as well as being a very strict disciplinarian, but those who knew him all agreed that underneath this stern exterior was the kindest heart imaginable'.

They had been happier at Harlestone House, in a village between Althorp and Northampton, where Frederick and Elizabeth were free from the obligation of overseeing the main estate, since Jack was alive, and yet had the benefits of living on Spencer land, with its beauty, its privacy and its history. Frederick's sister, Sarah, recalled in her old age,

There were often grievances formerly while your dear father and mother occupied that place [Harlestone]. But . . . though my eldest brother [Jack] was – in spite of his many noble qualities – V E R Y difficult to live with, and your father felt his faults too strongly, yet it was a happy affectionate time to all; and the removal from Harlestone was a grief in itself.

The regrettable strictness of the children's upbringing aside, it does appear that Frederick wanted only the best for all three of them. He had very firm views, one of which was that nails should not be cleaned with a nail brush, because to do so would spoil the shape of the nails. The result of this bizarre diktat was that both the children who lived to be adults had exceptionally beautiful hands.

There are several other stories which reduce this deeply contra-dictory character to the level of fallible, but well-intentioned man. One day his two younger children, John and Sarah, had just been given pogo sticks, and they were testing them out by the West Lodge at Althorp Park. Frederick spotted them by the brook, and, seeing that they had not got the courage to leap over the water, he lost his temper, and finally said he would show them how to do it himself. Apparently the children did not dare to show their amusement when his stick snapped in two in mid-air and he fell, fully clothed and full length, into the brook.

Another short snippet from the family folklore shows how Frederick's well-meaning interference extended beyond his own children. As head of the wider family, he believed it to be his duty to sort out problems among his dependants. His sister Sarah had a difficult son, Spencer Lyttelton, who was for many years the bane of his paternal and maternal families. He was always in debt, and he was perpetually squabbling in public with his wife. Frederick thought he had the solution to the latter problem, and invited the Lytteltons to stay at Althorp, having first of all ordered the removal of the bed from their dressing room, in order to force the couple to sleep together. The simplistic plan failed completely, Spencer Lyttelton refusing to speak to his uncle again until the latter was on his deathbed, so insulted was he by Frederick's clumsy meddling.

Frederick's perfectionism was famous in the family; indeed, it verged on the obsessive. When he was in the Navy in the 1820s, his mother, Lavinia, had written complaining that she found it hard to decipher his writing and told him with typical bluntness she would enjoy his news far more if she were able to read it. As a result, Frederick taught himself to write again from scratch, adopting a style unrecognizable from his earlier hand, but clear enough to gain his mother's approval.

His brother, Jack, died in 1845; Frederick was with him at Wiseton during his final moments. Jack spent his last conscious hours going through his will with his heir, 'talking over every point and explaining his wishes, as if it had been another's; and when all was done, and he had conversed beautifully with him, his countenance took an expression of perfect peace, and with a smile on his lips, he remained perfectly placid, and death came like a gentle sleep upon him like that of a child'.

Although Jack's death had been unexpected, Frederick would have found some small consolation in learning how exceptionally well his eldest brother had coped with the burden of debt he had inherited eleven years earlier: all the mortgages were paid off, and the Spencer estate was truly solvent for the first time since the heyday of the First Earl. Beyond that, Frederick had a wealthy wife with an income of her own of £5,500 per year.

According to Grandfather, Frederick was the only Earl Spencer to have possessed any business sense. He sold Wiseton and the villa at Wimbledon for good prices, and devoted his attention to the core family properties, leaving Spencer House and Althorp in as good a condition as they had ever been in. However, his thriftiness did result in some surprising decisions. In 1850, for his daughter Georgiana's coming-out party at Spencer House, he had the Ball Room redecorated in a beautiful red damask silk. Yet, out of a wish to economize, he had had no silk placed behind the paintings hanging in that room – the result being that it was impossible to put smaller pictures in their place, ever again, without the whole room being redecorated.

He was unsentimental about the individual objects that comprised his inheritance, selling a pair of large paintings by Lucarelli, of Jason and Hercules, that Sir William Hamilton had found for the First Earl, for 100 guineas each. The great chandelier from the Spencer House Ball Room was also disposed of, and some mahogany doors which he did not care for were sawn in half and transported to Althorp.

At the same time, he liked incorporating new ideas into the classical settings of his homes. Having particularly enjoyed seeing Queen Victoria's Persian carpet in the Indian department of the Great Exhibition, he had it copied by Lapworth of Old Bond Street, and had the result installed in the Library at Althorp to complement his father's splendid book collection.

He also collected porcelain; he had apparently acquired a taste for such things on his naval travels. This was a completely new departure for a Spencer, the First Earl in particular having a strong aversion to 'China and Japan'. However, Frederick's one true luxury was horses, not hunters, like many of his family, but race-horses – thus bringing back to Althorp a sport that had been absent since the time of William, Second Baron Spencer, in the early seventeenth century.

Frederick was a member of the Jockey Club, and at the time of his death his stud at Althorp included the famous Cotherstone, the first horse of note that he had bought, for the astronomical sum of £3,000, from Mr Bowes. Cotherstone had won the Derby, and in 1844 was the founder of the Althorp stud, standing at a fee of 25 guineas. The most successful horse sired by Cotherstone was Stilton, who won the Epsom Metropolitan as a three-year-old, beating Joe Miller in an epic race. However, Stilton's career was compromised in the most cruel way through suspected poisoning – not that that stopped the Prussian Government from buying him for £7,500, at the end of his racing career.

The other horses of note bred at Althorp during Frederick's earldom were Glenmasson, Farthingale, Pumicestone, Speed the Plough and Boadbil. The stud did not long out-survive the Fourth Earl, for his son was the most passionate foxhunting man that the Spencers ever produced, and he saw that the stables quickly reverted to catering for his sport and not that of his father.

Beyond his hobbies and his family, Frederick occupied his time in untaxing, but respectable, ways. He remained nominally in the Navy throughout his life, attaining the rank of vice-admiral shortly before his death. There was also a spell as a politician in the 1830s, when his brother Jack was in the cabinet. Frederick seems to have made less of an impression than Lord Althorp, *The Times* later writing that, 'He has represented Worcestershire and Midhurst with much silent effect.'

He subsequently became a courtier, following his elder sister, Sarah, into royal service. Sarah had married Lord Lyttelton at Wimbledon in 1813, but Lyttelton had died in 1828, leaving her a widow for the remaining forty-two years of her life. After a spell as a lady in waiting to the Queen, from 1842 she became governess to Queen Victoria's children. As the *Morning Post* remarked:

We need not point out that the duties of such an office far exceed those which are ordinarily comprehended in the term 'Governess'. They represent rather the position of one who stands 'in loco parentis', and it would be difficult to overrate the tact, the common sense, the intellectual power, and the qualities of disposition requisite to fulfil the requirements of such an office effectively. To say nothing of the pre-eminent station of Lady Lyttelton's pupils, she had the responsibility of supervising those who were selected to instruct them in this or that branch of knowledge, and, above all things, she had the duty of acting towards her pupils as a court of moral or intellectual appeal whenever they felt burthened with a difficulty or a grief.

Sarah was highly intelligent, with an active and wide-ranging mind. A formidable letter writer, although imbued with courtly discretion, she has left us pictures via her correspondence of the Queen and her consort, Prince Albert, away from the public gaze. In 1845, the royal couple returned from a foreign tour. It had been reported that Victoria had been suffering from *Verdriesslichkeit* – the appearance of being cross – during the trip, and it was agreed by the other courtiers that Sarah Lyttelton, being particularly close to the monarch, ought to inform her of this criticism. Sarah recorded:

Of course she listened with an air of meek endurance, as usual, and said she feared she might have looked cross from fatigue and shyness, before she reached Coburg, but that it was dreadful to have it interpreted into ingratitude . . . The Prince advised her (on her saying, like a good child, 'What AM I to do another time?') to behave like an opera-dancer after a pirouette and always show her teeth in a fixed smile. Of course he accompanied the advice with an immense pirouette and prodigious grin of his own, such as few people could perform after dinner without being sick, ending on one foot and t'other in the air.

In 1849 she left her post, Bertie – later Edward VII – being considered too old to require a governess. He wept on Sarah's departure, as did his siblings, and the link between governess and royal pupils remained throughout their lives, the surviving princesses reportedly deeply distressed at the news of Sarah's death, even though she had reached the age of eighty-two.

Frederick's time at court overlapped with that of his sister. From 1846, he was Lord Chamberlain, followed by a period as Lord

rederick, Fourth Earl Spencer, with
is dog 'Chatty' and his heir John,
ter Fifth Earl Spencer, *c.* 1855, in
ont of Althorp. Frederick was to die
ıddenly, soon after his eldest son's
ection to the House of Commons
ıd two months after the birth of his
·cond son, Bobby.

ady Sarah Spencer, by John Singer
argent, 1916. Sarah was the spinster
ster of the Red Earl, and half-sister
ɔ Bobby, Sixth Earl Spencer. Deeply
ıterested in the family's history, she
ʌas distressed that her brother was
assed over as prime minister after
ɨladstone.

*Left* John Poyntz, Fifth Earl Spencer, 1867. By this stage, aged only thirty-two, the Red Earl had been offered the leadership of the Whig Party and had become a Knight of the Garter.

*Opposite* A cartoon from the *Illustrated London News*, 30 January 1869, showing the Red Earl receiving the Freedom of the City of Dublin. His two spells as viceroy of Ireland could not have been more contrasting: the first revolved around dispensing lavish hospitality in Queen Victoria's name; the second was lived under constant fear for his life and that of his wife.

*Left* Charlotte, wife of the Fifth Earl Spencer, 1865. A renowned beauty with a charming character, Charlotte was popularly known as 'The Lady Lieutenant' during her husband's time in charge of Ireland.

*Opposite* The Red Earl with the Prince of Wales, later King Edward VII, in Dublin, 1871. As a boy at Harrow, the Red Earl was deeply embarrassed when the visiting Prince of Wales read in the school debating society records that he had proposed a motion 'That regicide is justified'. From such awkward beginnings developed a strong mutual respect.

Robert, Sixth Earl Spencer, by John Singer Sargent, 1916. Bobby Spencer was noted throughout his life for his dandyism. A gifted member of the House of Commons, his life was clouded by personal tragedy, and he was the only head of the Spencer family ever to quit Althorp through no longer being able to afford to live in it.

Lady Cynthia Hamilton, by John Singer Sargent, 1919. In the same year, Cynthia married Jack, who was to become Seventh Earl Spencer three years later. Her life of service to the community in Northamptonshire is commemorated by the naming of the county's hospice after her.

*Above* Jack, Viscount Althorp, later Seventh Earl Spencer, on his twenty-first birthday, 23 May 1913. A huge party was held at Althorp to mark Jack's coming of age, including a reception for the Spencers' many tenant farmers. Such hospitality was seldom possible after the First World War, which altered so much of England's social landscape.

*Above right* Jack, Viscount Althorp, later Seventh Earl Spencer, in uniform, by John Singer Sargent, *c.* 1915. Serving in the Life Guards in the First World War, Jack was shot in the knee and left for dead in no man's land, only to be saved by a daring rescue performed under fire by a brother officer.

*Right* A cartoon and poem from the *Northampton Independent* in 1913, on the occasion of Jack, Viscount Althorp's, coming of age. The Spencer family's history has always been closely bound to that of the Midland county of Northamptonshire.

**Northamptonshire to Viscount Althorp: Congratulations!**

Heir of a noble house and name,
Exalted on the roll of fame;
Godson of a gracious King.
Whom years to man's estate now bring;
We greet thee on this joyous day,

And join with heart and voice to say,
May time hold for thee in store,
Health and happiness more and more;
May the hopes enshrined in thee
Be all fulfilled abundantly.

H.

The Seventh, Eighth and Ninth Earls Spencer, May 1972, on the occasion of Jack Spencer's eightieth birthday. By this stage relations between Jack and Johnnie Spencer were fraught, largely because the old patriarch felt his son and heir might not be up to the job of running Althorp effectively when he inherited.

Park House, Sandringham, Norfolk. The birthplace of Frances Shand Kydd and two of her children: the Hon. John Spencer, who died soon after birth, and the Hon. Diana Spencer, later Princess of Wales. Until the Seventh Earl's death in 1975, Johnnie Spencer lived at Park House, in succession to his parents-in-law, the Fermoys.

Johnnie, Eighth Earl Spencer, outside Althorp, c. 1981. After suffering a stroke in 1978, Johnnie decided to leave much of the day-to-day running of Althorp to his wife, Raine. Approximately one-fifth of the house's art collection was disposed of in the subsequent decade and a half.

*Above* Johnnie, later Eighth Earl Spencer, in 1972 with his four children – Sarah, Jane, Diana and Charles. After his divorce from his first wife in 1969, Johnnie secured custody of the children, having them grow up with him in Norfolk.

*Right* Charles, later Ninth Earl Spencer, with sister Diana and nanny Mary Clark, 12 September 1972, the day he set off for boarding school at Maidwell Hall, Northamptonshire, aged eight.

Steward. In its obituary of Frederick, the *Northampton Herald* noted that the Fourth Earl had resigned the latter position just prior to his death, 'a place at Court, always uncongenial, it is understood, to his tastes . . .' The most enjoyable moment for him during his courtier days was when, dressed in knee breeches, he was complimented by Queen Victoria on having the best-shaped legs she had ever seen on a man.

It was largely due to his personal popularity with the Queen that he was made a Knight of the Garter in 1849. *The Times* of London took it upon itself to ridicule the award of such an honour to an aristocrat who in its opinion had done nothing to warrant it:

We have no wish to disparage the man whom the Sovereign delighteth to honour, but we cannot help asking, with nineteen in twenty of our readers, Who is Lord Spencer? When our readers see it announced that Lord Spencer is to have the vacant Garter, half of them will resuscitate for that honour the man better known as Lord Althorp. There was the venerable Lord Spencer, the scholar and bibliomaniac . . . But who is this Lord Spencer, and why is he to be enrolled in Victoria's first rank of valiant men?

*The Times* then disparagingly listed Frederick's achievements, naval and political, before concluding: 'Now the question is, Does Earl Spencer, the third of that title within a dozen years, come up to the mark? We cannot say that he does.'

It was an attack that sparked off great controversy about the general composition of the Order of the Garter, a rival newspaper stepping in to defend Frederick, while taking the opportunity to have a side swipe at other aristocrats whom it believed had been given Knighthoods of the Garter because of their social status, rather than as a result of individual achievement. Setting out the entire list of Garter Knights, the article continued:

And who of all the names chronicled above has done more than this for the country? We pick out Wellington, Anglesey, and Clarendon, and then defy the 'Times' itself to show us the fourth man among its motley lot who has half the claims of Earl Spencer to belong to the noble order

of the Garter. He brings honour to it even upon the showing of his low
and bitter assailant . . . We might ask for the particular and peculiar
achievements which have raised a Rutland, a Richmond, or a Salisbury,
to this pre-eminent distinction; – but we are satisfied to say they never
added any services to the country, to their political importance, to their
party. Earl Spencer has. He has gilded his title with new lustre, while
they have shone by the reflection of the lustre which their titles have
conferred upon them.

Frederick carried both the above cuttings with him in a notebook,
where they were found on his death.

The last years of Frederick's life were marked by family tragedies,
and also by a renaissance of romance. In 1846, he had built a third
vault in the family tombs at Brington church. Within five years, it
was to have its first occupant, for, in 1851, his wife, Elizabeth, died.
She had never enjoyed good health – indeed, Frederick had married
her in the knowledge that she might be too frail to have children
– but her death seems to have been avoidable. She had a blockage
in her uterus which, if attended to in time, could have been cured.
However, she found the subject to be one that she could not even
share with her husband, because it would have offended her genteel
sensibilities to have done so, and the penalty for this Victorian
coyness was death.

The family was surprised when Frederick remarried, and even
more so when they learned of the age difference between the
56-year-old widower and the 29-year-old bride, Adelaide Seymour.
However, the unlikely couple were besotted with one another,
Frederick choosing the best pearls from all the pieces of Spencer
jewellery to compose a row of rare perfection as a wedding present
for his young wife.

Adelaide, known as 'Yaddy', was from a distinguished fighting
family. Her grandfather was Admiral Lord Hugh Seymour. Adelaide's father, Sir Horace Seymour, was – as we have seen – not
the most gallant husband, but as a soldier he was exceptional. He
had served in the cavalry in the Peninsular War, against Napoleon's
armies, with enormous distinction, and was ADC to the Marquis

of Anglesey at the Battle of Waterloo, where he was wounded, having had three horses shot dead from under him during the day's fighting.

His son – the new Countess Spencer's brother – was Lieutenant-Colonel Charles Seymour of the Scots Fusilier Guards. He had entered the army in 1835, and then seen service in the first Kaffir War, in South Africa, in 1846–7. He returned to South Africa in 1852, as military secretary to Sir George Cathcart.

At the outbreak of the Crimean War, when the French and British allied against the Russians, Charles Seymour was very ill. However, he was determined to follow Cathcart into war, and managed to secure the post of adjutant-general to the Fourth Division.

At the Battle of Inkerman, already wounded, Seymour saw Cathcart without a horse and with the Russian infantry closing in on him. Seymour cut his way through the enemy in an attempt to help Cathcart escape, before trying to assist the general on to his own horse. As he did so, he was bayoneted to death by the Russians, and was later found with his body slumped over that of the slain Cathcart.

Another brother, Beauchamp Seymour, enjoyed lasting distinction. A naval officer, he was involved in the Burmese War of 1852. He led the Fusiliers in the capture of the Pagoda Pegu, was gazetted four times and received the Burmese medal.

The culmination of Beauchamp's career came much later, in 1882, when he was in his early sixties. By this stage he was Sir Beauchamp Seymour, supreme commander of the Mediterranean Fleet. He used his combined gunnery in the bombardment of Alexandria, destroying or knocking out of action all the forts, with very few British casualties sustained, either in terms of lives lost or ships damaged. For this success, he was awarded the thanks of Parliament, £20,000 and the hereditary title of Baron Alcester.

The new Countess Spencer was therefore from excellent fighting stock, and she needed to show her own strength and determination in order to overcome the reservations she met from members of her new family who resented her replacing Elizabeth at Althorp. The most difficult person to convince about her motives proved to be Sarah Lyttelton, the erstwhile royal governess. She was scathing in her criticism of the new châtelaine of Althorp, telling a younger relative: 'Yaddy was always (I daresay with good intentions) condescending and artificial; and if I had been a country neighbour, I should have been affronted by her continually.'

However, she did manage to produce two children. The first, Victoria, was born in 1855. It was thought a small consolation to Frederick to have another daughter, since Georgiana, the eldest child from his first marriage, had died of measles three and a half years earlier. There was one more child from this union – my great-grandfather.

Lady Stanley of Alderley went to stay at Althorp at the end of 1856. She reported to her husband: 'Lady Spencer is delicate . . . [she] never comes down in the morning and lies in the evening with her feet up. I suppose she is trying to make a little Spencer.'

She was proved correct, with the appearance of Charles Robert Spencer in October 1857. But father and son were not to know one another, for Frederick died quite unexpectedly, in what is now the Princess of Wales Room at Althorp, in December of the same year.

Even the local Tory newspaper, which had vehemently attacked Frederick's Whig views throughout his life, was shocked by the Fourth Earl's sudden passing:

In the death of Earl Spencer the country has sustained a great loss. We ourselves, often as we have been opposed to, have always been able to respect, the late peer. In dealing with him, every one felt there was no fear of petty subterfuge or underhand chicanery. Accustomed in early life to command, his position in the county may have sometimes led him towards the side of severity, but always, we fully believe, from a strict sense of duty, and never from personal feeling or pique. Characters such as this are rare, and valuable as rare. Few neighbourhoods can afford to lose a man who, elevated by his position above jealousy, and by a conscientious sense of duty above manoeuvring, can always be relied on in an emergency for an honest and straightforward course of conduct. Such a man this county has lost by the lamented death of Frederick, fourth Earl Spencer.

# 15. Father Ignatius

Jack and Frederick Spencer had had little in common and they had not been especially close. Bob had been popular with both of them. But there was another unifying link which bound the three of them together: their strong Christianity, learned from the earliest moments of their life from George John and Lavinia. And yet, it was the youngest son, George, who was to have religion not only as a support to, but as the cornerstone of his life, dedicating his existence to God in the most uncompromising manner imaginable.

There was only a year in age between George and Frederick, and they were initially brought up very much together, leaving for Eton the same day in 1808, when George was only nine. Their sister Sarah marked the impending departure of her young brothers with a letter to Georgiana, First Countess Spencer, their mutual grandmother:

Next Wednesday our two dear little boys go to Eton. I won't allow myself to think of it in as melancholy a way as I am inclined to do for I know my regret at it to be very selfish; they will be most satisfactorily situated in every way; and are I think too young to dread the event much. They have no conception of what it is to leave home, poor things, how little do they know the comfort of it!

A month later, Sarah reported that George John had gone to visit the boys, and had found them perfectly settled in at the school:

They are quite well, very much at their ease, and quite initiated already into the several mysteries of fagging, boxing, getting out of bounds, and buying trash at the pastry-cook's, which make up the character of a school-boy. Mr Godley, their tutor, is delighted with their docility and extreme simplicity of mind; they have not a notion of not doing and saying before him exactly what they would away from him; and they seem to wish for no intimate friends besides each other as yet; and the Latin hobbles on very tolerably.

The Reverend Richard Godley had been chosen by George John and Lavinia to look after their two youngest boys because of his reputation for being an extremely conscientious Christian. George later recalled: 'I must always account it one of the greatest blessings for which, under God, I am indebted to their wisdom and affection, that I was placed in such hands at so critical a time.'

Godley's religious teachings fell on receptive ears: George would remember for the rest of his life the introduction to the Christian faith he received on his sixth birthday, courtesy of his sister's Swiss governess. She took George aside, and told him about the joy of true faith, particularly of the qualities of the Church of England.

To what can I ascribe it, that I firmly believed from the first moment this truth, of which I was not capable of understanding a proof, that I never since have entertained a doubt of it, nor been led, like so many more, to universal scepticism; that my faith in the truth of God should have been preserved while for so long a time I lived, as I afterwards did, wholly without its influence.

This was the 'extreme simplicity of mind' that Godley had already detected, and to which he was to direct his own sincere beliefs.

Godley's prime aim with his charges was to keep them away from the other boys at the school as much as was possible. This perceived reluctance to mix with them spurred the Eton boys into a frenzy of bullying against the cosseted Spencers. However, the more they indulged in this brutality, the more convinced Frederick and George became that Godley was correct in keeping them separate from such oafs.

In 1811, when Frederick went to sea, George was left with Godley, and they spent a year constantly in one another's company. It was a seminal period of George's life, as he acknowledged in middle age:

I can now hardly give an account of what were the religious ideas and impressions which began so greatly to engage my mind, except that I took my chief delight in hearing Mr Godley speak about religion, that I had great abhorrence and dread of wickedness, thought with pleasure of my being intended to be a clergyman, as I was always told I would be, and admired and loved all whom I was taught to look upon as religious people.

However, George's parents became concerned that Godley was not sufficiently traditional in his Anglican beliefs, and they therefore moved the highly impressionable George into the main body of the school at Eton. He hated it, finding the conduct of his fellow pupils brutish and diametrically opposed to the principles that he had known at home, and had had reinforced by Godley. George could hardly believe that he had been placed in such a compromising position by his own flesh and blood:

But, alas! Little did my family suspect what a place was Eton; or, at least, if a suspicion came across parents' minds of what their children are exposed to in public schools, they generally persuade themselves that this must be endured for a necessary good, which is, to make them learn to know the world.

For the two years that he remained at Eton after leaving the security of Mr Godley's home, George did not pray once. He later bitterly contrasted this lapse with the much superior spiritual nurturing that he would have received, had he been brought up a Catholic child – an upbringing underpinned by religious principles that would have saved him from such oversights and omissions.

For the rest of his life, mainly because of his deeply unhappy experiences at Eton, George believed that parents had a duty to teach their own children, until the child had fully understood the overriding importance of virtue and piety. Only then could a public school be permitted to take a part in the education process.

At Christmas 1914, George left Eton with relief. He was then committed to the charge of Mr Blomfield, a priest on the Spencers'

Dunton estate in Buckinghamshire. Again, George John had placed his son in the care of a very able churchman. Blomfield was to rise to the position of Protestant Bishop of London.

Blomfield taught his pupil well, and George went up to Trinity College at Cambridge University in October 1817, his noble status more evident than his religious calling, since he arrived in the Spencer carriage, accompanied by his family's liveried attendants, as his father had done a generation earlier.

One of the chroniclers of George's life, Father Pius, took stock of his subject at this point in his youth: 'He was a young man, just turned eighteen; he had been brought up in splendour at home, and in a poisonous atmosphere at school. That he was not the vilest of the vile is to be wondered at more than that he preserved as much goodness as he did.'

Lavinia Spencer was all for her son becoming a priest, but she wanted him also to hone the attributes that she still believed to be important for his secondary role as a highly born young gentleman. She encouraged him to take up fencing. There was also, she said, something wonderful about the guitar; he ought to learn how to play it. Both of these recommendations he turned down. The only advice he took from his mother at this stage was to play cricket, a sport he had always adored, and which was to remain a 'mania' – his own word for it – throughout the rest of his life.

His elder brother Bob was to be of more value as adviser. When George, aged sixteen or so, confided in him that he found it very difficult to talk to girls at parties, Bob exclaimed, 'What a wretched false shame is that!', before berating him for thinking flirtation with women was an important pastime. After that, George later recalled, he was more appalled at the shame he had felt, than at his inadequacies with the opposite sex.

Of even more use to George was the advice Bob gave him just before he set off for Cambridge for his first term. Bob himself was about to leave for a tour of duty at sea, and, keen to protect his impressionable brother from falling in with the wrong sort of person when an undergraduate, he exhorted George never to laugh when those around him indulged in 'immoral conversation'. George set enormous importance by this brotherly guidance, marvelling in the honourable strength it revealed in Bob:

What rare advice was this from the mouth of a gay, gallant young officer; and if there were more of his character who were not ashamed to give it to their young brothers and friends, how many might be saved, who are now lost, because they do not see one example to show how a manly, fashionable character can be maintained with strict morality and modesty.

Without being diverted by the hedonistic pleasures that many of his fellow students pursued, George was able to forge ahead with his studies. Being the son of an aristocrat, he was excused the rigours of the normal seven-year degree that he would have been expected to sit, and was allowed to study for the two-year nobleman's degree. He came first out of all in his year sitting for the exam, achieving a first-class degree in mathematics and classics. Academic study was always something he excelled at. Later in his life his speaking and understanding of Italian and French were said to be 'perfect', and he had more than passable German.

His treatment as a young nobleman rather than as a potential priest continued after Cambridge, when he embarked on his own Grand Tour, in 1819, for a year. He was always to love travel, and the seeds of this passion were sown during this time. George John, Second Earl Spencer, was aware of the moral strengths of his youngest son, but he was also careful to warn him of the temptations that time away from home would present to him:

As to your conduct, George, I need not tell you how important it is for your future happiness and character that you should keep yourself from all evil; especially considering the sacred profession for which you are intended. But, on this subject, I have no wish concerning you but to hear that you continue to be what you have hitherto been.

At that time George began to become convinced that his life had been marked out for some special course – a theory reinforced when he and his companion narrowly escaped death while venturing too close to an active volcano in January 1820:

I went up Mount Vesuvius with Dr Wilson, when, as we were looking into the crater of the volcano, a discharge of red-hot stones took place. I heard them whistle by me as they ascended, and though it was of no use to attempt to get out of the way, I hurried back a few steps by a natural impulse, and immediately saw a lump of red-hot stuff twice the size of one's head fall on the spot where I had been standing just before. We immediately ran down the side of the mountain, and reached a place about a quarter of a mile distant from the mouth of the crater . . . Just then a grand explosion took place, which shook the whole mountain, and a vast quantity of these masses of fiery red stuff was spouted out from the crater, which in its return appeared entirely to cover the whole space over which we had been running five minutes before.

George's conclusion was straightforward: 'Here was an evident escape which, in a mind possessed with any religion at all, could not fail of awakening some serious reflections.'

Two years later a similar escape occurred. He was partridge shooting with his cousin, George Bingham, later Third Earl of Lucan, when the latter's gunpowder flask caught fire and exploded in Bingham's hand, severely burning him, and convincing George Spencer, who caught some of the blast himself, that only God had spared him from death.

It was at this stage of his youth that George Spencer started to put the trials of life into perspective, as being the will of God. He was prone to fits of depression. However, by giving these a religious provenance, he came to welcome them, for he believed God was giving him feelings of melancholy in order to teach him how there could be no happiness while he remained preoccupied with the superficial elements of life. He was later to chastise himself for his early inclination to follow the shallow and materialistic course expected of a young man of his privileged background:

Whatever I thought desirable in the world, – abundance of money, high titles, amusements of all sorts, fine dress, and the like, – as soon and as far as I understood anything about them, I loved and longed for; nor do I see how it could have been otherwise, as the holy, severe maxims of the Gospel truth on these matters were not impressed upon me.

Rejoicing in the trials sent down by God became a central tenet of George's belief. Accepting – indeed, almost wallowing in – feeling dejected in his early twenties was the first step down this road for the increasingly introspective young aristocrat. 'For if I have within me one bright, heavenly desire,' he acknowledged in later life, 'I owe it to these feelings, which first poisoned my pleasure in the world, and drew me at length to seek for it elsewhere, and now I wish never to have peace within my breast while one desire lives there for anything but God.'

This seems to have left more of a lasting impression on him than did his first brushes with the Roman Catholic Church. He travelled through several Catholic countries on his Grand Tour but, by his own admission, he was primarily concerned with his own pleasure, and, secondly, with absorbing what he saw and experienced as a tourist. In a distant third place, he made superficial observations about religion; an example being his view of Easter Day celebrations in Sicily, the fireworks, bells, fancy dress, flags and drums leading him to a dismissive view of Roman Catholicism: 'This religion is most extraordinary. It strikes me as impious; but I suppose it takes possession of the common people sooner than a sensible one.'

However, one of the most profound influences on the future direction of George's life was to take place during his foreign travels, and, although the setting was one of luxury and sophisticated enjoyment, it impacted directly on his religious consciousness in a manner that his direct exposure to Catholicism had failed to do.

While in Paris, in 1820, he twice attended the Italian Opera. On both occasions the opera performed was *Don Giovanni*, which tells the story of a legendary seducer and blasphemer, who attracts the wrath of men and God through his arrogant disregard for their conventions. George had felt weak even agreeing to attend the opera, since he believed he should have been living a modest life in preparation for taking holy orders. Going to the 'dangerous and fascinating' *Don Giovanni* was, he promised himself, the last occasion on which he would indulge himself in such a way.

It was the climax of the opera which was to have an unforeseen impact on his life – the irony of the venue for such a revelation not being lost on him:

The last scene . . . represents Don Giovanni, the hero of the piece, seized in the midst of his licentious career by a troop of devils, and hurried down to hell. As I saw this scene, I was terrified at my own state. I knew that God, who knew what was within me, must look on me as one in the same class with such as Don Giovanni, and for once this holy fear of God's judgement saved me: and this holy warning I was to find in an opera-house at Paris.

Such serious-minded reflection was typical of George Spencer, who seems never to have allowed himself truly to enjoy his youth, being too weighed down by his religious destiny. Reflecting on the occasion of his twenty-second birthday, he convinced himself that 'the best and happiest years of life are already past'. He made this the point at which a rededication of his energies was to be made, a focusing of his mind and body on matters which he felt he had wrongly neglected in the first part of his life:

God grant that I make those that remain more profitable to others, and consequently to myself. As to happiness, I think my temper and dispositions have prevented my having my share to the full of youthful pleasures; so I may look forward to the future for better circumstances: if I can but tutor my mind into contentment at my situation, and an engrossing wish to make my duty the leading guide of my actions. Indolence and irresolution are my stumbling blocks.

The early 1820s were a period of slow transition for George, in which his single-minded determination to serve God gradually gained strength. In December 1822, he took deacon's orders from the Protestant Bishop of Peterborough, thus taking the first step towards what everybody assumed would, given his family background, be a bishopric of his own, before too long. On 12 January 1825, he was appointed priest for Brington, the parish next to Althorp, by his father, in whose possession the living lay.

Although he was expected to lead a good life and be an example to others, strict religious devotion was not demanded of a gentleman-preacher like the Honourable and Reverend George Spencer; indeed, if he had chosen not even to live in the parish, that would not have been a matter for undue comment. A life of leisure could have been his, with the priesthood a mere career choice, not necessarily a vocation.

But George was becoming increasingly determined to dedicate himself to a sincere and rigorous life, where the appreciation of God was of core importance. He found, more and more, that he turned his back on his former pleasures. First, he decided not to visit the theatre again. This followed an embarrassing incident when he was at a play where the parson was depicted as a bumbling fool. George's fellow theatre-goers looked to see whether he had a sense of humour about this lampooning. He disliked the sensation of being put in an invidious position by people whose pleasure and concerns seemed so utterly shallow.

He also decided not to shoot again. This was not out of concern for the pain he was causing his prey, but because he despised the showing-off that was such an integral part of the sport, whereby an accurate or difficult shot evinced the acclaim of others.

Dancing was also a casualty of this period of reappraisal. When old, George had trouble with an ulcer on his leg. A religious colleague told him that he deserved to be lame, because: 'You made such use of your feet in the days of your dancing and sporting, that Almighty God is punishing you now, and the instruments of your pleasure are aptly turned into instruments of pain.' This was a judgement that George accepted fully, being in keeping with his entire philosophy as to how God rewarded self-indulgence.

However, despite such sacrifices, George had become convinced that his time as priest in Brington was lacking something. In 1826 and 1827, according to his biographer, Father Pius, 'He distributed

Bibles and blankets, prayer-books and porridge, and three of his best and most hopeful proselytes went mad, and were sent to the county lunatic asylum.' George himself noted, in one of his periodic bouts of critical self-analysis, at the start of 1827: 'I have found my mind so far from settled that I never saw myself more in need of God's grace. But I shall find it.'

The tensions between his social status and his religious beliefs were heightened with the building of an extremely large and luxurious new rectory for him in Brington, a structure thought fitting for someone of his heritage, with a substantial income of £3,000 per year, and the apparently limitless private resources of the Spencer family. Lavinia Spencer saw to it that everything inside the rectory – the upholstery, the linen, the furniture – was of the highest quality. All this while her son, the priest, was busy trying to help the poor and the wretched in his parish, outside the rectory's imposing gates. While his mother clucked around the place with ideas for grander decoration schemes, George would talk to his housekeeper, Mrs Wykes, about his wish to open his doors to the needy, converting the rectory into a hospital.

Lavinia wanted to see her youngest son married. At this stage there were no dynastic reasons for him to do so: Jack may have sunk into a life of bachelorhood, but there were still Bob and Frederick to keep the Spencer line secure. No, what Lavinia hoped to achieve was an end to George's obvious uncertainty about his lot in life; she wanted his 'metaphysical fancies' to be replaced by the realities of domesticity.

George did fall in love. He even went so far as to order his carriage down to Althorp, in order to seek his father's blessing to propose to the lady in question. However, when in the park and near the front door to the mansion, he stopped the driver and ordered him to return to the rectory in Brington. In his most far-reaching personal denial yet, he had resolved never to marry, invoking I Corinthians vii, verses 32 and 33, as his reasons: 'He that is unmarried careth for the things that belong to the Lord, how he may please the Lord: But he that is married careth for the things that are of the world, how he may please his wife.' One day, near the end of his life, he was asked what had happened to the lady he had meant to marry. George replied, without apparent self-pity: 'I passed by her house a few days ago. I believe her husband is a very excellent man, and that she is happy.'

Self-denial and generosity marked the few years of his Protestant ministry. When he made his rounds in his parish, he always had a bottle of wine in his pocket, together with as much money as he could afford to be without, to give to the ill and the poor. For the sick, he bought medicine, while the poor he helped to clothe, sometimes dressing the sores of the former, and giving the clothes off his own back to the latter. Concerned that the allowance he gave his son was being used unwisely, George John cut it back, but George simply adapted his own lifestyle, to ensure that he still had a surplus to give away: he stopped drinking wine and gave up eating puddings, while saving on the housekeeping expenses at the rectory, particularly cutting back on the laundry.

Eyewitnesses to his Christian generosity recalled how George would sometimes be approached by impostors, preying on his unquestioning open-handedness. If he did rumble them, he still gave equally liberally, and thanked God for the lesson in humility He was giving him by sending such people to him.

He dispensed with his horses, choosing instead to walk wherever he needed to go – to Northampton, five miles away, or beyond – his clothes in a knapsack, his stride purposeful and unfaltering, despite the mockery he attracted from people threatened or amused by his devotion to his beliefs. His housekeeper summed him up, during his Protestant priesthood: 'He was indeed the father of the poor, and a peace-maker, though meeting with many contradictions, particularly among the Dissenters. He bore all with patience and cheerfulness, and went on hoping all would end well in due time.'

His reward from his conventional and well-meaning father was not pride in a son's earnest endeavours, but a firm and wide-ranging rebuke:

I should not thus argue with you, my dear George, if I did not from my heart, as God is my judge, firmly believe that your welfare, both temporal and eternal, as well as the health both of your body and mind, depended upon your taking every possible means to follow a better course of thinking, and of study, and of occupation, than you have hitherto done since you have entered the profession for which, as I fondly hoped, and you seemed fitted by inclination, you would have been in due time, if well directed and well advised, formed to become as much an ornament to it as your brothers are, God Almighty be thanked for it, to those they have entered into.

George John was liberal in his beliefs, and this extended to Church matters. Both he and Jack fought for Catholic Emancipation, whereby barriers preventing Roman Catholics from being fully qualified citizens, with a right to hold all manner of public offices, would be removed. However, he had no sympathy with the teachings of the Catholic faith. As Father Pius noted, 'Lord Spencer was always favourable to Catholics, but it was in the spirit of generosity to a fallen, or justice to an injured, people.'

Moreover, the above communication makes it clear that he had not expected George to take to the most austere side of Christianity with such relish. Being God-fearing by nature was fine, but the goings-on at Brington were unacceptable – the sight of one of his sons fraternizing with the very poorest in society, and even appearing less well cared for than they, was embarrassing and threatening. As for Lavinia, she found that she could not even muster a civil word for George, so deep was her disappointment that her own Christian aims were being, in her view, subverted by a wilful son.

The problems were not simply related to conduct, though. George was also looking critically at the doctrinal inadequacies of the Church that he was serving. By the end of 1827, he was struggling with the text of the Athanasian Creed. This confession of the Christian faith started with a clear and strong message: 'Whosoever will be saved: before all things it is necessary that he hold the Catholic Faith. Which Faith except every one do keep whole and undefiled: without doubt he shall perish everlastingly.' The conclusion is equally clear-cut: 'This is the Catholic Faith: which except a man believe faithfully, he cannot be saved.'

George believed these statements to be in contrast to the general message of the Scriptures, as he understood them. The outright condemnation struck him as being at odds with the redemption which Christianity celebrated as one of its themes. This matter and others, George tried to resolve in long discussions with a fellow priest, Mr Allen, from the Spencer parish of Battersea. However, nothing Allen said could allay George's deepening suspicion that Anglicanism was deeply flawed.

If his fellow ministers from the Church of England were having little impact on George's faith, the opposite was true when he came into contact with Catholic priests. In March 1828, George welcomed Dr Fletcher into the rectory at Brington. Fletcher was a practised advocate for the Catholic faith, and he found George's state of doubt and confusion very promising; he could be a high-profile candidate for conversion.

It may well be that Fletcher arranged for a mystery correspondent to write to the troubled priest of Brington. Soon after, George received a letter from Lille, putting the case for Catholicism. He replied to it forcefully, but was surprised by the subsequent letter from the same source:

I expected only to convince him [the correspondent] that the Catholic Church was full of errors; but he answered my arguments . . . I discovered by means of this correspondence that I had never duly considered the principles of our Reformation; that my objections to the Catholic Church were prejudices adopted from the saying of others, not the result of my own observation. Instead of gaining the advantage in this controversy, I saw, and I owned to my correspondent, that a great change had been produced in myself.

There were three such letters from Lille. In total, there were thirty-two pages, and these were what finally made George's conversion inevitable. The argument that won him over was a simple one: that Scripture without Tradition cannot lead to salvation; that it is impossible for people to understand the composition, inspiration and interpretation of the Scriptures without that Tradition; that it is only through an unbroken succession of pastors to the present day that the Tradition can have been preserved, so only those pastors – the popes – can tell people with any authority what the Tradition comprises; that the creeds, liturgy, sacraments and jurisdiction of the Catholic Church are therefore the true Tradition of the teaching of Christ.

As the mystery correspondent said in the third letter:

It is certain that Jesus Christ founded a Church upon Earth for the salvation of man; where, then, is it? This is certainly the whole question among the different sects opposed to each other . . . I am persuaded the Catholics do not found their belief on the opinions and interpretations of men; their authority is Jesus Christ, God Himself.

It was only after his conversion that George learned the identity of the person who, through their letters, had brought him to the brink of becoming Roman Catholic. Mrs Dolling, who died a year before George took the final step towards his new faith, had been converted only a short time before she started writing to George. She had hoped to become a nun of the Sacred Heart, but her death prevented her from taking the veil.

When George gave an account of his conversion, in 1834, he attracted hostile ridicule from sections of the Tory press that had no time for Catholicism. Under the caption, 'The Hon. Priest Spencer', one editorial stated,

We were in hopes that he would at least have had the prudence to have kept silent, but he has thought proper to publish an account of his conversion, motives, etc., etc.; and we are compelled to assert that a more stupendous exhibition of ignorance and folly was never before put forth in the world.

It continued, with reference to Mrs Dolling's input, 'the immediate agent in his conversion was A LADY – a sort of "invisible girl", we suppose, for he never saw her. He was convinced by her "fine

Roman hand", that she was a lady; and he surrendered his faith to an unseen priest in petticoats!'

The final step for George had come at the end of 1829 through his acquaintance with the seventeen-year-old Ambrose Lisle Phillipps, himself a convert to Catholicism. A week's visit to Phillipps in Leicestershire in January 1830 satisfied George that he must leave the Protestant faith, and join the Church of Rome:

I saw how weak was the cause in behalf of which I had hitherto been engaged; I felt ashamed of arguing any longer against what I began to see clearly could not be fairly disproved. I now openly declared myself completely shaken, and, though I determined to take no decided step until I was entirely convinced, I determined to give myself no rest till I was satisfied, and had little doubt now of what the result would be.

After further deliberations, George felt an irresistible need to convert with immediate effect, telling Phillipps that he would declare himself a Catholic the following day.

The question now was how to break the news to his family. He was concerned that the shock would kill his father, whose health was floundering. As had happened at the time when he had considered marriage, so now a passage from the Scriptures gave him the strength to follow his conscience: 'He that hateth not father and mother, and brothers and sisters, and houses and lands, and his own life too, cannot be my disciple.'

The next morning, at nine o'clock, George Spencer publicly turned his back on the Church of England and embraced Catholicism. The Spencers were stunned, despite their forebodings about their son's recent behaviour. George, confident in the reasons behind his move, was unapologetic about, but sensitive to, the dismay he must have caused his family, writing to his brother, Jack: 'You and Fritz [Frederick, later Fourth Earl Spencer] and many more are my witnesses that I did not conceal my mind being staggered by the arguments of Catholics. And I wrote to my Father, the very first day that my resolution was taken.' In the same letter, he placed himself in George John's hands financially: 'I beg you will say to my Father, that whatever arrangement he pleases to make about me, I will agree to beforehand, for I have never found one cause to complain of him yet, and I am sure I never shall.'

He was right to retain confidence in his father. Like all of his family except his mother – who insisted on wearing black to demonstrate her grief at the news – George John took the view that George was quite mistaken in what he had done, but it was an error born out of the purest and most irreproachable of motives. A small income was allowed George by his father; and this continued during the earldom of his brother, Jack, and of his nephew, John. Frederick alone, the sibling who had been the closest to him in childhood, was to cut off the renegade priest, insisting that the money George would have received be given instead to charities of Frederick's choosing.

However accommodating his family might have been, George's overall financial position changed dramatically through the loss of his income as a priest. Just after his conversion, George had been advised by the Dominican friars of Hinckley that he could not continue to draw money from his Protestant benefice. The *Morning Herald*, reporting on George's new Catholicism, noted the monetary sacrifice implicit in such a move:

The conversion of so amiable and illustrious a nobleman in these eventful days, is in itself not a little remarkable; but what tenders it more so is, that by the change he will have to forgo a very large and lucrative church preferment, amounting to near three thousand a year. This fact, whatever may be thought of the change itself, is highly creditable to the honesty of him who has made so great a pecuniary sacrifice for the sake of his conscience.

George's was the most prominent of several conversions made around this time, in the aftermath of the 1829 Catholic Emancipation. Another newspaper, of 28 February 1830, put George's decision in context:

Lady Paget (the lady of Sir Charles Paget, Admiral on the Cork station) and her daughters, have been converted to the Roman Catholic Church; and so has a Reverend Gentleman at Leicester, a son of Earl Spencer, who, it is said, has become a Catholic Priest. – The late Dr Johnson, it is well known, had a 'sneaking kindness' for the Catholic worship; and Gibbon the historian took refuge at last in the bosom of that infallible Church.

Later, more hostile comment was passed on George's act of conscience:

Is this unfortunate man to be pitied as a fool, or despised as a Jesuit? Is he to be censured for publishing his folly, or thanked for showing to the world the art of manufacturing Popish Priests? – Altogether we are pleased. We have gained a lesson . . . and we have been spared the pain of having a weak (to say the least) and doubting man as Bishop or Archbishop of our Church – which we suppose Lord Althorp would have made him, had he remained one of our clergy.

George was oblivious to the sneering chorus of diehard Anglicans. He was, however, deeply offended by the spite exhibited by some senior members of the Church of England, furious at the loss of such a promising – and aristocratic – young priest. George wrote to his brother, Jack:

The Bishop of London has written to me, and says that he tells others as well as myself that I have not acted honestly. I will not resent this word from him, for he may be expected to be irritated; but he had better for his own sake, not use much more of such language, for he will have to recant it some day, when he hears more of my case.

There was little time for such local problems to trouble him, though, for George was sent to Rome to receive instruction in the faith whose beliefs he had found so irresistible. He embraced the strict life of his college there, marvelling at 'Such discipline and obedience, united with perfect freedom and cordiality, [which] is the fruit of the Catholic religion alone.'

A year and a day after his arrival in Rome, on 13 March 1831, George received the junior office of a subdiaconate. Accepting this involved a commitment to celibacy for life. At this point, the future of the Spencer family looked decidedly doubtful: Jack had shown no genuine inclination to remarry and produce an heir; Bob had died the year before; and Frederick's Poyntz bride was deemed unlikely to be able to have children, owing to the fragility of her health. The family sent a message to George, begging him not to proceed with the subdiaconate. However, as George responded, 'You spoke too late', for the plea only reached him days after his new vows were taken. Given the fervour which now possessed him, it is inconceivable that an earlier arrival of the Spencers' communication would have made any difference.

He stayed in Rome until July 1832, when he arrived at the Spencers' Isle of Wight retreat at Ryde, two months after being ordained a priest. Following a brief holiday with his family, he settled in West Bromwich, from where he attempted to convert Protestants to his way of thinking. In what was to become the defining thought behind the remainder of his ministry, he wrote to his friend Phillipps: 'Keep England's conversion always next your heart.'

The rest of his family had now not only come to terms with George's change of faith, they had had time to think through its implications for themselves. Jack, so progressive in his political thinking, proved to be disappointingly conservative in his treatment of his youngest brother. When Jack assumed the earldom, on the death of George John in 1834, the whole family gathered at Althorp. Jack, in one of his first acts as head of the family, forbade George from speaking to anyone on the estate unless they were of an equal social standing to the Spencers. He wanted to avoid the embarrassment of his Catholic brother trying to turn the tenants or servants away from the Church of England.

Sarah Lyttelton, however, the sister who was to be governess to Queen Victoria's children, was open-minded about the whole matter. In August 1835, George became dangerously ill, and began to spit blood. Sarah looked after him at her husband's family home, Hagley, showing him enormous tenderness and consideration – even arranging for a fellow Catholic priest to come to stay during his convalescence, to keep him company. George and she were to remain close throughout their lives.

When he recovered, George wrote a sequence of letters for publication in newspapers, stating clearly his religious beliefs, and defending them from other correspondents. These were doctrinal duels, with Protestants championing their creeds, just as he fought for the Catholic faith. Such 'controversies' were a popular feature of Victorian newspapers, and George's resolute logic and robust defence became well known to a national audience.

It was as a preacher, though, that he made a more lasting impact. In 1838 he dedicated himself completely to what had over the preceding half-dozen years become an increasingly important part of his life's work: praying for the conversion of England to Catholicism. George's simple yet sincere view was that, through prayer alone, this was an attainable goal. All that was needed was the rallying of Catholics in the lands around Britain to unite in this holy cause, and the result would be a return to the fold by the erring Protestants.

Later in life, George had three audiences with Pope Pius IX in which he lucidly explained the aims of his ministry: 'I am openly stirring the people of Rome to a third conquest of England,' he told the pontiff:

Rome conquered England once, under Julius Caesar, by the material sword. Rome conquered England a second time, more gloriously, under St Gregory I, by the Word of God. I am calling on Rome to undertake this conquest again, under Pius IX, when it will be a vastly more important one than heretofore, and by means more glorious and more divine, because referring more purely the glory of God, being chiefly holy prayer.

Apparently the Pope said nothing to George after this, but merely smiled. No doubt he was sufficiently realistic to understand that his priest's dreams would never be realized, while not wanting to undermine Spencer's praiseworthy passion.

The majority of the British press ridiculed George's efforts, seeing them as a blend of dangerous subversion and ludicrous superstition. Used to derision, George treated this criticism with a confidence bordering on the contemptuous, writing to the *Morning Chronicle*:

Public prayers of our days, at least in this country, have a power the influence of which, it seems, the highest and greatest must feel. It were well if those who wield this power always so wielded it as to make it a refuge to the weak under oppression, a terror to the strong oppressor, and an object of respect to all.

In the remainder of this letter, he laid out the background to his Catholic ministry, explaining his personal commitment to beliefs he accepted must be puzzling to others:

I am brother to Lord Spencer. I was once a clergyman of the Established Church. In the year 1830 I became a Catholic, and two years later a Catholic priest. My family and my countrymen generally must, of course, judge me to have been greatly mistaken in taking these steps; but I have never, I believe, been deliberately accused of dishonesty, or insincerity, on account of them. As an honest Catholic, I am bound to believe, what I do believe, what it is of infinite consequence, temporal and eternal, to the welfare of my countrymen as individuals, and as a nation, that they should return to the Catholic faith, and I have devoted my life to the object of leading them back to it.

George was aware that his beliefs must not impact negatively on the Spencer name, particularly while his brother Jack was so prominent politically. As a result George constantly stressed the fact that he was a loyal citizen, and his concerns were purely those of religion, not of politics:

I was once attacked by a staunch Church of England man, who had been an old sailor, and who had lost an arm in the service, for what he thought was unworthy of my character and family, leaving my colours and changing sides. I answered him thus: 'Suppose you, my friend, had entered a ship bearing the King of England's flag and pennant, and gone out and fought many a battle against French cruisers, but then found out by chance that the captain of the ship was an outlawed pirate, who had no right to the colours which he wore, and was making you fight for himself, not for your king, would you let me call you a deserter if the next time you came within hail of a true king's ship you jumped overboard and swam to her?' The good sailor seemed to understand me, and said no more about leaving my colours.

It was a good anecdote, and one that he often used in his days as a wandering preacher.

Technically, George was not a good public speaker. He lacked passion and verve, and many of the other qualities usually associated with skilful oratory. However, the power of his sincerity, allied to his patient tenacity, made him a curiously effective preacher. One lady who heard him recorded:

I saw him go into the pulpit; I heard him address the people, and I was waiting all the time thinking when will he have done talking and begin to preach, until, to my surprise, I found what purported to be a sermon coming to a conclusion, yet I can remember to this day almost everything he said.

The Catholic Church realized what an asset it possessed in a priest who could connect with an audience so completely – particularly one from such a rarefied background, who intrigued the public so. An announcement in an 1841 newspaper stated:

The Honourable and Rev. George Spencer, son of the late, and brother of the present Earl Spencer, preached two sermons yesterday at the Catholic chapel of the Royal Sardinian Embassy, Duke Street, Lincoln's Inn Fields, in aid of the funds of the chapel, which have been latterly in a depressed state. The chapel was so densely crowded, that numbers were unable to obtain admission.

But George was beginning to feel a similar unease to the sort that had preceded his switch from Anglican to Catholic. He increasingly questioned whether he was best serving his God by being an ordinary priest. He went into retreat in 1846 to decide what the best way ahead would be. When he emerged, his mind was made up: he would become a Passionist.

The Congregation of the Passion had been founded a century earlier by Blessed Paul of the Cross. Its work was centred on 'the uprooting of sin, and the planting of virtue in the hearts of the faithful'. It focused on the Passion of Jesus Christ, hoping to inspire Christians by his example, while reminding them of their everlasting debt to their saviour. On a practical level, the Passionists became troubleshooters for the Catholic Church as a whole. They could be deployed in a passive way, forming missions and retreats, but they could also be sent out as reinforcements, taking charge of parishes that needed a strong hand, and undertaking foreign missions at the behest of the Pope.

The day-to-day living was rigorous enough to satisfy even some-one as austere as George Spencer. Going to bed on straw, the Passionist had to rise shortly after midnight, to begin a day that revolved around services and meditation. Food intake was strictly controlled: there were regular fasts, and flesh could be eaten on only four days each week. Clothing was similarly harsh, designed to be without any element of comfort: George wore a coarse black robe, and had only open sandals on his feet, whatever the season.

The code of the Passionists was similar to that of St Paul, as stated in his letter to the Colossians, chapter I, verse 24: 'I rejoice in my sufferings, and fill up those things that are wanting of the sufferings of Christ, in my flesh for His body, which is the Church.'

Baptismal names were surrendered on becoming a Passionist. The new priest chose a fresh identity, invoking the example and guidance of a famous religious figure for the road ahead. George chose 'Ignat-ius', out of a desire to celebrate the muscular achievements of Ignatius Loyola, the founder of the Jesuits, whom he admired enormously: 'I intend to express my sense of obligation to . . . St Ignatius,' he wrote, 'by taking his name as my future designation, after I am admitted to the religious habit. So I hope in time I may come to be known no more by my own name, but by that of "Ignatius of St Paul".' It was the name by which he was known from his acceptance as a Passionist priest on 5 January 1847, until his death.

Despite this final rejection of all aspects of his temporal life, George was not shy of using his family background if it could help him in his constant fund-raising efforts for the Catholic Church. Once, having knocked uninvited at the door of a wealthy household, he was told by a servant that the master was out and the mistress was too busy to be disturbed by a begging priest. George retorted that perhaps the lady of the house was unaware that he was not as low-born as she had assumed from his garb; he was in fact the Hon. Mr Spencer. On being informed of this, the mistress of the house quickly appeared, offering him something to eat or drink. Father Ignatius declined, and said what he would like was money for his causes. She gave him £5.

If she had expected this donation to result in profuse gratitude, she was to be quickly disabused by the directness which was Father Ignatius's way: 'Now, I am very sorry to have to tell you that the alms you have given me will do you very little good,' he chided his benefactress. 'If I had not been of a noble family, you would have turned me away with coldness and contempt. I take the money, because it will be as useful to me as if it were given with a good motive; but I would advise you, for the future, if you have any regard for your soul, to let the love of God, and not human respect, prompt your alms-giving.' Having delivered his rebuke, he quit the house, and went on his way.

Being the son of George John, Second Earl Spencer, and brother to Jack Althorp, undoubtedly gave Father Ignatius access to influential people who would otherwise not have found the time to speak with a Catholic preacher. He was certainly able to play on his Spencer roots, which belied the simplicity of his appearance. As one newspaper said at the time:

Thus was constantly to be seen as a mendicant Friar, oft in the rude garb of his order, the descendant of the great Duke of Marlborough, and the son of an English Earl, Knight of the Garter, and the brother of two Earls, one of them a leading statesman and the other a Knight of the Garter also.

Certainly, Ignatius drew confidence from his distinguished ancestry. In February 1850, he strolled up to the door of Number 10, Downing Street, and requested an interview with Lord John Russell, the Prime Minister. Russell agreed to see Ignatius, on the condition that it was understood that, whatever answers he might give to the priest's questions were to be viewed as personal ones, and did not necessarily reflect the views of the government. Ignatius accepted this, and the private audience proceeded, both men enjoying the high quality of the ensuing intellectual and theological debate.

Six years later, in Paris, Ignatius was granted an audience with Napoleon III. He explained to the French monarch his mission of returning England to Catholicism. Ignatius certainly made an impact on Napoleon, the latter sending 1,000 Francs to his lodgings, to go towards the sum Ignatius was raising on yet another one of his European tours.

Father Ignatius was active throughout northern and central Europe. On one of his five trips to Germany, he bumped into Frederick, Fourth Earl Spencer, by complete chance, in Cologne. Frederick greeted his brother cheerily, with: 'Hilloa, George, what are you doing here?' Ignatius kept his reply succinct: 'Begging.' They then had an easy conversation, sharing reminiscences about their days at Eton together, neither commenting on what an extraordinary coincidence their chance meeting represented.

Despite their shared childhood, Frederick was severe on his younger brother after his conversion to Catholicism. From the time Frederick succeeded Jack as Earl Spencer, he banned Ignatius from visiting Althorp. This was not out of personal animosity, but because of a sincere belief that Ignatius's conversion could not be allowed to go unpunished. Whereas Jack had sought merely to avoid the embarrassment of his youngest brother trying to turn his staff and dependants away from the Church of England, Frederick believed, with unquestioning confidence, that it was not right to have the turncoat priest under his roof.

This exile from Althorp lasted twelve years, until the winter of 1857. Ignatius then sent Frederick a letter concerning a mutual acquaintance who was in financial need. It would be kind of Frederick, his brother said, to consider helping with a small donation. In passing Ignatius mentioned that he would be going from his present lodgings in Ireland to Bermondsey, in London, to open a mission, the following January.

When he replied, Frederick sent £3 for the needy friend and, more significantly, an invitation for Ignatius to stay at Althorp for a couple of nights, on his way between Dublin and London. Frederick pointed out that he was inviting Ignatius as a private friend, 'without seeing it necessary to hold spiritual communications with the people in the neighbourhood'. Ignatius gratefully accepted, and was greatly looking forward to seeing his brother and his family home once more. However, it was not to be. The day before Ignatius left Ireland for this homecoming, Frederick died.

Ignatius was deeply upset by the death, which he learned about from a newspaper article. The strange blend of unfettered emotion and strict Christian piety that was so central to Ignatius's life is revealed in his reaction to the bereavement. 'I gave myself up to three days' sorrowing for my dear brother Frederick, but I took care to thank God for the affliction,' he later recalled.

John Poyntz, Frederick's heir as Earl Spencer, treated his religious uncle with sensitivity and respect, giving him back his family allowance and making him a welcome guest at Althorp. It must have been an unsettling experience, staying at his childhood home, with all its luxury, after so many years of self-denial. However, Ignatius was able to take the contrast with his normal existence in his stride, delighting in the small details of his visits, telling Adelaide, Countess Spencer, about his first return 'home' for eighteen years, in a letter of June 1860:

I was to write to you an account of my visit to Althorp and of my impression of it . . . Perhaps you have heard that my visit there was not merely of a few hours, as intended, from Northampton to Weedon, but that I stopped the night . . . Accordingly I saw them at Althorp all retire to rest on the Wednesday night and witnessed the scene produced by those ladies (as they went thro' the anteroom to the tea room on their way to the only practicable staircase) being met there by a large rat . . . These ladies stood the shock decidedly with MORE courage and sangfroid than I have known displayed on some such occasions.

Two years later, Ignatius was invited by his nephew, the Fifth Earl Spencer, to be a house guest during a formal dinner for the Volunteer Corps, an amateur military body with which the young earl was closely associated. When Ignatius arrived, he was concerned to see how smart the other guests were in their dress uniform. He asked Charlotte, his nephew's wife, if she wanted him to wear something other than his Passionist garb that night. She would have none of it, and insisted that he remain in his usual attire – a gesture that Ignatius greatly appreciated for its thoughtfulness. He was also deeply touched when he found that, not only was he seated in the place of honour next to the Fifth Earl, but also he was invited to speak to the assembled group of guests after dinner. He felt truly accepted by his family once more.

These two visits to Althorp took place in a period, 1858 to 1864, when Ignatius was devoting his efforts towards what he termed 'little missions'. These were short, concentrated retreats, still revolving around his aim of reconverting England. For twenty-two weeks each year, he wandered from parish to parish, often on foot, expounding his beliefs. It was a gruelling schedule, with a daily routine that involved a 5 a.m. rise, the hearing of confessions, the observance of mass and office, followed by a lecture.

By this stage of his life, Father Ignatius was a deeply respected figure in the Passionist order. The novices regarded him as a saint, believing that he would qualify for such a position in the Catholic Church because he had reportedly performed miracles. One of these allegedly occurred as early as 1835, long before he became a Passionist, during one of his many visits to the sick. The then George Spencer had attended a child that had been ill for some time with a hideous affliction around the mouth. George had laid his finger on the child's tongue, then said: 'It will be well.' The child was apparently cured within half an hour of George's utterance.

Father Pius, his biographer, wrote of Father Ignatius's personal popularity among his fellow Passionists:

In recreation he was a treasure. We gathered round him by a kind of instinct, and so entertaining was he that one felt it a mortification to be called away from the recreation-room while Father Ignatius was in it. He used to recount with peculiar grace and fascinating wit, scenes he went through in his life.

It was a life that was slowly drawing to a close. As his own health became less reliable, Ignatius revealed an increasing appetite for helping dying Christians on their own deathbeds. During his final months he made a point of acknowledging that his ministry was coming to an end, stating that the current volume of his journal would be his last; when he completed it, that would mark the conclusion of his life as well.

He had one final ambition, revealed more than two decades before: he wanted to die like Jesus, without any care or fuss from his fellow man. As he said himself, 'How beautiful it would be to die in a ditch, unseen and unknown.' Eerily, it was a wish that was granted almost down to the last detail.

In September 1864, while changing trains at Carstairs Junction between 'little missions', Father Ignatius found he had some time before his connection would arrive. He decided to go to visit a godson of his who lived nearby, a man called Monteith. He walked along the drive to the Monteith house and, a hundred feet from the front door, in full sight of two children, he sat down for a rest on a tree stump, his ulcerous leg doubtless playing up. He never got to his feet again, dying instantly, so that his body was later found in its final, seated, pose. In the sack by his feet, his journal was discovered to be all but complete, only the last few lines of the volume remaining blank.

At his funeral the Right Reverend Dr Ullathorne gave the address:

Listen, then, dearly beloved, and hang your attention on my voice, whilst I speak of him who was once called in the world the Honourable and Reverend George Spencer, a scion of one of the noblest houses of the nobility of this land, but who himself preferred to be called Father Ignatius of St Paul . . . How beautiful, how sublime was his departure. Father Ignatius had often wished and prayed that, like his Divine Lord, like St Francis Xavier, and like his dear friend and master in the spiritual life, Father Dominic, he might die at his post, yet deserted and alone. God granted him that prayer.

The acclamation from Ignatius's family was sincere, and tinged with admiration, John Poyntz, Fifth Earl Spencer, writing to his uncle's superior:

I assure you that, much as I may have differed from my uncle on points of doctrine, no one could have admired more than I did the beautiful simplicity, earnest religion, and faith of my uncle. For his God he renounced all the pleasures of the world; his death, sad as it is to us, was, as his life, apart from the world but with God.

His family will respect his memory as much as I am sure you and the brethren of his Order do.

## 16. The Red Earl and the
## Fairy Queen

John, Fifth Earl Spencer, was the only son from the first marriage of Frederick, Fourth Earl Spencer and Elizabeth Poyntz. He was born in October 1835 at Spencer House, and received as a second name the surname of his mother's family. My grandfather always referred to him as 'Uncle Poyntz', but, to the rest of those who have ever needed to invoke his memory, he has become known as 'the Red Earl', on account of his vast auburn beard.

Sent away to be educated at Harrow, the then Viscount Althorp was there when he learned of his frail mother's death, writing to his father with a maturity far exceeding his fifteen years: 'The sermon we had from the Bishop of Ripon yesterday was very consoling; to think of the hope of the blessed saints (and among them my dear mother) hovering about and seeing the world from Heaven in all its vicissitudes.'

It was while at Harrow that he experienced a moment that he recalled in old age as being one of the most awkward in his life. The Prince of Wales – Queen Victoria's son, later Edward VII – came to visit the school, and John was one of the pupils chosen by the headmaster to be present in the Vaughan Library. The Prince stopped to look at a book that minuted the school debating society's recent topics. By chance, he opened it on a page which recorded a debate, '"That regicide is justifiable", moved by Viscount Althorp'. It was noted by those present that John Althorp was extremely distressed, but the Prince said nothing, merely smiling. It was not an occasion that the future Red Earl was ever to forget.

After his death, a contemporary of John's wrote that as a Harrovian he was 'a general favourite and much respected. In boyhood, as all through his life, his manners were delightful, genial, friendly, perfectly simple.'

John's education was identical to that of his grandfather, George

John, in that he went from Harrow to Trinity College, Cambridge. There the similarities ended, for John showed none of the intellectual promise that had marked out George John as an exceptional undergraduate. Indeed, John's tutor advised him against taking an ordinary degree, suggesting that he would not attain one; so he plumped for a nobleman's one instead.

After graduating in 1857, John stood as Whig candidate for the southern division of Northamptonshire. He was not ashamed to play on his family associations and traditions, writing to voters an electioneering letter, dated 6 March, which said: 'It will not be, as you know, the first time that one of my name has aspired to this honour, & I am glad to be able to come forward on the same general liberal principles which my Uncle the late Lord Spencer [Jack] held when Member for this county.'

The Whig or Liberal interest of Northamptonshire had not been represented in Parliament since Jack Althorp had succeeded to his seat in the House of Lords, a generation earlier. However, the news brought to Frederick Spencer, resting on a bench in front of Althorp, was of his son's electoral success.

John had little interest in culture, and he eschewed the conventional Grand Tour for a trip to the United States. He set off in July 1857, on a ship that was also carrying the American showman Phineas Taylor Barnum (John reported to his father that he was 'full of tricks and jokes'), and for three months travelled across the States, dipping into Canada.

John's observations of tensions and prejudices in the run-up to the American Civil War proved highly perceptive. In New York, where he went after arriving in Boston, he first encountered 'the terrible thundercloud ever ready to explode and separate the North and South' – the different attitudes to slavery. The observation of this young English aristocrat was that:

Things are now comparatively quiet but the press keep up a warfare of the most violent and agitating description; the Northernmen are so imprudent and the Southern so obstinate that if any more agitation takes place in the North, I fear the consequences may be very serious: the ill feeling is so great that many of the Southerners who used to fly with their families to the New England watering places from the awful heat of the South, now prefer going to Europe or even remaining in their dangerous homes to coming among the Northern people.

John was concerned that Northern interference, although understandable to him as an opponent of slavery, might actually prove to be counter-productive. He was convinced that the Southern slave owner would become more obstinate, and fight harder to preserve the practice of slavery when, otherwise, it would die out naturally as a result of economic forces. As he wrote to his father:

Missouri has returned a Republican, and they there have found out how much more profitable free is to slave labour. This will be the real means of overturning slavery, the tide of emigration throws free labour nearer the slave states, and the marked difference in the wealth and prosperity of two districts so differently cultivated is the strongest argument to the Slave owner against his favourite institution, for it touches the pocket.

He was aware that the question of slavery's continuation was bound up in the voracious appetite of British industrial might. While on board the ferry *Baltic*, sailing between Memphis and Natchez on the Mississippi, he wrote to his father:

The fact is that, we in England are the great indirect supporters of Slavery for Manchester and the Cotton Manufactories require so much raw Material and that can only be supplied by Black labour, for the white never can stand the Southern climate: but this does not prove that the labour must be slave labour. Free black labour is I feel sure available, if the negro is trained for independence, but now the Planters are prejudiced and obstinate. They dare not educate their Slaves because once intelligent and enlightened, they will cast off their Slavery; the result of this will be that one fine day Emancipation will be forced upon them, [and] they will have a dependent helpless set around them with no prospect of improvement for many years . . .

As well as grappling with profound matters of human rights versus those of socio-economic forces, John was also intrigued by a more mundane matter: the differences and similarities between the North American and the Englishman. His views are those of a young man from an extremely sheltered and privileged upbringing. One can feel him struggling to come to grips with the very different emphases placed on everything from diction to courting, while attempting to remain broad-minded, aware as he was that he was merely a guest in this continent, an ocean away from home.

Again writing to his father, John described how,

It is curious how superior the Lady seems in manners to the Man, a few of the men are what we should call gentlemanlike in manner and talk as we do but most men have the twang and are unmistakably not Englishmen, whereas the best American ladies could often be taken for Englishwomen. I do not though dislike the men. Far from it, they are kindness itself, VERY WELL educated and when you get over their short manner and their nasal talk you find them very agreeable ...

Having passed his adolescence in the stultifying formality of early Victorian British high society, John was particularly struck by the apparent freedom enjoyed by the unmarried women of North America. There is no record of how Frederick Spencer reacted to the following passage from his son and heir, extolling the sort of freedom that the Fourth Earl would doubtless have considered both disgraceful and provocative:

The liberty young ladies have seems strange, but I believe it is a wise plan. They get to learn the tricks of the world by themselves before they marry, become much better managers of husbands and themselves than if tied too closely to their chaperone, and they say such a thing as a girl going wrong is never known, and they evidently make most loving and devoted wives ...

John would return to the United States several decades later, one of the grand old men of British society and politics. However, the

1857 trip was his last venture abroad as Viscount Althorp. Moreover, he was destined never to make a mark in the House of Commons, since his father, Frederick, died soon after John's return to England at the end of the year.

His first consideration was what to do with his stepmother, the 32-year-old 'Yaddy', so recently delivered of her second child, Bobby. Sarah, Lady Lyttelton, Frederick's sister and governess to the royal children, was keen to get Yaddy out of Althorp and ready to contemplate remarriage, so that she could be sidelined by the Spencer family at the earliest opportunity. Known for her charm throughout her early years, Sarah now revealed a waspish side that became more pronounced in her middle and old age:

She will, I think, be removed from many little temptations to interference and worreting by not being actually at Althorp. She will, I daresay, always be more or less a trial . . . Much will depend on the footing upon which you put your intercourse with her at first starting. There should be no fixed habit of daily meetings nor any UNDERSTOOD RULE of inviting her on every occasion – that you often wish to be alone . . .

There was no obvious justification for such a harsh attitude towards somebody as inoffensive and essentially good as Yaddy Spencer. Sarah may have been driven by a misguided loyalty to the memory of her brother's first wife, Elizabeth. Whatever the reason, Yaddy proved to be no trouble to the new Earl Spencer, devoting her remaining years to her and Frederick's two children, to charitable works, and to remaining a thoroughly respected Northamptonshire lady. John's affection for his stepmother is shown by a will he drew up in the 1870s, in which he bequeathed an allowance of £200 per year to Yaddy, 'as a mark of my great love and esteem for her, and a return inadequate as it is for the obligations I feel for the devoted love to her husband my father and her Motherly kindness to my sister and myself'.

Yaddy's death, twenty years after Frederick's, saw her still single, in defiance of Sarah's assumption that she would quickly remarry. She had worn black throughout her widowhood, living quietly at

Guilsborough Hall, where she died. John arranged for her body to be brought the few miles back to Althorp, where his stepmother lay in state in the Saloon, the doors draped in dark-blue curtains embroidered with the Spencer 'S' in gold, and hot-house plants surrounding the coffin itself. From there it was removed to Brington, on foot, Yaddy's insistence on the plainest and least expensive funeral possible being obeyed; as was her request that her coffin not be screwed down for two days after her death had been pronounced, in case she came alive again.

Among the chief family mourners was John's beautiful wife, Charlotte, who was known, in dual reference to her looks and to the poem by Edmund Spenser, as 'Spencer's Fairy Queen'.

Charlotte Frances Frederica Seymour was a cousin of her husband's stepmother, as well as being the youngest of the three daughters of Lady Augusta and Frederick Seymour. Her maternal grandfather was the First Marquess of Bristol, and she spent much of her childhood at Ickworth, the Bristols' estate in Suffolk. Her two elder sisters, Lilah, later Lady Clifden, and Augusta, who married Lord Charles Bruce, were also celebrated beauties, each being blessed with a wonderful complexion, dazzling eyes, a neat aquiline nose and exquisite lips. Of Charlotte it was said: 'There was probably never a face that so reproduced and reflected the goodness, the inherent nobleness of nature, the inward beauty of the soul, so much as hers.'

Charlotte had met John Althorp early in 1854. Both their families were frequent guests at the Hampton Court home of the Dowager Lady Clinton, their mutual aunt. There was much family rejoicing when John summoned up the courage in May 1858 to ask Charlotte to marry him. On the day of the engagement, Charlotte humbly wrote of her fiancé: 'He is so good and everything that I could possibly hope for, that I feel it is far more than I deserve.' The wedding took place on 8 July 1858, at St James's Church, Piccadilly, despite John still being in mourning for Frederick, his father.

Charlotte introduced her new husband to her passion for travel, but the Red Earl was always happier among his ancestral acres than elsewhere. Before they set off on a nine-month honeymoon, he wrote to Charlotte: 'I wonder whether we shall be satiated with our foreign expedition or get the contrary desire of always travelling? I do not know what you think but I am always happier at home and settled . . . but I may be converted by you and we may become roamers; I hope not.'

The irony of the remark was to become evident as the Red Earl's political life took on an energy of its own, involving him in extended tours of duty overseas. For now, he carried on with the obligations of a courtier that his father had found so irksome. At first, the Red Earl was Groom of the Stole to Prince Albert, Queen Victoria's consort, from 1859. However, he had held the position for only a short time when he received a letter from Lady Mary Biddulph, wife of the Master of the Queen's Household, sent in haste from Windsor:

I write one line from my Husband's room in the Castle, to tell you VERY VERY bad news – All the household have just been up to the Prince's room to see for the last time him who is fast sinking – The doctors say there is no hope – not the slightest – of his Royal Highness's life being spared, but none can say how long it may go on – The Queen is composed and perfectly aware of the state of the case.

Albert died later that night.

The following year, the Red Earl was asked to become Groom of the Stole to the Prince of Wales – the man in front of whom he had experienced crimson embarrassment as a schoolboy. Extending the invitation on Queen Victoria's behalf, Sir Charles Phipps wrote: 'Her Majesty attaches much importance to the appointment in His Royal Highness' Household being fulfilled by Gentlemen of acknowledged high character in every respect . . .' The Red Earl remained Groom of the Stole to the Prince for six years, when he took up an active role in politics.

As early as 1866 the Red Earl was first sounded out by fellow Whig grandees as a possible leader of the party. Lord Elcho tried to persuade him to accept the challenge with a stirring letter:

You have a hereditary title to the headship of the Whig or Constitutional as opposed to the democratic Liberals. You have station, wealth, and a large well known Whig house in the centre of London. Personally you are very popular. You have plenty of ability and business experience . . . In taking this position you would be doing a great public service . . . You would at the same time, if ambitiously inclined, be doing the best thing for yourself.

But the Red Earl was devoid of personal ambition. As one of his parliamentary colleagues was to note,

No man of high social station or low was ever more disinterested, more unselfish, more free from the defects incident to either patrician pride or plebeian vanity. He was of too lofty a nature to have a trace of the covetousness of place that disfigured the patrician Whig caste even down to such days as these.

It was therefore in character for him to reply to Elcho as he did:

Though I entered Parliament very young, various things, my father's death, my Court appointment, my journeys abroad, have taken me away from active Politics.

I have no experience of official life; I have never publicly handled any question of general Politics.

I thus, though anxious to be of some political use to the country, feel strongly my need of experience without which I should have no confidence in myself.

By the time he rejected the Whig leadership, at the age of thirty-one, the Red Earl had already become a Knight of the Garter, an honour usually reserved for much older men, after a lifetime of distinguished public service. It was, again, something he had sought to avoid, claiming it was an award he had done little to merit. However, the Prince of Wales and the Prime Minister, Palmerston, pressed him to accept; the Prince particularly so. He had recommended the Red Earl for the Garter when the latter was only twenty-nine, so impressed was he by his steady, sincere personality. Edward also wanted Spencer's public-spirited generosity to be acknowledged: in 1864, the Red Earl had decided to give Wimbledon Common to the nation.

It was a gift of such importance that it warranted its own Act of Parliament to enshrine it in the nation's annals for all time. The Act stipulated that the section of the common situated between the Kingston Road and Wimbledon Village must, in perpetuity, be a public park with its own lodges. The magazine *Punch* celebrated the Red Earl's munificence in its issue of late November 1864:

> There is for us, and shall be, one retreat
> If but the only, saved stucco-free;
> Wimbledon, ever more for pilgrims' feet
> Kept sacred, noble Spencer, thanks to thee!
> Thy generous charter gives us scope to flee
> Still thither from the hubbub and the heat.

While the Red Earl was establishing himself as a man of spotless character in public life, at home Charlotte was showing herself to be a natural châtelaine of Althorp and of Spencer House. In April 1859 the newly married couple had returned from their honeymoon to a rapturous welcome from the tenants and labourers of their 27,000 acre estates. The Red Earl wrote to his sister with pride that: 'Charlotte was delighted & did her part admirably, her reception was most cordial and enthusiastic.'

Charlotte's charm and elegance, combined with her down-to-earth nature and her genuine love for her husband, entranced the people of Northamptonshire. However, these attributes were sources of aggravation for the increasingly cantankerous Sarah, Lady Lyttelton. In November 1861, the ageing Spencer aunt took it upon herself to deliver a rebuke to Charlotte. It must have been all the more devastating, given the pretence at civility that shrouded the rude attack on a young woman trying to establish a home for herself and her husband. The letter started: 'Now my dear kind niece, you are going to pay a fine for being so very kind and dear, and encouraging me to be afraid of nothing when I have a hint to give or a bit of advice to lay before you . . .' Sarah then recounted how, while staying with friends, she had been dismayed to hear, 'quite in a roundabout and unexpected way', that Charlotte was

in danger of becoming unpopular in the County from being thought FINE and not ready enough to invite, and notice, and visit the old habitues among the Althorp neighbours – that you and Althorp [the Red Earl] seemed to prefer the YOUNG people and neglect the old; and that HIS popularity and yours might suffer . . .

Now I need not say what is most entirely true that I don't suppose y'ore fine or proud! Moreover your manner to the people of inferior rank is ALWAYS quite REMARKABLY good – and I know that you wish to do all your duty as a country lady most honestly.

At this point, having deployed insult and hypocrisy, Sarah switches to condescension:

It is, however, a duty which must be quite new to you and may often be very irksome. But it is quite worth your while to do it THOROUGHLY and in a manner which except during Althorp's dear Mother's time never has been practised in earnest.

Throughout all the material I have read about Charlotte, I have never come across any reference to her having been anything other than the epitome of considerate hospitality. It appears that 'Aunt Sarah' wanted to vent her spleen at her young, beautiful, highly capable niece, for running the Spencer homes with such aplomb. This calculated attack was her way of inflicting pain while appearing considerate.

Charlotte spent much of the 1860s and 1870s imposing her taste on Althorp. In doing this, she drew on her childhood experiences, making the Northamptonshire gardens mirror the sophistication and detail that she had known when growing up at Ickworth, instead of maintaining the more rural look favoured by the previous two generations of Spencers. Intricate flower beds were cut into the lawns, and cypress trees were planted on the north and west sides of the mansion. Inside, the cloakroom to the right of the main entrance was transformed into a breakfast room, and it was planned to move the dining room from the current South Drawing Room to a purpose-built extension.

In all these improvements, Charlotte showed herself to be exactly what was hoped for from a Victorian aristocrat's wife: an apparently effortless hostess with superior taste and an eye for perfect detail. Between them the Spencers were seen to possess the gifts and qualities that would lead to responsibilities far removed from the confines of their London and Northamptonshire residences.

The Spencer family knew the Gladstones through George William, Fourth Baron Lyttelton, son of the lady who had written so hurtfully to Charlotte about her perceived failings as châtelaine. The Fourth Baron Lyttelton married Mary Glynne, whose sister, Catherine, was married to William Gladstone.

Mary and Catherine's father, Sir Stephen Glynne, ran into huge financial difficulties in 1847 after an unsound business venture collapsed. He was left with debts amounting to £450,000, and the probability that he would have to sell the family estate of Hawarden, on the Welsh border.

It was agreed that, although approximately half of the debt would be met through the disposal of Hawarden land, such a sale should take place within the confines of the family. Then, if the Glynne family could recoup its lost money, buying back the land would not be difficult. William Gladstone and his father bought half the land, while Lyttelton agreed to purchase the rest. However, to his embarrassment, Lyttelton found himself unable to raise the necessary sum, and turned to his uncle Frederick, Fourth Earl Spencer, for help. Frederick obliged, buying that part of the estate known as Queen's Ferry.

Despite the Spencers' acquaintance with the Gladstones, there was still general astonishment when the Red Earl was selected by William Gladstone, during his first premiership, to be the Lord Lieutenant — or Viceroy — of Ireland. True, the Red Earl was a man of undoubted integrity, and his wife was an accomplished hostess, so the basic requirements for occupying Dublin Castle on the monarch's behalf were both met in full. However, Spencer had held no official post previously, and he had no knowledge of Ireland. It later emerged that the Red Earl was only the third choice for the Lord Lieutenancy.

The two main Irish issues revolved around the questions of religion and of the relationship between native farmers and their predominantly English landlords. The former was not an area of expertise for the Red Earl: he was a solid, unquestioning, member of the Church of England. Perhaps Gladstone hoped that Spencer's reputation as a conscientious landowner might help with the second sphere of his duties?

The prime role of the Lord Lieutenant was to control a troublesome province, and with this responsibility went real power. Lord Carnarvon, who held the post in the mid-1880s, opined in his diary: 'It is remarkable how all government of the whole country centres in the Lord-Lieutenant.'

Although pageantry and lavish hospitality were important adjuncts of the viceregal position, London was relying on its man in Dublin to exercise authority as swiftly and as thoroughly as the situation deserved.

The Spencers' first term at Dublin Castle was relatively undemanding. They proved to be generous hosts, far exceeding their £20,000 allowance from the public purse, giving dazzling balls and overseeing opulent gatherings. A 'drawing room' was regularly held, where up to 1,000 of Ireland's grandest and most influential citizens assembled to pay their respects to their Lord Lieutenant. Part of Spencer's duties involved kissing all the ladies presented to him at a drawing room, which forced the Red Earl to retire periodically to have his beard brushed clean of all the glitter and make-up that accumulated in its bushiness.

The Red Earl found himself popular with the leisured classes who largely shared his passion for foxhunting. He even paid for several of his old hunting friends to come out from England's Midlands for a taste of the sport, Irish style. Meanwhile, Charlotte's beauty and charm won over all who met her, the newspaper *Freeman's Journal* giving a typically positive report of her in January 1874: 'The Countess looks her best – amiable, graceful, dignified – a presence as fair and gracious as ever shone within the walls of Dublin Castle.' She became affectionately known as 'the Lady Lieutenant'.

The Spencers quickly became aware of the very real problems faced by the less privileged sectors of Irish society. Charlotte wrote to her sister, Augusta, in 1869:

The atmosphere seems tainted with the breath of injustice – everything is crooked and out of joint. The marvel is how things can have gone on as they are so long. I don't for a moment pretend to say that the Church question is the cry of the poor, but I believe nevertheless that it is at the root of all the troubles of this country.

The Red Earl tried to oversee a fairer system of landlord–tenant relationships, sending reports direct to Gladstone. The Prime Minister, for his part, thought Spencer's recommendations were too interfering, and did not give him the support necessary if the cabinet was to follow the Red Earl's recommendation as how best to settle the rampant problem of agrarian crime.

Gladstone also refused to listen to Spencer's argument that a simple way of gaining more control over Ireland would be for a member of Queen Victoria's direct family to reside there in an official capacity. In July 1871 the Red Earl submitted a report which concluded:

I have frequently expressed my opinion that the effect of a Royal Residence in Ireland on the people would be excellent. It would remove a sense of neglect which they undoubtedly feel; it would give a good example to those Irish proprietors who do not live in the Country; it would make the Irish people realise by acquaintance the good qualities of the Royal family and it would enable the Royal family to know the true character of the people.

It was too bold a suggestion, and Gladstone's cabinet decided to postpone a decision indefinitely on the matter.

Overall, though, Gladstone appreciated the qualities that the Red Earl brought to the Lord Lieutenancy of Ireland, writing to him towards the end of his first administration: 'It has been a great thing for us to have in the Viceroyalty that remarkable union of striking excellence, high position, and every popular quality, with solid judgement and indefatigable industry, which have been exemplified in your person . . .' On being replaced as Prime Minister in 1874, Gladstone offered Spencer an elevation from the title of earl to marquess, but the Red Earl preferred his earldom, and declined the honour.

Gladstone headed four administrations, with Spencer having a prominent role in all of them. The Red Earl twice served in the important but relatively uninteresting post of Lord President of the Council, but his talents were destined for Ireland again. During a meeting of the Privy Council in 1882, he found himself in the bizarre position of publicly announcing his own reappointment to the Lord Lieutenancy of Ireland. In her diary that night, Queen Victoria noted that Spencer appeared 'much impressed with the difficulties of the task before him. He hoped he was right in undertaking it . . .'

This was, as the Red Earl had so rightly anticipated, a posting far removed from the one he had previously experienced in Dublin. Ireland was seething with discontent, the terrorist movement of the Invincibles causing particular concern. It whipped up nationalist feeling against the British, promising from its formation, in 1881, to concentrate on the assassination of British officials in Ireland. There was also grave dissatisfaction in the ranks of the Royal Irish Constabulary, as well as a mutiny in the Metropolitan police force. As *The Times* recorded in 1882: 'Over half of the country the demoralisation of every class, the terror, the fierce hatred, the universal distrust, had grown to an incredible pitch . . . The very foundations of the social order were rocking.'

On 6 May 1882, Spencer arrived in Dublin Castle, Lord Lieutenant again after an absence of eight years, leaving Charlotte in

England to follow later. In the Red Earl's retinue, as his chief secretary, was one of his closest friends from his schooldays at Harrow, Lord Frederick Cavendish, a direct descendant of Georgiana, Duchess of Devonshire, and a Spencer cousin. Along with their assistant, Mr Burke, the two kinsmen held a meeting in the castle after lunch that day, after which the Red Earl decided to ride back to the viceregal lodge across Dublin's Phoenix Park, with his mounted escort. The other two elected to walk.

As Cavendish and Burke ambled back, past a polo match, they were suddenly attacked by a group of Invincibles with knives, and were stabbed to death a few yards apart. The cuts in Burke's gloves, and the agonized look on his face when his body was retrieved, showed that he had tried to defend himself, but Cavendish can have known little about his death, his expression one of peaceful sleep rather than of conscious terror.

The Red Earl later recorded:

When I reached the lodge I sat down near the window, and began to read some papers. Suddenly I heard a shriek which I shall never forget. I seem to hear it now; it is always in my ears. The shriek was repeated again and again. I got up to look out. I saw a man rushing alone. He jumped over the palings and dashed up to the lodge, shouting, 'Mr Burke and Lord Frederick Cavendish are killed'.

The news that reached England was garbled, and Charlotte feared that her husband had also been caught up in the grisly outrage. She called the time between receiving the first news of the deaths and confirmation that her husband was safe, 'the most terrible and longest day of my life'.

Spencer wrote a letter to Charlotte later that day, disjointed with shock:

We are in God's hands. Do not be filled with alarm and fear. I was alone and have no apprehension.

God knows how I feel, this fearful tragedy – two such men at such a time.

I dare not dwell on the horror for I feel I must be unmanned.

I am very calm.

Do not, loved one, come unless you feel more unhappy in London than here.

There is no danger really whatever.

The last point was clearly unrealistic. Above all, there was a suspicion that it was Spencer himself who had been the true target of the assassination, since he and Cavendish looked alike, with similarly lush facial hair, and this added greatly to the consternation felt by those charged with protecting British officials in Ireland.

At the same time there was widespread public revulsion at the cowardliness of the attack on two unarmed officials by terrorists. Solidarity with the victims' families was demonstrated by all parties of the House of Commons – 300 of whose Members, including Gladstone, trekked to Chatsworth for Cavendish's funeral.

It was decided to try to crush those who had brought about the so-called 'Phoenix Park murders'. Several of the Invincibles stood trial and were hanged. The ringleader of the murderers, James Carey, traded evidence against his co-conspirators for the sparing of his own life, taking advantage of Spencer's own controversial witness protection scheme. But it did him little good, for he was recognized by a fellow Irishman on his way to a new life in South Africa, and was shot dead by his compatriot on the ship taking him from Cape Town to Port Elizabeth.

Spencer was confronted with a bitter dilemma. Brought up a Whig, his instincts were to be liberal in all matters, and yet the crisis British rule now faced in Ireland demanded extremely tough measures. He was reviled by many in Ireland for his perceived harshness at this time, the extreme Parnellites accusing him of 'striking murderous blows at the people', and of having a 'cruel, narrow, dogged nature'.

However, Spencer was applauded by those who believed he had no alternative but to be vigorous in his seeking out and destruction of dangerous dissident elements. Lord Morley judged that the Red Earl:

brought the most inflexible determination to stamp out murder and outrage, a calm disdain of the fiercest and foulest personal attacks levelled against a public man in our generation, and an unswerving desire to do good to Ireland. He conquered by his character and his bearing. He punished the guilty. He saw the thing through.

After the Phoenix Park murders, everyday life for the Spencers changed dramatically. They were forced to travel with armed guards wherever they went. A tour of west Ireland undertaken by the Red Earl in September 1882, which would previously have involved protection from a couple of policemen and a token cavalry officer, now involved an escort of eight hussars, eight mounted police, and four armed detectives. Even trips back to Althorp involved bodyguards sleeping near to the Red Earl, much to his chagrin. Despite his protests, this level of protection was realistic; the police believed even Dublin Castle might be attacked by nationalists at any time.

The castle became almost a prison, in total contrast to the pleasure palace of the Spencers' first viceregal stint. Charlotte exercised by walking in the Pound of the Castle. This area could only be accessed via a guarded iron door, with a spiked metal gate, followed by a heavily guarded bridge, with yet more spikes and locks. She never complained about this depressing turn of events, mirroring the unflappability of her husband. As Gladstone remarked of the Red Earl in a letter to Queen Victoria from this time, 'He possesses all the fine and genuine qualities of his excellent Uncle Althorp, and exercises them with heightened powers.'

Neither Prime Minister nor monarch ever understood how much Spencer hated dispensing harsh justice to the Irish people. Two decades later, extremely ill, the convalescent Red Earl sat talking with his half-brother, Bobby, about this period, when he felt obliged to send so many to their deaths:

We talked about the precautions for his safety that had been taken, an A.D.C. having to sleep in his dressing room. I reminded him of the police sleeping on his and my door mat in the Westfort Hotel. Then about our luncheon at Ryburn and Mrs Walsh kneeling before him praying for her son's life, almost the most agonising thing that could happen. I recollect everything about it, 23 years ago. Spencer in the outer porch, framed by the porch. Mrs Walsh kneeling in front of him in agony of sorrow. Spencer tried to raise her, and with his reserve quite overpowered by the emotions of the Mother's anguish.

After 1882, the Spencers remained in Dublin with ever decreasing enthusiasm, their private thoughts clouded with worries: their personal safety; the expense of being Lord Lieutenant, on an inadequate allowance; the virtual halving of their own income, through the agricultural depression in England; and the desire to be back at Althorp and Spencer House, which they felt they had neglected for too long.

The Red Earl confided to his Devonshire cousin, the Marquess of Hartington, in June 1883:

In many ways it would be a great relief to be turned out of office and I sometimes wish for release from this place, but I don't know that one ought to wish for it on public grounds . . . it is a banishment from friends and associations, and at times the worry and responsibility are dreadful.

A year later, resigned to a life of continued public service, the Red Earl considered applying to become Viceroy of India, in the wake of Lord Mayo's assassination. This was out of an understanding that such a position would be considerably less expensive than its Irish counterpart. Hearing of this possibility, Gladstone said: 'Of course Lord Spencer has only to hold up his little finger in order to have it placed absolutely at his disposal.' However, the thought of the heat and the risk of disease – the Red Earl was, like his mother, cursed with wretched health from an early age – eventually dissuaded Spencer from pursuing the idea, and he remained in Ireland. Charlotte was highly relieved, telling her mother: 'I am thankful that Lord Northbrook has accepted, and that we have not had the option. I can imagine nothing more detestable – 5 years banishment and a hateful climate – with a chance of assassination or death from fever – and a terrible responsibility.'

Responsibility and risk from assassination remained constant factors in Dublin. From 1883 to 1885, Irish-American terrorists mounted a bombing campaign in England and Scotland which had symbolic targets – the Houses of Parliament and the Tower of London – as well as ones of a more practical nature, such as the Underground network. Scotland Yard countered by setting up a Special Branch, whose brief was to undermine and eradicate the terrorist organizations. Nevertheless, the Red Earl came gradually to despair that enforced British rule could ever prevail in Ireland.

Until this point in his life, the Red Earl had been a solid supporter of the Establishment line on almost every issue, but he could not advocate a policy which he sincerely thought both unsustainable and likely to lead only to ever greater discord. His conclusion was simple: 'I believe that if we had to wait until we convinced the Irish people that they would not get Home Rule we should have to wait until the crack of doom.'

This was an opinion shared by his most trusted and knowledgeable officers. In September 1884 he received a letter from Edward Jenkinson, who was in charge of fighting secret organizations in Ireland, which ventured that Home Rule was the true solution of the difficulty. Jenkinson, like Spencer, believed that English distrust of Home Rule was the result of pitiful ignorance; it was up to those who understood the situation to promote the Irishman's right to self-governance. Jenkinson pleaded with his Lord Lieutenant 'to consider earnestly whether it might be possible to take a new departure, and so to initiate a Policy which in the end may rid us of this troublesome Irish question'.

Spencer looked at alternatives. He returned to his earlier suggestion that a royal residence be established in Ireland, but Queen Victoria thought it a ludicrous idea. Hearing of the Queen's rejection of his proposal, the Red Earl despaired, telling a friend: 'I feel inclined to throw up the sponge and retire to my plough in Northamptonshire.'

In the summer of 1885, the Red Earl's direct involvement in

Irish affairs came to an end when he returned to England at the
conclusion of his second and final spell as Lord Lieutenant. *The Times*
reported on 28 June: 'Lord Spencer yesterday formally resigned the
office of Lord Lieutenant of Ireland, which he had held during
three of the most eventful years in the history of the country.'

His perceived success in exceptionally testing circumstances was
marked by a dinner given in his honour by 200 Whig members of
both Houses of Parliament. In his speech that night, he gave a
candid view of what he felt to be his political *raison d'être*: 'I am
but a poor soldier in your army. I was enlisted for a special service.
I was enlisted for the service of Ireland.'

After returning to Althorp, he went to Northampton to make
his first public address in the county for several years. 'I need not
tell you,' he said to his cheering audience, 'how rejoiced I am to
find myself once more among old friends in Northamptonshire, to
see well-known faces again, and to be able to take part in the county
business and country pursuits which are so familiar and agreeable
to me.'

The two periods spent in Ireland by the Fifth Earl and Countess
Spencer were interludes of genuine power and responsibility in an
existence that was otherwise similar to that of many aristocratic
families in the latter half of the nineteenth century.

They had almost no understanding of money, finding finance
an embarrassing subject to raise even with their professional advisers.
It was also a confusingly scarce commodity, as agriculture failed to
provide the income they had previously taken for granted. This
was particularly the case after 1878. One major problem was the
increased influx of grain from the North American prairies. Another
was the fact that families such as the Spencers rarely had other
commercial enterprises on which to fall back, whenever agriculture
failed to perform.

When newly impoverished aristocrats did face up to their change
in circumstances, it was often with the bemused realism that Spencer
betrayed in a letter of August 1886 to Lord Rosebery: 'We have
given up all travels and mean to live in a hut without servants. We

have given notice to nearly all our servants. It is a great bore but inevitable and it is better to face it at once than return to narrow means in 6 months.' However, the Spencers were typical of their class in being unable to maintain for long such a thrifty resolve.

The Red Earl's obsession with foxhunting was a very costly pastime. For much of his time at Althorp, he was Master of the Pytchley, a pack jointly kennelled at Althorp and at the nearby village after which the hounds were named. It was considered correct form for a man of the Red Earl's apparent wealth to bankroll the sport for his fellow foxhunters, and so we find Spencer, whose keenness to fulfil social obligations frequently exceeded his bank balance, in April 1879 seeking a loan for £15,000, 'on account of the excess expenditure for the Hounds, 1874/8'.

In return, the Red Earl expected total respect on the hunting field. It was customary for the other riders to have the courtesy to allow the Master to lead the field. However, approaching an awkward jump one day he was amazed to see a stranger cut in in front of him, and clear the obstacle first. Initially speechless, his face redder than ever his beard had been, he then shouted to the offending rider, 'I'm much obliged to you, sir. Upon my word I am. Did you come far to do this?'

Spencer's enjoyment of foxhunting was famous throughout the aristocracy and royalty of Europe. His reputation brought Elisabeth, Empress of Austria, as a guest in 1876 and 1878. The Empress was noted, not just for extraordinary good looks, but also for her eccentricities: she stuck to a rigorous diet, but enjoyed beer or port, and transported a gym around with her on her frequent travels. At Althorp she provoked astonishment from her fellow guests by lighting herself a cigar after dinner one night.

There is a large and handsome portrait of Elisabeth in the Billiard Room at Althorp, flying over a fence on her mount, riding side-saddle, beautiful and fearless. The Red Earl was concerned about how to protect his imperial guest in the field, as much from herself as from any other dangers. As he told his cousin, Lord Granville, 'The responsibility of piloting her is awful.'

The Red Earl relied on certain assumptions as host to the Empress, and one of these was that she viewed the pursuit of the fox, as he himself did, as a pastime that should not be interrupted by everyday matters – or even by matters of state. One day the Pytchley met at Stanford Hall, not far from Althorp. Stanford's owner, Lord Braye, had just been informed that Pope Pius IX had died, and he told Spencer that he was going to pass the news on to Elisabeth. The Red Earl thought this a poor idea, and told Braye: 'You need not tell her just yet; she would have to go home and not finish her day.' Perhaps this attitude helps explain why Elisabeth wrote to her husband, the Emperor Franz Josef, about the Red Earl: 'I like him very much. He is so nice and natural and I think that if he ever pays us a visit you will like him too.'

It was not until he was close to sixty that the Red Earl could bring himself to retire as Master of the Pytchley. He told Charlotte of his decision in January 1894: 'I wrote yesterday to give up Hounds. It is a bitter thing to do as it is what I care most for as amusement in the world. But I dare not face the cost . . .' In 1890 he had spent over £5,000 on his horses; the following year, in excess of £4,000.

Financial worries had come back to haunt the Spencer family again. Just as Jack Althorp, on succeeding his father, had been forced to concentrate on settling debts, so the Red Earl realized that he must address the accumulated shortfall on his income occasioned by the expense of his Irish Lord Lieutenancy and of funding the Pytchley. There were also the expenses of living at Althorp, Spencer House and the shooting lodge they maintained on the Norfolk estate, North Creake.

In 1886, the first drastic cutback was made when the Red Earl decided to find a tenant for Spencer House. Being in office then, he was able to occupy an official residence when in London, so this was a logical and relatively painless economy. One of his early tenants was Barney Barnato, born in the East End in 1852 who, by the 1890s, had become perhaps the wealthiest and most influential financier in South Africa. In the summer of 1895, he was calculated to have earned £5 for every minute of his working day.

'Flamboyant' is the adjective usually trundled out to describe

Barnato; but it seems too simplistic. He was unique, particularly in his confidence. When the Red Earl told him with trepidation that the rent for Spencer House was £2,000 per year, Barnato made an immediate payment of the first two years. He was soon heard to comment of his new residence – one of the great private palaces of London, bordering Green Park, and a symbol of classical elegance – 'It's not a bad position: exactly half-way between the Prince of Wales in Marlborough House and the PM in Arlington Street.'

The atmosphere of the house changed dramatically. No more was it a bastion of Whig politics, but rather the rented accommodation of a multi-millionaire freed from the social obligations the Spencers had always felt so keenly. Barnato held open house for his coterie of actors, horse trainers, boxers and impresarios. He objected to paying the butler and the footmen, whose purpose he could not fathom – to him, they stood around far too much. What was more, they seemed unable to enjoy themselves. When Barnato wanted to practise his boxing with them, he was astonished to discover that the beautifully mannered Spencer staff simply would not fight back. As Barnato said, disappointedly, 'It's no fun punching a bloke who bows and thanks you as if he's afraid of losing his ruddy job.'

Being freed of the cost of Spencer House was a help, but it was not enough to solve the crisis. The Red Earl decided to do something that his uncle Jack had so assiduously avoided, half a century before: he sought a buyer for the Spencer Library, so expensively assembled by George John, the Second Earl.

He wrote to his half-brother, Bobby, who was also his heir:

I feel it much, now that it has come, but I do not alter my view that it was my duty to do it. I could not have gone on as I have been for the last 12 or 13 years . . . It will make a vast difference to my financial position, and relieve me of what at times was intolerable, the feeling that I had no right to go on even in the very reduced way which we have adopted for some years past: and I saw no way out of the difficulty.

His hope was to preserve the books in one collection, and in

Great Britain; the hope being that they would be readily accessible to British scholars. Only a few books were to be kept back from the sale: the Bible of Sarah, Duchess of Marlborough, and Ben Jonson's masque, performed at Althorp for Anne of Denmark in 1603, among them. Everything else – the Caxton bibles, the early psalters, the foreign classics – went.

It was an unfortunate business transaction. The Red Earl's preference for a British buyer made him settle for the offer of Enriqueta Rylands, the widow of a businessman from Manchester, who wanted to establish a memorial to her husband, John. If the Red Earl had followed up the expressed interest of the New York Public Library, he would have learned that the Americans were prepared to pay £300,000 for the Library. As it was, when he signed the contract in 1892, Spencer had settled for £220,000.

There was to be good news for Spencer, in the same year of 1892. Gladstone won the general election, and he considered making his trusted supporter of a quarter of a century the Home Secretary. However, the Red Earl received a post that he had hoped would one day be his: that of First Lord of the Admiralty. As Queen Victoria noted in her diary for 18 August 1892: 'I saw Lord Spencer who seemed pleased to go to the Admiralty, though all was new to him, as his father and uncle had both been in the Navy, and his grandfather First Lord of the Admiralty in Nelson's time and even had recommended him for employment.'

The Prince of Wales followed up the appointment with a letter of congratulations: 'Nothing has given me greater pleasure than to know that you have been appointed First Lord of the Admiralty, and I know it is a popular one in the Navy. That it is pleasing to yourself I can easily imagine . . .' This marked the Red Earl's re-emergency into royal favour after several years which must have been deeply hurtful to a man whose constant aim in public life was merely to obey his conscience and his considered judgement.

In the late 1880s the question of Home Rule for Ireland had become one of the bitterest in the political arena. Charlotte's brother maintained that the debate 'developed into a social war. It invaded the hearth and home with unprecedented acrimony. Even in the preliminary fencing in the Houses of Parliament the buttons had been removed from the foils. The controversy assumed almost a religious tinge.'

Feeling was strong enough to split the Liberal Party, with the Unionists deserting Gladstone. Gladstone and Spencer were united in their belief that this was an issue that needed to be dealt with honestly and conclusively. Gladstone knew little about Ireland, having visited it only briefly in 1877. Indeed, his ignorance had astonished the Red Earl's half-brother, Bobby, who reported: 'I had luncheon with Mr Gladstone . . . I was much struck by the evident way he thought Ireland was as quiet really as here with only a row or an outrage every now and then.'

The Red Earl, by standing by his old friend in the face of so much withering aggression – some of it from former allies of theirs – gave Gladstone and his cause credibility. At the same time, he became a social pariah to many of his class, who failed to see the drive for Home Rule as anything other than an underhand, treacherous way of depriving the British sovereign of control over his or her dominions. The Duchess of Teck was typical in her unquestioning contempt for the Red Earl's stand on the issue, writing to a friend: 'We have heard that Lord Spencer, of <u>all people</u> is a convert (<u>pervert</u> I think I ought to say!) to Home Rule.'

Sir Dighton Probyn, of the Prince of Wales's household, joined in the chorus of disgust:

I am worried over Lord Spencer. I have always looked upon him as being an honest Englishman, and a Gentleman . . . But he has fallen into the traitor's clutches, and is lending a helping hand to a fearful Civil War . . . A man of that sort advocating Communism shakes my belief in anything mortal.

Sir Rainald and Lady Knightley of Fawsley, distant Spencer kinsmen in Northamptonshire, made their condemnation of the Red Earl and Charlotte clear at a dinner party in 1886, Lady Knightley recording: 'Saw Lady Spencer, both R. and I greeted

her with MARKED coldness – publicly and privately I do feel
so angry with them.'

Queen Victoria also felt let down. She confronted a slightly
flustered Red Earl about his apparently sudden conversion to a
cause that he had fought against for so long, noting that, 'He
continued that he certainly had changed his opinion very much
tho' he must confess he had for some time had a sneaking feeling
that "something of this kind would have to be resorted to" . . .
Altogether I thought his explanations very unsatisfactory and weak.'
She stopped asking the Spencers to Windsor. Even more crushing
was the decision of Lord Frederick Cavendish's family not to invite
the Spencers to Chatsworth – a ban that stood for twelve years.

After such a bleak period in the social and political wilderness,
the appointment as First Lord of the Admiralty was doubly welcome.
The Red Earl brought the same qualities to the post as his grandfather
had done, in particular through his insistence on a hands-on style
of management. Moreover, he took the helm at a time when the
Navy was facing something of a crisis: not warfare and mutiny, but
a definite feeling of grave doubt as to whether it had the capability
to fight a war on anything like the superior footing it had been
used to for ninety years.

The French and Russians had been improving their fleets in the
1890s, and the British were nervous about either or both matching
or surpassing their seapower. The Russians were causing concern
through their aggression in Afghanistan, and the French were
proving to be problematic in Egypt. There was also a perceived
problem with the standard of senior officer in the Royal Navy,
many of whom had failed to understand how much warfare had
moved on since they last fired their cannon in anger: the advent of
the submarine, the seamine and the torpedo had all to be digested
and mastered.

The Red Earl decided his best chance of making the necessary
improvements in the Navy was to deal directly with his admirals.
(As was the case throughout his public life, he wrote nearly all his
correspondence himself, in fairly diabolical handwriting, eschewing
the services of a secretary.) During his period at the Admiralty,

from 1892 to 1895, Spencer saw to it that: naval personnel was increased by 6,000; the problem of there being too few stokers was solved; the number of quick-firing guns was added to; the élite blue-jackets and marines were armed with magazine rifles; and extensive harbour works at Gibraltar, Portland and Dover were begun.

His main responsibility was to prepare the estimates relating to naval expenditure in the following year, to be submitted to his cabinet colleagues for their approval. Given the worries expressed by his Sea Lords, which reflected the mood throughout the country, at the end of 1893 the Red Earl submitted that the Navy should be reinforced by ten first-class battleships. Gladstone was almost alone in opposing the recommendation, fearing the cost was unsustainable, and that the continued escalation of firepower would result in war. The Prime Minister asked Spencer to revise his department's estimates, but the Red Earl was assured by Admiral Fisher, one of his most able Sea Lords, that any fewer than seven new battleships would severely compromise national safety. The impasse between Gladstone and Spencer was one that the two friends could not resolve, and was one of the main reasons why Gladstone resigned in March 1894.

The Red Earl felt remorse that his inability to back down on a point of political principle had resulted in the end of Gladstone's premiership, writing to him:

I cannot conceal from myself that the policy which I proposed for the Navy has had a marked influence in bringing you to the decision of resigning at this moment. I most earnestly wish that I could have modified my proposals, or given place to someone else whose views would have agreed with your own . . . This position has been most painful to me for I owe my political career entirely to you, and I have always and still do admire your political principles and action and if I may be allowed to say so have a real affection and veneration for you personally.

It was testament to the two old colleagues' regard for each other that, despite their cabinet quarrel, Gladstone had resolved to

champion the Red Earl as Prime Minister, during his resignation
meeting with Queen Victoria. Harcourt and Rosebery were the
two front-runners, as successors, but Gladstone thought Spencer
would be better than them, recording in a memorandum:

Less brilliant than either he has far more experience . . . he has also
decidedly more of the very important quality termed weight, and his cast
of character I think affords more guarantees of the moderation he would
combine with zeal, and more possibility of forecasting the course he
would pursue.

However, the Queen broke with unwritten custom and talked
about many subjects with Gladstone, including his eyesight and
hearing, but not about his views as to the best future Prime Minister.
She had already made her mind up and asked Rosebery to form an
administration.

The Red Earl continued as First Lord under Rosebery, and his
time in office was seen as a successful one. Queen Victoria wrote
to Salisbury after the Liberal defeat in the general election of 1895:
'Lord Spencer has been very successful not only as an Administrator
but from his personal and social position which has lent prestige to
what is our national service.'

Doubtless of more value to the Red Earl would have been the
assessment of one of his Sea Lords, Fisher, who wrote to the
departing First Lord: 'I am confident you will live in the annals of
the Navy as amongst the best and greatest of First Lords . . . I
sincerely hope I may yet be able to serve under you again.'

Freed from political office, the Red Earl was able to indulge his
wife's taste for travelling. The Spencers had visited Europe throughout their married life, primarily because of the Red Earl's health,
which resulted in frequent trips to spas, where his lungs and his eczema
could be treated. The voyage they undertook in 1895 and 1896 was
altogether more ambitious, taking them to India, Ceylon, Singapore,
Hong Kong, Japan, Canada and the United States.

The Red Earl was intrigued by India, and deeply impressed by
the devotion and ability of the Indian Civil Service, in contrast to

the revulsion he felt at the arrogance of his fellow countrymen working there, 'who talk as if every Indian interest must bow to the Britisher, and the native only exists to minister to his wealth, pleasure and convenience . . . It is very wrong, for we cannot forget that we have seized the natives' country and are governing it for them.'

In Japan, the Spencers were received at a private audience by the Empress. The Red Earl's impressions of the country were very positive, both with regard to its beauty and its people:

Japan is delightful, lovely scenery at palaces with wonderful Parks of trees such as we never see. Then the people are wonders of energy, and ability, swilling wholesale the newest of our ideas of Government and civilisation. They are ahead of us in many ways, some very odd ways.

A decade later, his enthusiasm for Japan undimmed, Spencer would be one of the more enthusiastic proponents of the new Anglo-Japanese agreement between the two nations' governments.

The Red Earl was pleased to see North America again after nearly forty years. In May 1896, Spencer gave his first ever newspaper interview, to the *Manitoba Evening Bulletin*, while later, he and Theodore Roosevelt discussed their political theories with one another at a meeting in New York.

The Spencers were treated with great respect wherever they went, the Red Earl having earned an international reputation as a grand old man of British politics. He was still mooted as a possible Prime Minister, whenever a solid compromise candidate was thought desirable, and his views on matters at home and abroad always carried weight, even if they did not hold sway.

When the British decided to swallow up the Afrikaaner regions of South Africa, the Red Earl could see the injustice of the British cause and the dangers of antagonizing such a proud people. He knew the Boers, under Kruger, would fight if pushed. He wrote at the very start of the 1899 Boer War: 'I have lately come to the conclusion that if the Government could show conclusively that Kruger never intended peace on reasonable terms, the Government would be greatly justified, but I cannot see that this contention is proved . . .'

He was appalled when the war that followed proved to be one that the British were incapable of winning quickly; or, as a consequence, of fighting cleanly. In an effort to bring the Boer guerrillas to their knees, the British had instigated a policy of burning their farms and resettling their families in centralized prisons – the first concentration camps. In October 1901 the Red Earl gave his opinion of these British inventions:

The Concentration Camps carry with them their terrible toll of death. I look on them as the dire consequence, it may be, of the farm burnings, but if they were a necessity, surely the authorities never provided what was essential for keeping them efficiently, by way of food, nurses, doctors, tents, etc. The mortality which still continues is appalling.

While the Red Earl increasingly assumed the role of elder states-man, at home Charlotte Spencer's health was beginning to wane. She had enjoyed all the benefits of a robust constitution – apart from contracting malaria while on honeymoon in Italy – which had led to an active life, primarily as hostess at Althorp, Spencer House, Dublin Castle and the Admiralty, but also as a perpetrator of good works.

Her most important charitable efforts were in league with eleven other concerned ladies, each of them adopting an area of London's East End and helping to fight the fall-out of dire poverty. This campaign, fought through 'The Women's Association', had its successes, and is noted for having been one of the earliest schemes for dealing with the East End's problems in such a concerted and applied manner.

As for her primary role – that of châtelaine and hostess – despite constant reminders, from the 1870s onwards, that she and her husband had not the money to entertain as lavishly and often as they had been accustomed to in the first part of their marriage, when the opportunity did present itself for a proper party, Charlotte refused to stint.

The largest party Charlotte gave in her latter years was a ball supper in 1899, in the Picture Gallery at Althorp, when all the Marlborough silver was displayed. The newspapers that covered the event focused on the novelty of the use of electric lighting, contrasting the 2,000 lbs of candles used with the 120 lights which, it was calculated, gave off the same illumination as a further 1,620 candles.

Three hundred and fifty guests were welcomed to Althorp, the house thick with plants, flowers and evergreens from the gardens overseen by Silas Coles, who, two years later, amazed the horticultural world with his invention, 'the Spencer Sweet Pea', whose first examples were termed 'the Countess Spencer' after Charlotte. Coles was famed for his ability to use his flowers to transform a room, and his blooms were apparently more striking than the jewellery of the female guests, or the silver of the Red Earl.

Charlotte, though in late middle age by this point, was still remarkably fine looking, and she danced to the music of the band, called 'Mr Kinkee's' after the conductor. The guests feasted on tortoise soup, pheasant, *foie gras*, lobsters, prawns and *marrons glacés*, all prepared by a famous London-based chef, Monsieur Emile Beguinot. It was a lavish reminder of the days of high entertaining she had regularly dispensed in the Queen's name in Ireland.

Three years later, in 1902, Charlotte, who had been feeling unwell for some time, was diagnosed as having cancer, and was made to have an operation without delay in Spencer House. Her surgeon was, unusually for the era, a woman, Dr Mary Scharlieb, who had been one of the first students at the London School of Medicine for Women. The Red Earl knew of Scharlieb, and had a high regard for her skills. Certainly it seemed as though the operation had been a success, Charlotte being allowed to return to Althorp in January 1903.

Over the next few months her convalescence took place, her usual retinue of dogs – predominantly dachshunds – padding round after their mistress, as she made an almost daily walk from the mansion down to the side of the Round Oval lake that she had created in the gardens, before sitting quietly under the arch of the temple at the far end of the water, enjoying fresh air after her many weeks of being confined to bed.

On Charlotte's return, a service of thanksgiving was held in the Chapel at Althorp for her apparent recovery, attended by relatives and close friends. However, the period of tolerable health granted to her was brief. In June 1903, returning from Northampton railway station in an open carriage, Charlotte was caught in a rainstorm and contracted pneumonia. Four days later she had what appears to have been a stroke, leaving her paralysed down her right side and incapable of speech. Charlotte's last few months were spent in silent confusion, each day faithfully chronicled by the Red Earl. His entry for 31 October 1903 read: 'At 12.50, "sorrow of sorrows". She left us in a sleep of perfect peace and beauty.'

The widowed Red Earl was a pathetically lonely figure. He and Charlotte had been unable to have children, and so he was left alone at Althorp, the presence of his half-brother and his young family, several miles away in Dallington, only partially able to compensate for his own solitude. There was also a maiden sister, Lady Sarah Spencer, named after Sarah, Duchess of Marlborough. An active Liberal herself, she was a great friend of Sir William Gladstone's, often reading to him after his eyesight had dimmed. Gladstone noted: 'Many kind friends have read to me; I must place Lady Sarah Spencer at the head of the proficients in that difficult art; in distinctiveness of articulation, with low, clear voice, she is supreme.'

This was not, however, a talent that was to secure her a husband, and Lady Sarah devoted much of her energy to helping the Red Earl in his public life, never overcoming her disappointment at her elder brother's failure to replace Gladstone as Prime Minister, thinking him perfectly suited for that task.

Lady Sarah was intrigued by the Spencer family and its history, spending an enormous amount of time chronicling the history and provenance of the heirlooms to be found at Althorp and in Spencer House. She lived next door to the latter, but was not averse to leaving her spinster's home to enjoy her single life.

A keen rider with a reputation for daring, she went to Algeciras in Spain, at the age of seventy-one, and encountered trouble while riding a donkey too fast. Thrown by her mount, she broke a leg. A member of a nearby picnic party, Rear-Admiral Foley, gallantly escorted Lady Sarah back to her hotel. Unfortunately for the admiral, he too chose a donkey as his mode of transport to return to the picnic he had so suddenly left. He was thrown as well, and broke his leg too.

Lady Sarah lived until 1919, when she was eighty-one. In the congregation at her funeral in Great Brington was Mrs Emma Garderton, who had been a pall-bearer at the funeral of her and the Red Earl's sister, Lady Georgiana, who had died of measles in 1852.

In the early 1900s, there were final calls upon Spencer from political allies, again looking to him as a potential caretaker leader of the Whigs and Prime Minister. Edward VII had recorded his happiness at the possibility of his former Groom of the Stole becoming Premier in 1902. In 1904, it appeared probable that Spencer's moment had come. In January several publications were contemplating the real prospect of a Spencer administration, and later the same year the Red Earl's young cousin, Winston Spencer-Churchill, came to consult him about how to effect a desertion from the Conservatives to the Liberals, with the assumption that the Red Earl might very well then be his party – and national – leader.

The Red Earl was still an imposing presence, even with his seventieth birthday approaching. Edmund Gosse, librarian of the House of Lords, met Spencer at this late stage of the earl's active life in that chamber:

I found him very intimidating; one looks up in despair for his face at the top of the white cliff of his great beard. He was possibly shy, he certainly made me feel so, but he gives the great impression of great dignity, and the temper of a very fine gentleman. I admire him intensely, but he is certainly the most alarming figure I have yet encountered here.

The same year as this observation, 1904, saw Spencer laid low by a heart attack. Although the Red Earl did rally briefly from its effects, Edward VII decided then that Spencer was not physically strong enough to be considered for the position of Prime Minister. However, the rest of the political classes were unaware of the King's private decision, and only ruled the earl out in October 1905, when he suffered a serious stroke while out shooting on his Norfolk estate. The local doctor reported on a scrap of paper: 'Block of a small vessel in the brain producing loss of speech but no loss of power in limbs, perfectly conscious.' Winston Churchill, thinking that Spencer had been within an ace of achieving the highest office in the land, wrote to Lord Rosebery: 'Poor Lord Spencer, it was rather like a ship sinking in sight of land.'

A man who had been a byword for quiet dignity was now reduced to an unpredictable invalid, sometimes speaking in barely distinguishable tones, at other times showing the greatest confusion as to his whereabouts and his identity. There was relief among those who knew him in those final years when the end came, a further stroke delivering him from his pain and discomfort. On 13 August 1910 he died, his half-brother Bobby kissing his head before recording:

He is now at rest, my dear S. [Spencer.] And I must face the horrid domestic difficulties as I best can. Looking back, I can see the thing that he lacked was children – yet he took mine to himself. His delight and pride in them was really great: and so was Charlotte's . . . My dear S. looked most 'digne' and fine lying on his bed, a weary warrior at rest. R.I.P. – My dear old Brother.

## 17. More than a Mere Dandy

I found Bobby Spencer's diaries in a bank vault five years ago. They had been there since his death, placed in privacy and safety by the executors of his will in accordance with his final instructions: nobody was to open their pages for at least twenty-five years after his demise. Indeed, because they were forgotten when that period of time had elapsed, it is probable that I am the only person apart from him ever to have laid eyes on their contents. They constitute a sharp and intriguing insight into the mind of a man who felt keenly that he was presiding over the death throes of his family as people of influence and property, particularly after the First World War.

Bobby had been born two months before the death of his father, Frederick, Fourth Earl Spencer, in 1857. He had one full sister, Victoria Alexandrina, known as 'Va', who was a goddaughter of Queen Victoria. They shared three half-siblings, almost a generation their senior. Bobby and Va's mother, Yaddy, was given a house at Guilsborough, in Northamptonshire, for her widowhood. It was a period of their lives that her two children were always to remember with fondness, revolving around riding their ponies, gardening and piano-playing. Their favourite game as children was playing at Ivanhoe in the laurels.

Bobby was always of delicate health. He was sent to a boarding school in Sevenoaks, Kent, followed by several years at Harrow. Because of his fragility, he was not pushed either academically or on the sports field. Nevertheless, he seems to have enjoyed his time at school, and at Harrow made friends for life with the Earl of Crowe and Lord Desborough. His studies were interrupted once after a bad concussion sustained when out hunting, which led to his being sent with his uncle, Admiral Sir Beauchamp Seymour – later Lord Alcester – on a long recuperative voyage.

After his return, he went up to Trinity College, Cambridge, in 1877, and showed little flair for his studies, although he revealed what was to be a lasting interest in music, the fine arts and drama. He took a nobleman's degree, less, apparently, because he wanted to, but more because they were in danger of being discontinued, and he believed that it was therefore his duty to help to perpetuate them if he could.

The Red Earl was a hugely important influence in Bobby's life, becoming a blend of brother and benign uncle. He was the guiding force in his public life, seeing in Bobby a way of extending Whig influence in Northamptonshire, after a gap that went back to his own elevation to the House of Lords in 1857. Since then the Southern Division of Northamptonshire had become a safe seat for the Tories. As the Red Earl's election agent, John Becke, reported to his political master in January 1874: 'It is my firm conviction, which is shared by all the sober minded men of the party, that there is no hope of considering with success the Southern Division unless we have a "Spencer" to bring forward.'

In 1880 the Red Earl's lungs were causing him much distress, and he was sent to Algiers to benefit from its dry heat. However, his absence did not stop him from pushing forward his young half-brother, fresh out of Cambridge, in the general election of that year. Although the Red Earl had hoped to train his brother longer before the youth embarked on a political career – he had advised Bobby to train as a barrister in order to help his public speaking – the opportunity of having a Spencer once again in the House of Commons was one that galvanized the Red Earl into action, as energetic and focused as if he had been fighting the campaign for himself.

Having decided that it was still futile to try to wrest the Southern Division of Northamptonshire from the Tories, the Red Earl told Bobby to stand for the Northern Division – not traditional Spencer territory, but still within the family's sphere of influence. The Red Earl wrote to all the landowners in the area, asking them to support his young half-brother. The reply from Henry Nethercote, one of the Red Earl's hunting friends but an avowed Tory, was typical of the response that was given by many to the request: 'Had any other Candidate stood I should have opposed him with all my might. As it is, my attachment to, and my respect for, the House to which Bobby Spencer belongs keeps me quiet, and I shall not vote at all.'

The result was that Bobby was elected, ahead even of Lord Burghley, whose family was the largest landowner in the Division, and who had widely been expected to head the poll. Bobby wrote to the Red Earl to thank him for the virtual gift of the seat: 'I am so pleased and happy and feel now more than all is due to you and your being so respected and cared for in the county.'

Bobby Spencer, at twenty-two, was the youngest Member of the House of Commons. T. P. O'Connor, MP, writing in the *Sunday Times* forty years later, remembered his first sighting of Bobby in his new official capacity:

I never will forget the feeling of perplexity I experienced when I saw, on the floor of the House of Commons crowded with members waiting to take the oath, a strange figure that stood out in almost ostentatious and astounding contrast to the rest of the people around him. He looked so ridiculously young – so absolutely babyish, that I thought for a while he was a son of one of the members – still probably at Eton – who had been brought in by mistake or by some exceptional privilege given to the swells of the new House. But the boy was a member right enough; Northants had chosen him.

To begin with, Bobby's youth meant that he was not taken seriously by the rest of the Commons; even less so when it was assumed, from his dandyism, that he was more interested in his sartorial splendour than in politics. A parliamentary sketch writer wrote of Bobby at this stage: 'It was said of him in those days that he always had his blue books bound by Zahnsdorff in blue morocco; it was said of him that he always carried a laced pocket handkerchief to his nose after the manner of a modish French "abbé" of a last century salon.'

And then there was the matter of his collars . . . Although high collars were in fashion in the 1880s among the gilded youth, nobody had ever seen collars as high, or as immaculate, as Bobby's. As O'Connor noted: 'Bobby's collar was to the ordinary collar of the dandy as the Matterhorn to Mount Snowdon.' And it was not simply the collars that provoked incredulous comment:

The spats were of spotless white that might make snow blush in rivalry, and, of course, the boots were blinding in their brightness. Nobody among the middle-aged and elderly men who then usually formed the majority of the House of Commons could take such a palpable boy seriously; and for years Bobby did not overcome the under-estimate provoked by the Alpine-heighted collars.

Indeed, one evening in the Commons an irate Irish member promised to keep the debate going for as long as it was necessary, to push through his point; and that could be 'until Bobby Spencer's collar gave way'.

But there was more to Bobby than an outlandish dress sense. As he became more established as a Member of Parliament, so his qualities grew more obvious. He was noted as a highly accomplished speaker, occasionally quite brilliant, with a dry wit. Once, when taking part in a debate on a Small Holdings Bill, Bobby stood up, his collar tall, his coat and waistcoat immaculate, his hair combed back and slicked down to reveal his smooth, aristocratic hauteur, and started his intervention in the proceedings with the phrase: 'I am not an agricultural labourer . . .' The House dissolved into an uproar of laughter, some Members apparently so convulsed by mirth that they were 'nearly sick', before the imperturbable Bobby put forward his case on behalf of his predominantly agrarian constituency.

His quickness of wit was well known; as, indeed, was his measured courtesy. Once, when he was addressing his constituents, a heckler shouted out at Bobby: 'Mr Spencer, do tell us how you get into them collars?' Without missing a beat, Bobby calmly replied: 'My friend, you are much mistaken if you think I shall lose a single vote by your being rude.' The acclamation that greeted this retort was strong enough to force the heckler to slope off into the darkness, his barb deflected.

Once the meeting was over, Bobby returned to his carriage. As he stepped into it, he saw a hand held out to him, and realized it belonged to the heckler. 'Mr Spencer,' the man said, 'I'm sorry I was rude. I've always voted blue before, but you shall have my vote this time.'

Bobby was greatly respected for the way in which he supported his half-brother during the Red Earl's second term as Lord Lieutenant of Ireland, one newspaper remarking, 'Mr Spencer is not a mere dandy, however, and the pluck with which he rode and walked about Dublin with his half-brother, Earl Spencer, as if it were St James's Street, was quite a public service.' Indeed, such loyalty nearly cost him his life – not from any subversive elements, but because the drains at Dublin Castle gave him a serious bout of typhoid fever. His condition was critical for several weeks, and only the nursing of his half-sister Sarah, his full sister Victoria and his sister-in-law Charlotte carried him through.

Gradually he obtained the respect that was to lead to his becoming a government whip and parliamentary Groom in Waiting in 1886. Whips have traditionally been people of firm views, prepared to make their Members perform the party's bidding, by whatever means; the line between persuasion and bullying has often been blurred. This was not Bobby's style at all. A contemporary newspaper observed that: 'Members find it more difficult to excuse themselves for indiscipline or absence under the soft application of Mr Spencer's gentle and caressing whip than when bidden by the harshest and most blustering of the officers of the party . . .' He was still not thirty years old.

The irrepressible Bobby – 'so young, so lighthearted, so glad he is alive' – met his life's love in 1887. Margaret Baring was only a teenager, and he was eleven years her senior, but he was sure this was the woman he would wed. They married after a one-month engagement, on 25 July of the same year.

Margaret was the second daughter of Edward Charles Baring, Baron Revelstoke. The Barings controlled one of the great banking dynasties of late nineteenth-century Britain. The founder of the firm had been Francis Baring, the son of an immigrant from Bremen. Francis had originally been a cloth dealer, but he appreciated the growing importance of banking – a trade that took off during the Continental and Napoleonic Wars. It was a wise career move. The Prime Minister, Lord Shelburne, referred to Francis Baring as 'the Prince of Merchants', while, at the time of Francis's death in 1810, Lord Erskine dubbed him 'the first merchant in Europe'.

Francis left £2 million in his will. He had five sons and five daughters, of whom the most successful proved to be Alexander, who banked on an unprecedented scale. Once he secured a loan for France which 'freed France from the incubus of the Russian, Prussian and Austrian occupation'. This transaction led the French Premier to claim: 'There are six great Powers in Europe – England, France, Russia, Austria, Prussia, and Baring Bros.' This was borne out by the head of the family becoming known as 'Alexander the Great'. When he died, in 1848, he had been raised to the peerage as Baron Ashburton.

The next head of the firm was Alexander's nephew, Thomas Baring. In official circles the respect for the Barings, and for their financial nous, was underlined through Lord Melbourne's decision to appoint Thomas Baring as Chancellor of the Exchequer.

It was Thomas's nephew, Edward, who was Bobby's father-in-law. In 1885, he had been given the title of Baron Revelstoke, joining his brother, Baron Northbrook, in the House of Lords. Margaret was, through her mother, a great-great-granddaughter of the same Lord Grey who had fathered Georgiana Devonshire's love child. Among her brothers, Margaret numbered: one Director of the Bank of England; a war hero from Sudan – who was subsequently military secretary to the Viceroy of India, Lord Curzon; a diplomat; and an army officer, severely wounded in the Boer Wars, who lived in New York. Francis Baring's progeny were so conspicuous in the success and diversity of their careers, that it seemed that Lady Ashburton was justified when she said of the Barings: 'They are everywhere.'

The *Daily Reporter* was effusive in its praise of the couple on their wedding day. About Bobby, it reported: 'In Parliament he is known as the most popular member of the House of Commons; and in London society is an especial favourite.' Then, approvingly, it noted: 'The bride arrived at the church very punctually. She looked sweetly pretty, her personal charms enhanced by the exquisite dress she was wearing. It was of white satin, with a long train, completely covered with rich 'Point d'Argentan' lace, trimmed with lovely orange blossoms.'

Bobby festooned his bride with wedding gifts, the jewellery dominated by diamonds: a tiara, a brooch for her hair, two bracelets; also an emerald and diamond ring, a moonstone and diamond necklace, a pearl necklace; as well as an old Berlin tea service, a 'Venus Martin' box and two Dresden snuffboxes.

The honeymoon was spent at Althorp, by invitation of the Red Earl and Charlotte. Given that the couple had known one another for such a short while, this was the first time that Margaret had seen her husband's family home. One hundred estate and park staff pulled the carriage from Althorp station to the mansion, under an arch with 'Long Life and Happiness' written on it. Children from the park lodges threw flowers on the lady they assumed would one day be the mistress of Althorp.

Married life for the Spencers centred on Dallington House, which was then a mile from Northampton. It was a separate estate from the other Spencer land in the county, and had been bought by Jack Althorp. The house itself was of a suitably large and grand design to be home to a couple who were heir presumptives to the Spencer title since it was evident the Red Earl and Charlotte were not to have children. However, it was considerably less forbidding than Althorp.

The photograph albums from Bobby and Margaret's Dallington days show a deeply contented late Victorian/early Edwardian household, the living rooms filled with luxuriant potted plants and crammed with paintings of the burgeoning family the parents so adored. In accordance with the tastes of the time, furniture was crowded into every available space, with pride of place going to the piano: this was a highly musical family, with Bobby a keen pianist, and Margaret a highly accomplished violinist – a gift she passed down to the eldest child, Adelaide, known as Delia. The children often accompanied their mother, giving concerts for the benefit of local causes, while Bobby would lead the entire family in enthusiastic performances given at Spencer House. There were five children after Delia: Jack – my grandfather, Cecil, Lavinia, George and Margaret.

Margaret was much respected in Northamptonshire. A local newspaper commented that 'She was the good angel of Dallington, and of her small and numerous family.' Another claimed that she possessed 'the gentle loving kindness of a lady who would have been noble if the first breath of her life had been drawn in a miner's hut'.

She was a loyal wife, helping Bobby in his electioneering and becoming President of the Northamptonshire Women's Liberal Association. Above all Margaret was a warm and loving mother, more than usually involved in the minutiae of her children's upbringing, and not prepared merely to hand them over to nannies.

Her particular charitable interests were the Northampton Crippled Children's Fund and the Northamptonshire Nursing Association, both local concerns with which she was fully involved. She was also a keen supporter of the RSPCA and patron of the Band of Mercy Section, the latter being an organization established to appeal to the young, and to teach them how to act with kindness in all they did.

The Reverend W. N. Martin later recalled of Margaret that she 'used all her ability – and that was great – all her influence – and that was not slight – to do the very best that she could for everyone that she knew was suffering or had a claim on her'.

With the responsibilities of a large family, and of the post of government whip, the ebullience that had marked Bobby's youth slowly ebbed away, being replaced by a growing maturity. As a parliamentary sketch writer noted in 1892: 'To be Whip to a political party is to be a serious statesman, and to be a serious statesman one must be serious, "quel diable". And so Mr Spencer has become serious, dimming the bright gloss of his dandyism thereby, and gaining, in return, fame.' He also became, in that same year, a Privy Councillor and Vice-Chamberlain of the Royal Household – the latter position giving him a prominent role in the wedding of the Duke and Duchess of York, later King George V and Queen Mary.

Bobby's public life now started to follow two quite different courses, one of which would eventually have to surrender to the other: those of politician and of courtier. He sat as an MP from 1880 until 1895; for North Northamptonshire from 1880 to 1885, and then, when the county was divided into three constituencies, for Mid-Northamptonshire for the following decade. In 1895, he was one of many Liberal casualties in the general election, despite the Red Earl's continued assistance for his cause.

There followed five years away from the Commons. Bobby missed his political life enormously, and even stood in East Hertfordshire in 1898. His chances were known to be almost non-existent: the seat had only become vacant through the death of the Conservative MP; it was a solidly Conservative area; and his opponent was Evelyn Cecil, a grandson of Lord Salisbury. Bobby was apologetic about even thinking of standing in such a vain cause, writing to the Red Earl: 'I hope I have not done too foolishly to consider it, but when the offer came for the party's sake I confess I panted to fight, knowing the hopelessness of it all the time.'

However, revelling in the role of underdog, Bobby excelled in the campaign, and was delighted to reduce the Conservative majority from 1,236 to a mere 268. On the day the results were made public, he again wrote to his half-brother:

You will have received a telegramme announcing the poll in East Herts. It surpassed my wildest dreams. Our people were mad with excitement, and I really am enchanted. Never did I expect to win but I hoped to run them close, and the Tories' faces when the numbers were declared were very low and depressed.

In 1900 Bobby recaptured the Mid-Northamptonshire constituency, but his hopes of achieving high office were impeded by his being the Red Earl's heir. T. P. O'Connor wrote of Bobby, in 1920: 'A good, sometimes even a brilliant, speaker, with strong convictions tenaciously held, Bobby might have been a big Parliamentary figure: but the doom of an inevitable earldom . . . hung over him, and he subsided into a great courtier.'

Bobby did not want to leave the Commons. He believed he had much still to do there, and he had little enthusiasm for the life of a courtier. However, he felt a sense of duty to obey his monarch's wishes and, after the Red Earl's debilitating stroke in 1905, Edward VII decided it was time to promote Bobby in the royal household, and to recognize his position as heir to the Spencer title. Thus Bobby was created Viscount Althorp in his own right, and became Lord Chamberlain in December 1905. Although Bobby put a brave public face on these developments, his diary reveals his utter disappointment at being removed irrevocably from the Commons:

I said that I would accept the position if the King wished it. And there is the end of my political life in the House of Commons. I cannot say how I regret it, and I am by no means sure that we shall not lose the seat; but there it is – Heaven help me . . . I feel very depressed about it.

It was clear from the start that Edward VII was looking to Bobby to provide some relief from his more stuffy courtiers. Bobby's diary entry for 12 December 1905 reveals:

At 11.40 I was sent for by the King, who greeted me most cordially. Said as an old friend he wanted to talk to me about the Ld Chamberlain's department . . . Then he talked about S. [Spencer – the Red Earl] and heard all I had to say. Was most sympathetic and kind . . . Said that I was to come and see him often, my duty was to do so. I tried to go away but he kept me and talked. At last he ended the audience saying that next week I should probably kiss hands. I had asked him about his cough. He said it was only the fog, and one ought to have oxygen to breathe. He hoped to find less fog at Welbeck.

Apart from the responsibilities appertaining to the Royal Household, the Lord Chamberlain was also the censor of plays destined for public performance in Britain. As a contemporary noted with disapproval, 'A tick of his pencil was law; despite the Liberalism that is supposed to be in him, he loved that autocratic weapon.' However, by the time that Bobby was wielding this power, the public mood had started to turn against blithe acceptance of the Lord Chamberlain's moral judgements on its behalf. Petitions were signed against his authority and, by the time of Bobby's resignation, it was clear that the petitioners had won: he was to be the last of the old-style censors.

The period 1900–1910 was perhaps the decade most redolent with family grief in the entire Spencer history. In 1903, Charlotte had died; 1905 saw the end of the Red Earl's effective life, as he settled into five years of dotage before his own death in 1910. But there were two other deaths in the intervening period which rocked the remaining Spencers more than either of the above, for they were of two ladies who had seemed still too young and healthy to be considered candidates for an early grave.

Bobby's sister Va had always been particularly close to her brother. They had survived a childhood together without knowing their father, and living very much as a secondary Spencer family at Guilsborough, with the Red Earl residing at Althorp and Spencer House.

The siblings shared the same politics in adult life, Va becoming an active member of the Women's Liberal Foundation. In 1881, she had married William, Lord Sandhurst, and accompanied him during his term as Governor of Bombay from 1895 to 1900. Va and Bobby had missed one another enormously during the five years of absence, and had made a point of meeting regularly on the Sandhursts' return from their posting. However, towards the end of 1905, Va started to feel unwell.

To begin with, nobody was overly concerned by Va's condition. The first note of alarm comes in Bobby's diary, on 1 January 1906: 'Got up to find a letter from Sandhurst saying that Va was still unwell, and that Barlow was to be consulted. Flurried me a good deal. I pray that there is nothing really wrong . . .' There was: the consultant discovered that Va had cancer of the liver, and that it was so far advanced as to be terminal.

Va, a devout Christian, showed enormous courage over the next two months, as she slid rapidly towards death. The last time she was able to talk to her brother was on 3 March, and he was distraught at the ravaged form that greeted him that day: 'I went in. Va smiled at me. I kissed her twice, blessed her, and came out, saying I hoped she would sleep. She said, "I think so". She looked very very thin, her neck shrunk to nothing, her right hand perfectly bloodless lying on a cushion.' Va never regained consciousness.

On 12 March, it was decided to try to prolong her life by up to three months, by operating on her, with a mixture of ether, laughing gas and chloroform as anaesthetic. When she was cut open it was discovered that her stomach was half the expected size. Her physical reserves were similarly reduced. Bobby was by her bedside at 8.55 p.m. the following evening, when Va shivered, took two or three deep breaths, before sighing her life away: 'We used my watch to see if there was any breath, then a looking glass, but there was none.' She was fifty years old.

This bereavement, keenly felt though it was, acted as a mere prelude to the most tragic event of Bobby's life, which took place three and a half months later.

Margaret had been advised by her doctor not to add to the five healthy children she had produced. However, when she fell pregnant at the end of 1905, it was decided to proceed with the pregnancy. Margaret rested as much as she could during the intervening months, and all seemed to be on course for another addition to the family when, on 4 July 1906, she went into labour. As Bobby recorded in his diary:

M. was restless getting up . . . so I called Mrs Ingram. We sent for Blacker by telephone, at 2.35 he arrived. I was outside hearing very unusual noises, at 3.20 a baby girl was born – soon after 3.45 Blacker came out and asked for Reid to be sent for. Jamie soon came, and reassured me, but M.'s heart failed far too much. They tried everything. About 4.45

she asked for me so I went in, and her colour terrified me. I held her while the oxygen cylinder was tried. She was conscious but I felt it was hopeless . . . I lifted M. up. She asked for relief from suffocation . . . She said 'Delia' but said she must not be frightened. Then 'the Boys'. Then she was propped up with pillows, but all useless, and at 5.55 my darling breathed her soul away in my arms. God help me.

The rest of the entry for that day is fragmented by the grief and horror of the scene he had just witnessed. The triteness of their dialogue was recalled: 'She had said to me, "Am I dying?" I had answered, "I don't think so – why should you?".' And then the realization of the devastation that this death signified for him and his children began to sink in:

I closed her eyes and with them all that belonged to youth and lovely ideals. My own Margaret, how can I live without her? But I must for the children . . .

My children, our children, how can I bring them up? I have no knowledge of children. M. trained them so well. God help me. Nothing earthly helps one, the future is the only stable thing . . .

The following morning Bobby went to see the Red Earl at Spencer House. Addled though the old man's head was, he tried to comfort the distraught Bobby: 'He was so dear. Kissed me, and nearly broke down.' From there Bobby returned to Althorp. He read the children some stories and put them to bed – only to find all of them, apart from baby Margaret, later congregated in the Picture Gallery, 'sobbing'. Bobby wrote: 'My poor motherless ones. I can't comfort them as M. could have done. Felt hopeless . . .'

The coffin was sent to Althorp Park station by train, the door of the carriage being opened to reveal 'a bank of blossoms, wreaths piled upon wreaths, sweet messages of sorrow and affection'. Members of Lord Althorp's Volunteer company – reserve soldiers who had Bobby as their honorary commanding officer – bore the coffin to Brington church, Bobby walking behind, solitary in his grief.

The Spencer children were excused the pain of the funeral service, and therefore did not hear the priest exhorting the congregation 'to sympathize and sorrow for the family that had been for so many centuries associated with the parish, and to all of you must come the thought of how frequently during the past few years you have seen the clouds of heavy sorrow breaking over that house . . .' A simultaneous service was conducted for Margaret in the Chapel Royal – ordered in the King's own hand, and seen by one courtier as 'a rare mark of esteem' for the 38-year-old viscountess.

The *Northampton Reporter* listed Margaret's accomplishments for its readers, before opining:

. . . but it was in home life that she was at her very best. And greatly as she will be missed by the public, deep as will be the sorrow evinced by the outside world, it will be as naught compared with the grief in the home. For her bereaved husband the fullest and the most generous sympathy will be felt; and for the children, the eldest 17 years, the youngest a day, the people at large will mourn as for their own.

Bobby's summation of his grief, and his utter feeling of despair, was:

My M. gone, my whole life broken. God help me. I must live on for our children, but shall I ever be able to do it without my own M.? – Va gone. My sister, that was hard enough to bear; but now my beloved M., my constant loving help meet for nineteen years gone too, how can I go on? I must and so I suppose I shall.

Bobby's spirit was broken, and it was never to recover. Every anniversary – of Margaret and his initial meeting, of their engagement, of their wedding, of her birth, of her death – set off a stream of profound grief in his diary entries for the remainder of his life. He was the saddest of widowers – genuinely inconsolable. On 25 July 1914, he wrote:

Tired and sad – 27th anniversary of OUR wedding day. Can hardly believe THAT. It began the nineteen blessed years. Now I know that those years were my life. These 8 last years have been only an existence. I miss Her. I doubt my getting to Her in the hereafter. The loneliness seems very very great.

The only time he appeared glad that she was not alive was when their two oldest sons, Jack and Cecil, were on active service in the First World War. Nearly every day brought news of casualties, among them the sons of Bobby's friends. It made him fret endlessly about his own boys' safety: 'My eldest Boy on land and my 2nd on the sea. Would be beyond endurance. I feel thankful She has not this anxiety.'

Both survived, although one was wounded and only saved from death by a brave brother officer; the other becoming a highly decorated hero in his own right. As an act of gratitude to God for sparing them, and out of a wish to establish a lasting memorial to his wife, Bobby decided to give Dallington to the people of Northamptonshire as the 'Margaret Spencer Convalescent Home', together with five acres of gardens.

Dallington had been an auxiliary military hospital during the war, with nearly 2,000 wounded servicemen passing through it between November 1915 and May 1919. It was now decided that it would serve twenty male and twenty female patients, with priority being given to prisoners of war and ex-servicemen. Bobby opened the new facility on 1 December 1920 with the words:

My gift of this house is a small token of my sense of the Divine mercy which has brought my sons safely through the war, and it was in my mind when I first thought of giving this home that it should be in memory of a period of existence which I cannot believe could be equalled in happiness, peace, and contentment . . .

In private, he confided to his diary that night: 'Spoke. Not well. My own M., it was about you. Of the radiant happiness of our life at Dallington. It was hard work getting through it. I left at once, choking a good deal.'

In 1919 'Mr Gossip', from the *Daily Sketch*, gives us a vivid snapshot of Bobby in late middle age:

I have just seen the best-dressed man in the world, in a tall hat and a mackintosh. Earl Spencer, clad thus, was taking a stroll along Piccadilly and St James's Street early yesterday morning. He is a bit greyer than he was in his 'Bobby Spencer' and House of Commons days, but he is still slim, aristocratic, and immaculate, his collars are still hugely high, and his cravats spotlessly white, and he doesn't, by ten years at least, look his 62. It is refreshing in these Bolshefied days to find remaining so perfect an example of the good old school.

Although Bobby's outward appearance suggested otherwise, 'Mr Gossip' had been eyeing a deeply impoverished man. Around this time he had been forced to sell four of Sarah Marlborough's surviving estates: Sandridge, the original Jennings patrimony, in Hertfordshire; Elkington, in Northamptonshire; Stantonbury, in Buckinghamshire; and Theddingworth, in Leicestershire. None of the three latter estates fetched so much as twice the price Sarah had paid for them nearly two centuries before, so depressed were land prices in the late 1910s.

Spencer House was again let out, this time to an American millionairess, Mrs Leeds, who later married Prince Christopher of Greece. Economies were made at Althorp, the gardeners who had been killed in the war remembered in stone plaques, but not replaced, the house staff reduced to a handful. And yet it was not enough.

On 8 October 1921, the *Daily Telegraph* reported:

Our Northampton Correspondent states: Earl Spencer, K.G., has closed Althorp House for an indefinite period, as he finds himself so impoverished by high taxation and the increased cost of living that his trustees advise him that it is impossible to maintain the estate under present conditions. He left Althorp yesterday for his Norfolk home at North Creake, and after a short tour abroad will spend most of his time at his town house in St James's Place, close by Spencer House . . .

Bobby had spent the preceding week bracing himself for the pain of separation from Althorp. He drove to Brington to say goodbye to the family tombs, feeling anger and sadness that 'I have to leave my home. My own M.'s resting place. My 2 sisters, my old Brother and beautiful C. – R.I.P.'

He returned to Althorp, for a final, melancholy tour:

Went round the rooms. Long Gallery. All the best bedrooms. After tea, parting from the dear pictures. It will be a relief to get off tomorrow. But shall I ever get back again? I feel it so very much, and my loneliness makes me dread living anywhere else. This old family home so woven into my life. Hard indeed to have to part with it. God preserve it.

# 18. The Curator Earl

Bobby died in the summer of 1922, leaving the remaining Spencer land, as well as Althorp and Spencer House, to his thirty-year-old eldest son, Jack, and his wife, Cynthia. At this stage, we move from the historical to the near-contemporary, for I can clearly remember my grandparents, as well as some of the great-aunts and -uncles who were their siblings.

Grandfather was a figure of awe; his moustache bristled, his stomach bulged under outsized trousers, and he had the uncompromising air of a man who had no time whatsoever for fools. However, Viscount Palmerston's view of John, First Earl Spencer – 'The bright side of his character appears in private and the dark side in public' – applied equally to the Seventh Earl.

Jack had been brought up at Dallington, going to Harrow at thirteen, a few months before his mother's death. Bobby had been very worried that his sensitive eldest son would be picked on by the older boys, but noted in his diary for 3 March 1906, on the occasion of Jack's first exeat: 'A bright spot seeing the precious Boy, who told me that he was not bullied, no one was now. And that all was well. He said that he found the food bad.'

By this early age, Jack had already made his first political speech, on behalf of the Liberal Party, in Dallington. However, his interest in politics was confined to his youth, and he was the first Spencer, in the direct line, who was eligible for political office but did not actually hold one, since the First Earl of Sunderland, three centuries before.

By the time of Jack's coming of age in 1913, Bobby and his children had been occupying Althorp for three years. It was decided to turn the birthday celebration into an enormous party, with 1,000 guests from the tenantry of the Spencer estates in Northamptonshire, Hertfordshire, Buckinghamshire, Warwickshire and Norfolk. They were all given lunch and tea, and there was an air of easy privilege about the afternoon of the sort that was snuffed out the following year with the advent of war.

My grandfather became a Life Guard, eschewing the family's naval traditions. His life was nearly brought to an end when a German bullet lodged in his knee-cap, leaving him immobile in no-man's land. He thought that he would bleed to death, but a brother officer – my father told me his name was Henry Boyd Rochford – ran out, slung Grandfather over his back, and brought him to safety, and to surgery. The wound fortunately proved serious enough to keep him out of the front line for the remainder of the Great War.

I have often heard that my grandfather suffered from strong jealousy over his two younger brothers. Certainly Cecil, exactly two years grandfather's junior, was the sort of young man it would be easy to envy. Very good-looking, he had a reputation even as a naval cadet for being devastatingly attractive to women. He was a close friend of the Prince of Wales – later Duke of Windsor – when they were together at naval college.

Cecil was, by all accounts, utterly without fear. It was therefore no surprise to the family when he emerged as something of a hero during the First World War. His proudest moment lay in the capture of Zeebrugge harbour, when his coastal motor boat purposefully drew much of the hostile German fire, in order to help the more powerful Royal Navy vessels to penetrate the enemy defences. Indeed, as Vice-Admiral Sir Roger Keyes reported in his official dispatch of events on the night of 22 to 23 April 1918:

C.M.B. No. 23 (Lieutenant the Hon. Cecil E.R. Spencer) escorted 'Vindictive' close inshore, and kept touch with her until 'Vindictive' gave 'the last resort' signal, on which C.M.B. No. 23 laid, and lit, the million candle-power flare, by whose light 'Vindictive' eventually found her way in.

For his bravery, Cecil was awarded a bar to his Distinguished Service Cross. By the end of the war he had a plethora of foreign decorations as well. They are displayed with pride in their own case at Althorp, the White Ensign from his torpedo boat hanging in the entrance hall.

His gallantry in battle made his ultimate demise – being thrown by his horse after a polo match on Malta, in 1928 – even more pathetic. His coffin was laid to rest off the Maltese coast, not far from that of Captain Sir Robert Cavendish Spencer, his great-uncle.

My grandfather's youngest brother was George, the baby of the family before the late arrival of Margaret. Reading Bobby's diaries, it is clear that George was something of a favourite. Whether he was spoiled or not as a child, he was always represented to my father's and my generation as a black sheep – to the extent that my sisters and I were never allowed to meet him. My father told me that Uncle Georgie had the dubious distinction of having been the only man in British service history to have been dishonourably discharged as an officer from both the Army and the Navy; but I have no idea if that was simply family folklore. The intimation was that he drank and spent freely. However, I have spoken to con-temporaries of his who claimed he was one of the most charming of men. It would appear that it was this natural allure that was the cause of my much more awkward grandfather's envy.

There were three sisters, too. Aunt Delia, born in 1889, seemed impossibly old to me, as a child. She was tiny – bent over by age, but her mind still sharp. She had, as a seventeen-year-old girl, filled the gap left by her mother's death as best she could, both with regard to the other children, and frequently acting as companion to her father on official functions. When she announced her engage-ment in 1913, the local newspaper said: 'There is no more popular lady in Northamptonshire, in whatever circles she moves, than Lady Adelaide Spencer . . .'

Perhaps because she had had to be so mature from such an early age, she married a much older man – Sidney Peel. He was forty-three, she just twenty-four. Eighty years earlier, their fore-fathers had fought hard in the Commons, the Whig Jack Althorp versus the Tory Sir Robert Peel. The newspapers noted that the two families had produced three Chancellors of the Exchequer in the 1830s, Francis Baring being the third.

My father told me the sad – and unverifiable – story of how one of the senior staff at Althorp gave Delia as a wedding present some elasticated underpants, so that they could expand when she became pregnant. The sadness lies in the fact that Aunt Delia never achieved that state, although she adored children and was believed to want them passionately.

A gifted musician, especially with the violin, Aunt Delia was a memorable person, full of intelligence and wisdom, but with a discernible steeliness about her which her younger siblings always respected and bowed to.

Lavinia I never met, for she died in 1955, aged fifty-five. She was, apparently, a vibrant character, always in trouble, one of the last of the Spencer children to be brought up in any large measure at Spencer House. Her special childhood friend was Lady Elizabeth Bowes-Lyon, later the Queen Mother. In the summer of 1998, one of the visitors to Althorp was a man in his nineties who had worked in the Stables as a boy, and who claimed to have caught these two young ladies clandestinely smoking together round the back of the carriages.

She had a reputedly difficult marriage with Lord Annaly, who lived across the valley from Althorp at Holdenby, Charles I's one-time prison, and she would discuss at length the problems she had with him, with my ever receptive grandmother. Lavinia's son, the Hon. Lukie White, represented England at international cricket after the Second World War, in the so-called 'Victory Tests' against Australia.

Aunt Margaret I knew very well. She was the little girl who was born the day her mother, also Margaret, died. There are many reasons for regretting her death, a couple of years before I started researching this book, but her vast knowledge of the Spencer family largely died with her – and that is partly my fault. I had often tried to persuade her to record her memories, and, thankfully, she did write down lyrical snippets of her early memories in *A Spencer Childhood*. However, this was just a tantalizing taste of her wider recollections.

The family myth was always that her father, Bobby, had never forgiven young Margaret for 'killing' her mother, and had effectively banished her to be brought up by the house staff, away from the rest of the family. Indeed, until I read Bobby's diaries, this was a record of events that I had always believed to be so. However, so affectionate are the father's references to all his children – Margaret included – that I doubt this to have been the case.

Aunt Margaret was a life-enhancing force, her deep and generous laugh always at the ready, a passion for gossip evidence of an enquiring, rather than a malicious, mind. To visit her in her small cottage in Burnham Market, between the Spencer estate in Norfolk and Nelson's native village, was to experience humour of the greatest breadth, and intelligence of a rare intensity. The local community was fiercely protective of their 'Lady Margaret'. Few were not bewitched by her mischievous chuckle. I loved her dearly.

It seemed barely conceivable to me that someone so spirited and modern could be from the same generation as my thoroughly Edwardian grandfather. I believe he was weighed down from an early stage by the responsibilities of taking on a family estate that was teetering on the brink of collapse. His father had always been honest about the parlous state the finances were in, noting in his diary for 2 October 1916: 'After luncheon a long and comfortable talk to Jack about the family difficulties. I fear they arise from my ignorance & perhaps from being too easy going!'

The end of the Great War resulted in a rush of couples becoming engaged. Some would have gone ahead earlier, but had chosen to wait until the risk of death in battle had passed. Others rushed into it, egged on by the euphoria of finding themselves still alive after the onslaught. Perhaps my grandparents were from the latter group. Their genuine joy at becoming betrothed was recorded with pride by Bobby, who had met and greatly liked his future daughter-in-law, the Duke of Abercorn's daughter, Lady Cynthia Hamilton:

I was stopped by Jack coming in to tell me he had proposed to Lady Cynthia and was accepted. He said, 'How pleased Mummy would have

been', which went through me . . . Rushed in to greet Cynthia – Flew
to telephone for her to tell her parents. She did and the Duke said 'yes'
. . . What a day. My Boy coming to tell me in his happiness has pleased
me more than I can ever say – and his remembering his beloved Mother
at that moment. It was so wonderful to me. Bless him and Cynthia. She
was so good when I said I feared he would be poor.

My grandparents married on 26 February 1919. One hymn,
'Perfect Love', reduced Bobby to tears, and it was a deeply emotional
day for the widower, who felt a pang at Cynthia's becoming Lady
Althorp – the first to carry that name since his Margaret. In the
vestry, while the choir sang a Brahms anthem, Grandfather leant
over to kiss his father, who then in turn embraced his daughter-in-
law. Afterwards they made their way in the rain to a reception at
Hampden House. That night Bobby wrote in his diary: 'So they
went off in a motor to begin, as I pray, the divine "vie a deux".
May my Boy be as happy as happy – oh so happy.'

Grandfather and Grandmother moved into Althorp in 1922, after
Bobby's death from a heart attack. The house soon became the
passion of Grandfather's life. He had the mind of a curator, and he
loved nothing more than hand rinsing the china, or dusting the
books in the Library. A member of the Standing Commission on
Museums and Galleries, he was also chairman of the Royal School
of Needlework. During the middle years of the twentieth century,
he was the ideal tenant of the family's possessions: highly appreciative
of their heritage importance, while living modestly enough to
minimize the need for sales.

His one serious miscalculation was agreeing to the disposal of
Holbein's only portrait from life of Henry VIII. Grandfather took
the view that he needed cash, in order to be able to pay for
his children's education. Negotiations were conducted through a
London dealer in the 1930s. Eventually it was sold for £10,000, to
the Thyssen family. At the time, this was thought a good price for
the tiny painting. However, it was valued in the 1980s as being
worth £30 million, and is now one of the masterpieces of the

Thyssen collection in Madrid, where I visited it four years ago, with a pang of regret.

After decades of neglect, Althorp's maintenance needs also required funding. Bobby had had no money for even the most basic work, and the House was in as poor a state as it had ever been, when Grandfather began a steady programme of restorative work in the 1930s. By the early 1940s he was in despair. The task was so massive and unrelenting, that he feared it would prove impossible to complete. It was an assessment that led him to contemplate handing the property over to the National Trust.

In June 1942 Captain Hill, the National Trust surveyor, came to inspect Althorp, to see whether he would accept its gift from my family. At first, during a meeting in the Estate Office, he seemed interested. However, Grandfather was determined to give him an unadulterated picture of the problems that had led him to ponder Althorp's disposal, and so he showed the captain the dry rot. This infestation was particularly virulent outside the Long Library, but was not confined to that area — it seemed to be everywhere.

The captain thanked his host for his honesty, and reported back to his superiors. The National Trust then told Grandfather that, given the circumstances, he could keep his ancestral home, and the unenviable expense of cutting out its cancerous flaws. The Trust's reply reached Grandfather as he was going round the top floor rooms, putting down foot baths to catch the rain water that was seeping through the roof.

Spencer House also came to be viewed by Grandfather as an ancestral burden. Again, it was a place he treasured for its history, and even more for its beauty, but one that he hated for its expense. He had no need for such a huge residence in London, and the cost of maintaining the building — let alone the staff's wages — persuaded him to quit it. He gave a final dinner party there in the 1920s, having the splendour of the occasion photographed for the family records. He then resigned himself to the fact that he would never occupy it again, allowing a succession of tenants to use it, a practice that has continued to this day, with the string of companies controlled by Lord Rothschild enjoying opulent surroundings, thanks to the huge sum of money that they have spent restoring it to its original splendour.

Credit should go to Grandfather for not following the trend in the 1920s and 1930s, when Devonshire House, Dorchester House, Aldford House, Chesterfield House and Brook House were all pulled down by despairing owners. The aesthete in Grandfather would never have contemplated such a move. He did, however, come very close to a sale in 1943, when the Bath Club and the Royal Society expressed serious interest in acquiring Spencer House. The price discussed was £250,000, and over tea one afternoon, Queen Mary encouraged Grandfather to take the money and sell.

He hesitated, not wanting to be the Spencer who finally surrendered one of the family's two principal homes. It was with relief then, that in mid-1944 he received an application from the auction house, Christie's, to rent Spencer House. Their King Street premises were destroyed by incendiary bombs, and they needed to find somewhere suitable in the St James's area, to continue their business. Grandfather negotiated a lease for £5,500 per year, for five years. It was testimony to his spirit and to his sensitivity to the importance of heritage, that he did not meekly accept the money, and shed his responsibilities.

That said, Grandfather did not like the idea of leaving Spencer objects behind during his tactical withdrawal from London. From the 1920s until the Christie's lease, he oversaw the gradual transferral of all the contents of Spencer House to Althorp. When the pictures, furniture and china had been removed, it was the turn of the doors and fireplaces. The extraordinary richness of the fittings of Althorp is largely thanks to its having cannibalized the innards of its urban sibling.

From 1939 to 1945, Althorp was – in common with many other large ancestral houses – made to do its bit for the war effort. Oak trees in the Park were cut down for use in naval construction. At the same time a searchlight battery was established a few hundred yards from the House. Also in the Park, the family cricket pitch was handed over to soldiers billeted locally, for them to use for football matches.

Inside the House itself, the main bedrooms were used to store the Law Society's picture collection. However, cunningly, Grandfather saw to it that Althorp's interior was not handed over for the use of servicemen. In July 1943, when 900 Royal Artillery personnel and 100 vehicles streamed into the Park without warning, Grandfather complained with such vigour at the invasion of his patrimony that the entire force was gone within eight weeks. There were to be no repetitions of this sort of mishap: Grandfather was happy to help his country, but the contents of Althorp had first call on his loyalties.

The same was not the case with the Shooting Box at North Creake, the Norfolk home where the Red Earl was taken when he suffered his stroke in 1905. This became a land girls' hostel, and was treated with such a wilful lack of respect that after the war my father believed it to be irreparable, and had it pulled down. Grandfather was aggrieved at this decision, having faced far greater challenges with Althorp and Spencer House, and having dealt with them with gumption.

Grandmother was very loving, and was greatly loved. I have never heard anyone ever say a word against her memory, and she is still very much alive as a paragon of sweet nobility, in the recollections of everyone I have spoken to about her. The word most widely used to describe her is 'saintly'.

She showed an enormous affection for people of all backgrounds, frequently visiting the ill or the bereaved in the villages and on the farms around Althorp, an easy presence in total contrast to the bristling tensions of Grandfather.

Grandmother was beautiful, sensitive and utterly without pride or snobbery. The young girl who had shown no concern when her future father-in-law had warned her that she was marrying a pauper never complained about the straitened circumstances of the once wealthy family she had married into. She drove her weathered little Morris around the county, happy for Grandfather to enjoy the luxury of the chauffeur-driven Rolls-Royce that he would not surrender, even when he clearly could not afford to run it.

One day Grandfather told her that he needed to be driven to

London, and she would therefore have to take the train. She agreed readily. The train crashed, Grandmother was thrown hard against the side of the carriage, and her head was badly damaged. It was on the same part of her brain that took the impact of this blow that she later developed the growth that turned into a malignant tumour, causing her death in 1972.

The royal family mourned a charming and popular courtier, who had assisted the Queen Mother as a Lady of the Bedchamber with energy and sparkle. But Northamptonshire felt the loss more keenly, knowing that somebody very special, who had done an enormous amount of unsung voluntary work for the community, was gone for ever. As a mark of respect, it was decided to name the county's hospice after her.

I remember Grandmother's memorial service. The whole family gathered at Althorp, and I came over for the day from my nearby prep school, aged eight. The most vivid memory I have is of breakfast that day, a troupe of mainly elderly relatives sitting glumly round the table in the Tapestry Dining Room, most of whom I had never knowingly met before.

Grandmother's brother, 'Uncle Jimmy', sat chain-smoking on one side of me and then, with an absent-minded flourish, stubbed a cigarette out in his uneaten grapefruit. It was an act so fantastically thrilling to me, barely out of the strictures of the Nursery, where even elbows on the table resulted in punishment, that I instinctively warmed to the charming old duke, who showed his contempt for petty convention in the extinction of his early morning smoke.

The other underlying memory of that winter's day was the feeling of genuine grief that a truly outstanding life had come to an end. My father looked utterly devastated; and even Grandfather, who had not been close to his wife for many years, seemed shaken to the core. I wish I had known her for longer.

Grandfather never attained his wife's popularity. He induced respect in many, and fear in almost all. John Richardson, who has worked on the Estate as a forester since I was born in 1964, still recalls with a shudder how 'the old Earl' would drive around his land, checking

how everything was looking. One day he found the foresters at
work, and stopped to watch them. John can still recall how he
could barely move, so terrified was he by this silent inspection.
Grandfather sat there, motionless, attentive, unintentionally menacing, before driving on, without a comment.

There was something about Grandfather that enjoyed antagonism. My father told me about his sadness, on taking over Althorp,
at finding file after file of letters that Grandfather had copied out,
to keep for ever. They were often combative, sometimes abusive,
and largely regrettable. It was a fault Grandfather was aware of, but
could do little about.

In 1929, he found himself alone at North Creake with my father,
then aged five. Grandfather decided to take this opportunity to
start a notebook, writing down observations on subjects or people
that he might from time to time find interesting. In the foreword
he noted: 'I know I am inclined to be most critical about people
so my views will be perhaps more unfavourable than they ought
to be but I think I can discern their good points though I am afraid
I am more likely to notice their bad ones.'

His special prejudices were engaged by the ignorant, particularly
if they failed to show sufficient interest in his beloved home – a
sorry fact demonstrated by countless entries in his diaries: 'Waited
about until 4.10 when the Youth Fellowship from St Mary's Far
Cotton came 40 minutes late. The 22 young people were very
dumb, so it took just an hour to go round the house . . .' 'Opened
the house & at 2.30, 29 wounded American soldiers came to see
the pictures. They were very nice & liked looking, but knew
nothing.'

One of Grandfather's other regrettable characteristics was his
reluctance to engage in easy conversation with those who worked
for him. He particularly did not enjoy banter with his chauffeur;
the desired silence being encouraged by the glass screen between
himself and the driver's seat.

On the drive between London and Althorp, before the motorway
was opened, Grandfather would sometimes find it necessary to tap
the glass; a signal that he needed to stop for a call of nature. One

day he was on the road's verge, half-way through his business, when the wind blew and slammed the passenger door shut. The chauffeur knew that the slamming of the door meant that his lordship was back in his seat, ready to resume the journey, so he drove on. Apparently he did not once look behind him during the remaining stretch from mid-Bedfordshire to Althorp, aware that Grandfather did not enjoy being glanced at in the mirror.

After sweeping in to the front yard of the House, the chauffeur got out and held my Grandfather's door open for him. It was only then that he realized something was seriously wrong; and only when my Grandfather arrived in the car of a senior member of the Bedfordshire Constabulary that he knew he was in for a distinctly difficult time with 'Old Lordy'.

However tricky Grandfather may have been, he was not an evil man. This, though, was how he was portrayed by a national newspaper after it deliberately misconstrued a typically thorough and practical piece of housekeeping by him, labelling him 'the Anti-Christ'.

When the vault in the Spencer Chapel at Great Brington was chiselled open to receive Charlotte Spencer's body in 1903, the resident agent, A.L.Y. Morley, took the opportunity to write a report on the condition of the enclosed coffins. The results made distressing reading for the family, as it became clear that centuries of neglect were depriving generations of Spencers of dignity in their final resting place:

The coffins lie in two chambers; those in the western chamber are all leaden ones, and nearly all are those of the Earls of Sunderland, who were also Barons Spencer, and their families. The coffins live in bad and irregular order, one on the top of another, some of the lower ones being much crushed, and in at least one case bones are visible . . . There are four or five name-plates lying loose on coffins, but there is no certainty to which coffins they belong.

This sorry picture remained with Grandfather throughout the next half-century; he even copied Morley's report into his own crested notebook. He then decided, in middle age, to address the problem in an intelligent but slightly startling manner: the lead of the coffins would be used for repairs to the church roof, and the bodies would be individually cremated, the ashes being given their own individual urn.

Grandfather was present when each coffin was opened. He later recalled how the majority of early Spencers were small men, by modern standards, with red beards that had continued growing after they were interred. Once exposed to air, they quickly started to wither into powdery disintegration.

The newspaper in question, which has long been established at the bottom end of the tabloid market in England, decided this was an opportunity to portray a member of the aristocracy as a depraved gravedigger, disturbing the bones of his ancestors in an inexplicably macabre manner.

The only other time that Grandfather was treated with such inaccuracy by the press was during the scandal surrounding the Prince of Wales's affair with Wallis Simpson. In compiling a profile of Simpson, one newspaper correctly named her first husband as being 'Earl Spencer'. However, when the photograph accompanying the article showed Grandfather, instead of an American naval commander with the first name of 'Earl', his sense of humour came to the fore, and he enjoyed the ridiculousness of the error with his family.

Grandfather was capable of a lighter side. After Grandmother's death he used to enjoy having my eldest sister, Sarah, to stay at Althorp. He would delight in spoiling her – letting her wear some of his Spencer jewellery, and revelling in the naughtiness of his teenage granddaughter smoking in his presence. They had an easy rapport which, if they had witnessed it, many would not have believed possible of a man mockingly known as 'Jolly Jack'.

My last memory of Grandfather stems from 20 May 1975. It was my eleventh birthday, and he appeared in his Rolls, with the whippet-like chauffeur, Mr Hutchings, at the wheel, to give me my present: four very academic books on the weapons and uniforms of the British Army. I remember being aware that this old man, with his slicked back hair, his suit fitted so the waistline came in at the ribs, covering his mighty belly, was essentially a very kind person. You could see it in his eyes.

Looking back, I genuinely believe that the death of his mother at such an impressionable age, combined with the undiagnosed depression that his father slipped into, impacted hugely on him, making it easier to hide behind bluffness and apparent aggression, rather than having to allow gentler emotions to come to the fore. He was difficult in order to scare off people in a way he could justify to himself, rather than risk the agony of trying with others, and then being rejected. We said a rather formal farewell to one another that afternoon.

Less than three weeks later, I was walking around the front of the school, preparing for our daily compulsory exercise programme – seventy-five boys in six lines doing stretching exercises, the whole ordeal called 'drill' – when I saw the headmaster and his deputy talking quietly in the corner, then both turning simultaneously to look at me. There was something very eerie about that look. The headmaster came over to me, and asked if he could see me after drill, in his study.

I did not need him to tell me, for I knew it in my bones: Grandfather was dead. There had not been a hint that he was even unwell, when I had seen him. I just knew.

# 19. From My Father to My Children

My father and Grandfather had had a difficult relationship, which had enjoyed intermittent periods of understanding and mutual appreciation.

There were only two children in my father's generation: himself and his older sister, Anne. My sister Jane has always felt that this was a pity in itself, for growing up at Althorp in such a small family must have been very lonely for everyone concerned. More children might have lifted the feel of the place.

Aunt Anne was born in 1920. We sadly saw little of her when I was growing up, as my father and she were not close in middle age. By that I do not mean there was anything approaching coolness, let alone hostility; it just seemed that whatever bond there was, was not strong enough to result in frequent contact between the two siblings. This was particularly the case after my father's remarriage, when my stepmother failed to encourage my father to see people who were part of his life before she appeared on the scene in the early 1970s.

Aunt Anne had five children, the product of over fifty years of marriage to Christopher Wake-Walker, a naval lieutenant she had met while serving in the war as a Third Officer in the WRNS. Aunt Anne broke the news of her engagement to Grandfather when she chanced upon him in St James's Street, one day in November 1943. As he recorded in his diary: 'We went to tea at Stewarts & later met Christopher at the English Speaking Union, where Anne is staying. He was very shy & silent but looked very nice.'

They married on 10 February 1944 at Westminster Abbey, in the presence of the Princesses Elizabeth and Margaret, Grandfather dressed in the uniform of Honorary Colonel of the Northamptonshire Regiment. As Christopher Wake-Walker's father was an admiral – one who was partially responsible for the successful sinking of Hitler's pocket battleship, the *Bismarck* – the reception was held at the Admiralty. Because of the general shortage of luxury items during the war, the families drank the couple's health from the one bottle of champagne Grandfather had been able to procure. He recorded how everyone was obliged to drink 'nasty cider cup' for the rest of the reception.

My father's childhood memories – at least, those that he shared with me – were not happy ones. It is clear from his diaries that Grandfather felt he was tolerably close to his son; however, my father felt the *froideur* of a parent not fully engaged emotionally in their relationship.

School for my father started at Wellesley House, in Kent, where he boarded from the age of eight. Being quite good at sport, and having inherited his mother's enormous charm, my father was a popular boy, excelling at cricket, and conscientious academically. He used to dread the train journeys home at the end of term, though, and told me how he would hide in the shadows of the train carriage, hoping his father had forgotten to collect him, until he was convinced he was hoping in vain.

At Althorp, whenever he felt the atmosphere tightening, he would climb up on to a false ceiling in the bathroom next to the Old Nursery, and wait up there, his terriers as companions. I fear these solitary moments were relatively frequent.

In 1937, my father went on to Eton, again enjoying moderate success. His forte was soldiering and, since most of his time at the school was during the war, it was the right discipline to excel at. It was also here that his talent for photography began to emerge, as he chronicled with his Box Brownie the bomb damage inflicted on the venerable school buildings.

Certainly, my father had a great affection for Eton throughout his life, and enjoyed sharing his knowledge of the customs, the slang and the history of the place, before taking me there for my new boys' tea party, in September 1977. I always found it slightly disappointing that he subscribed to the view that 'your schooldays are the best time of your life', since this has never been a philosophy I could share.

After Eton my father went into the Army. He was not sure which regiment to join, but he did know that the cavalry was his preference. In February 1942, Grandfather decided to get some advice for his son, and went to St James's Palace to see an old friend influential in such matters, the gloriously named 'Wombat' Howard-Vyse. It was decided that my father should join the Scots Greys.

During the years from my father's emergence from adolescence until after his marriage to my mother, there seems to have been a relaxation in the two men's relationship, resulting in joint visits to the theatre, the cinema, restaurants and cricket matches. Grandfather's happiness with his son was no doubt partly born out of pride in his military prowess.

One Sunday at the end of September 1943, Grandfather got up early to take the tube to Waterloo, then the train down to Camberley. There he was overcome to find his son taking 'the whole Church Parade as Battalion Commander – he did it very well with the voice of a bull'. Three months later Grandfather returned with his wife, daughter and Christopher Wake-Walker. 'Maj.-Gen. Briggs did the passing-out & made a very good speech, partly drowned by aeroplanes overhead. Johnnie was called out & given the belt as best cadet in his troop – it was thrilling!'

My father did not speak much about his time in the war. I know he landed the day after D-Day, and that he had under his command four Sherman tanks, of which only the one he was in survived the war. He saw his best friend, in one of his other tanks, disobey his order to keep his head down, and pay the penalty when a German sniper shot him dead. At some stage, my father was mentioned in dispatches, for bravery.

After the war he served as ADC to Lord Norrie, Governor of South Australia, before becoming a courtier. He served as equerry to the Queen, accompanying her on a tour of the Commonwealth in the early 1950s. His respect for the monarch aside, I got the impression that he found many aspects of his duties less than exciting.

★

We now get into territory that has been trawled through by every pop psychologist and profiteer who has tried to analyse my sister Diana and her life: my parents' marriage, their subsequent divorce, the apportionment of blame thereof, the custody battles for us children, and all the other things that should remain private between the parties. It is not for me to wade publicly into such difficult territory.

I would say, though, that we had very loving parents, who cared for us in their separate homes with devotion, humour, honesty and respect. With my father, the homes were bigger, the life more formal. There was always a full house staff, and both Park House, Sandringham, where we were until 1975, and Althorp, were enviably situated, in the midst of some of the most beautiful parts of the English countryside.

My mother lived in London, and a succession of country houses: one, briefly, in Berkshire, followed by three years at a modern house near Itchenor in Sussex. Ardencaple, where she moved to in 1972, was on the west coast of Scotland, a magical place which Diana and I adored for its wild beauty and the fun we had on the sea, lobster-potting and mackerel-fishing.

We had two very different step-parents: Peter, always self-effacing, humorous, generous, spontaneous and exciting; and Raine. Of course, their different characteristics influenced our enjoyment of the two family homes, during the weeks of holiday we enjoyed away from school. The variety was intriguing and, in retrospect, I am glad we had the balance of glorious but stuffy Althorp, and vibrant and welcoming Ardencaple. I feel truly lucky to have had two parents who did so much for us; both had immense qualities.

My sister Diana's marriage to the Prince of Wales in 1981 moved us as a family from the shadows of the landed aristocracy into the role of bit-part players in the soap opera fantasy world that the media has foisted on to the British royal family.

I often wonder what would have happened if this marriage had not taken place. Certainly, this book would have generated less interest, and fewer sales; and Althorp would have remained just another stately home on the tourist trail, rather than one of the most popular in the country, visited by scores of thousands keen to pay their respects to a Princess far from forgotten for the good she did in her all too brief public life.

I suppose the truth is that the aristocracy in Britain is perceived as an anachronism, with a minimal percentage of people able to distinguish between the different ranks of the peerage, and nobody particularly interested in the plight of the dozens of decent men and women who struggle to keep their family heritage together, in the face of ever increasing expense and diminishing reserves – both financial and emotional.

It has been a fascinating exercise, researching and writing this book, learning how a family such as the Spencers has survived hard times, and profited from a combination of hard work and good fortune, from sheep farmers to wealthy beneficiaries, from seventeenth-century roguishness to Victorian respectability.

I have had the instinctive responsibilities of being the latest in a long bloodline reinforced by my studies, of course; it would be unnatural not to be humbled by such a rich and diverse heritage. However, it has also confirmed to me the necessity to move forward whenever possible, and not simply to fight an ever more desperate tactical withdrawal.

I may never be in the position to buy great art for Althorp, like Robert Sunderland or John, First Earl Spencer. I certainly will not emulate the political careers of Honest Jack Althorp or the Red Earl. However, I do know that there is a way in front of me, just as there is a history behind me, which may well be more modest than previous generations of Spencers may have expected for themselves, but which is important for the continuation of the family name. Above all, I hope that when my children take over from me, they will feel able to add a chapter to this book without any twinge of shame or regret, for a lot of what I do today I do for them.

# Selected Bibliography

Baring, Maurice, *Cecil Spencer: A Memoir* (privately published, 1928)

Bartlett, William A., *History of Wimbledon* (Simpkin, Marshall and Co., 1865)

Bentley, Michael, *Politics Without Democracy* (Blackwell/Fontana, 1984)

Biddle, Sheila, *Bolingbroke and Harley* (George Allen and Unwin, 1975)

Broughton, Lord, *Recollections of a Long Life* (John Murray, 1909)

Camden, *Britain* (Edmund Gibson, translated by Philemon Holland, 2nd edition, 1637)

Carlisle, Georgiana, Countess of, *A Description of Holywell* (privately published, n.d.)

Chancellor, Beresford, *Lives of British Architects from William of Wykeham to Sir William Chambers* (Duckworth & Co., 1909)

Churchill, R. S., *Winston Churchill, Vol. 2: Young Statesman, 1901–1914* (Heinemann, 1967)

Clifford Smith, Harold, *Sulgrave Manor and the Washingtons* (Jonathan Cape, 1933)

Coward, Barry, *The Stuart Age: A History of England 1603–1714* (Longman, 1980)

Cradock, J., *Literary and Miscellaneous Memoirs* (Gregg International, 1973)

Devine, Pius, *The Life of Father Ignatius of St Paul, Passionist – the Hon., And Rev.*

*George Spencer – Compiled Chiefly from his Autobiographical Journal and Letters* (James Duffy, Dublin and London, 1866)

Dibdin, Rev. Thomas Frognall, *Aedes Althorpainae* (Shakespeare Press, 1822)

*Dictionary of National Biography* (Oxford University Press, 1996)

Duggan, James, *The Great Mutiny* (André Deutsch, 1965)

Evelyn, John, *The Diary of John Evelyn* (Headstart History Publishing, 1994)

Fea, Allan, *James II and His Wives* (Methuen & Co., 1908)

Foreman, Amanda, *Georgiana, Duchess of Devonshire* (HarperCollins, 1998)

Gordon, Peter (ed.), *The Red Earl* (Northamptonshire Records Society, 1985)

Gotch, J. Alfred, *The Old Halls and Manor Houses of Northamptonshire* (Batsford, 1936)

Harris, Frances, *A Passion for Government: The Life of Sarah, Duchess of Marlborough* (Oxford University Press, 1991)

Holland, Clive, *Warwickshire* (Adam & Charles Black, 1906)

Hood, E. P., *A Visit to Althorp* (privately published, 1884)

Howell-Thomas, Dorothy, *Duncannon* (Michael Russell Publishing, 1992)

Jackson, Stanley, *The Great Barnato* (Heinemann, 1970)

Jones, J. R. (ed.), *The Restored Monarchy* (Macmillan Press, 1979)

Lander, J. R., *The Wars of the Roses* (Sutton Publishing, 1990)

Le Marchant, Sir Denis, *Memoir of John Charles, Viscount Althorp* (Richard Bently and Son, 1876)

Locke, Amy Audrey, *The Seymour Family* (Constable & Co., 1911)

Lucy, H., *A Diary of Two Parliaments* (Cassel & Co., 1885, 1886)

Lyttelton, Sarah, *Letters from Sarah, Lady Lyttelton* (Spottiswode & Co., 1873)

Macky, John, *A Journey Through England* (published anonymously, 1732)

Metcalfe, Walter C. (ed.), *The Visitations of Northamptonshire, Made in 1564 and 1618–19* (Mitchell and Hughes, 1887)

Money, Walter, *The Popular History of Newbury* (Simpkin, Marshall, 1905)

Murray, Alexander (ed.), *Sir William Jones* (Oxford University Press, 1998)

Nevill, Ralph, *Light Come, Light Go: Gambling – Gamesters – Wagers – The Turf* (Macmillan, 1909)

Nichols, John, *Literary Anecdotes of the Eighteenth Century; Comprising Biographical Memoirs of William Bowyer . . . and Many of His Learned*

*Friends, etc* (New York, AMS Press; Kraus Reprint Co., 1996)

Passavant, Johann David, *Tour of a German Artist in England, with Notices of Private Galleries, and Remarks on the State of Art* (London, 1836)

Pevsner, Nikolaus, *Northamptonshire* (Penguin, 1961)

Pevsner, Nikolaus, *Warwickshire* (Penguin, 1966)

Pinny, T. C., *The Spencer Family* (privately published, n.d.)

Plumb, J. H., *The Growth of Political Stability in England 1675–1725* (Macmillan Press, 1967)

Prestwich, Michael, *The Three Edwards: War and State in England 1272–1377* (Weidenfeld & Nicolson, 1980)

Rosebery, Lord, *Chatham: His Early Life and Connections* (A. L. Humphreys, 1910)

Seymour, Frederick, *Charlotte Spencer: A Memoir* (William Mark, 1907)

Shelley, Lady Frances, *The Diary of Lady Frances Shelley, 1787–1817* (John Murray, 1912)

Shirley, Evelyn Philip, *The Noble and Gentle Men of England* (Westminster, 1859)

Shute, Nerina, *The Royal Family and the Spencers* (Robert Hale, 1986)

Simpkinson, Rev. J. N., *The Washingtons* (Longman, 1860)

Sinclair, Andrew, *Death by Fame* (Constable, 1998)

*Spencer Family Bible, The* (private papers)

*Spencer Genealogy* (private papers)

Spencer, John Charles, Third Earl, *Autobiography* (privately published, n.d.)

*St James's Westminster Register*

Steinman, G., *Althorp Memoirs* (privately published, 1869)

Stone, Lawrence, *The Crisis of the Aristocracy, 1558–1641* (Oxford University Press, 1967)

Sykes, Chistopher Simon, *Black Sheep* (Chatto & Windus, 1982)

Wasson, Ellis Archer, *Whig Renaissance: Lord Althorp and the Whig Party, 1782– 1845* (Garland, 1987)

*Wimbledon Parish Register*

# Index